I'm Not in Kansas Any More! Love, Dorothy

By
Dorothy Dale Kloss

Book cover design by
Ken Prescott

Cover Photo courtesy of
Dirk Halstead

BearManorMedia.com

I'm Not in Kansas Anymore! Love, Dorothy

 Published in the USA by:
BearManor Media
P.O. Box 1129
Duncan, OK 73534-1129
www.BearManorMedia.com

ISBN: 1-59393-232-4
ISBN-13: 978-1-59393-232-9

Printed in the United States

Design and Layout by Scot Penslar

CONTENTS

All photos have been either taken by the author or used with permission given by the stars or their representatives.

To
Craig, Joni, Jamie and Megan — my family
Love Ya

Ken Prescott —
You are the sunshine of my life!

Dancing, singing, performing,
traveling and laughing!
We've had a great run, and
we're not done yet!

THE ENDLESS DANCE
(For Dorothy)

In such a woman lies that special glimmer

A beacon shining from afar

And even as our days grow dimmer

We seek the brightness of her star

With grace and poise she moves serene

A flower of spring devoid of frost

And all her silver gold and green

Reminds us of the springs we lost

She is the miracle of enduring youth

An angel treading life's gossamer stage

Carrying the essence of eternal truth

A million steps have brought her here

Fresh and beautiful to our door

To lay the mystery of what is dear

That flame of life we hunger for

How she makes us shine forever

Caught in the mist of time's romance

Paints our hearts with sweet endeavor

This golden lady of the endless dance.

— David Cadden

December 2009

Dear Judy:

From one showgirl to another —

Hope you enjoy my first adventure as an author —

Love,

Dorothy

Martini Bar with Doris. She said, "Why don't you write a book?"
I said, "Let's have another drink."

Foreword

Writing a book is not all periods and commas. It's very personal, especially if it's "all about me" book. Going back in my life brought forth important memories, and how they have affected my life. One change in direction and you're on another path.

My path in 2009 took me to "The Falls Martini Bar," across the street from The Follies. Doris Bennett was from New Jersey, and she had a timeshare in Palm Desert. Doris loved to play golf and attend "The Follies." Every year, she would arrive around Valentine's Day, and stay for two weeks. She would hitch up with several friends from New Jersey, who were also here for the season.

I believe I met Doris in 1997. She usually came to The Follies two or three performances and would stop to say "hello" when I was shaking hands in the lobby of the theatre. After a couple of years, she asked me to lunch and our friendship began.

Back to "The Falls Martini Bar." She and another friend, Margo Mayer, met me there after the show one evening. Never at a loss for words, I was telling stories and we were all laughing. Suddenly, Doris and Margo said, "You should write a book!"

I said, "Are you nuts?"

"No," they chimed in, "And write it just the way you talk!" Well, it was a scary prospect, but Doris went home and would not let it go. She e-mailed me nearly every day. "Did you start the book?" gently nudging. So, one day, I turned on the computer and the rest is history. Well, maybe not HISTORY, but my history. So here it is, "I'm Not In Kansas Any More," and I'm still kicking at 88, and maybe even beyond 89. I don't believe I have a second book in me, maybe some people will probably say, THANK GOODNESS, so get it while it's hot. Time waits for no one.

Through the past 15 years, during my arduous performance schedule, I was periodically asked by the "powers that be," in a rather condescending tone, "Where would you be if you weren't here?" This was implying that I had neither the wit, nor the talent or intelligence to do anything else.

Well, my answer to them? On the stage, television, and enjoying being a published author.

But first, let me tell you where I have been. And to my cherished fans who have taken time to read this, and are ready to embark on my literary remembrances of the past, present and my exciting future, I hope you enjoy the journey through my personal "Oz!" So let's get started, and "click our heels!"

Curtain going up! Exciting things are in my future and whichever way the wind blows, I'll go with it!

Love,

Dorothy

Dorothy and Ken, *The Guinness Book of Records* Certificate, 2009

"THE OLDEST LIVING, WORKING SHOW GIRL IN THE WORLD"!

Chapter 1: St. Louis 1923

I'm sure my mother named me Dorothy because she knew I would be "clicking my heels" from the beginning of my life to my "finale." At this time in my life, my "last curtain call" could happen at any time, but I do hope I can give this book "my big finish" before I'm finished; so let's go for it.

My Oz was St. Louis, Missouri. October 27, 1923 on Grand Avenue. No hospital for me! At 6:20 p.m., I came into this world and gave my parents a look that read, "Here I am, so deal with it!" I was welcomed by my mother, Alice Donnelly Hunn, my father, Vincent D. Hunn, and two brothers, John and Vincent. John was ten years older and Vincent was seven years older. I had it made! They all adored and loved me forever more. How lucky can a girl get!

My dad was an artist turned sign painter to support our family. In those days, unless you were Van Gogh, it was difficult to make a living. So, like many other professions, you move on, but the talent is still there. And you hope someday you will be able to prove yourself. My mother was a homemaker. After I was born, we moved several times. My mom was a real mover, and I mean that in the nicest way. She loved sunshine and lovely things around her, so if we moved into a house and it was dark, she had to get out. That's why we moved to a bright, cheerful apartment on St. Louis Ave.

Boy, do I have memories of that house. One of the most vivid was when I was three years old. I was sitting next to my mom in our home as she was sewing a dress for me. My mother was an accomplished seamstress. I was watching her, when suddenly we heard a loud noise. She grabbed me and we waited, as the sound of wind swept through the house. The roof was blowing off the second floor apartment! Mom found a corner where we waited for the quiet, all the time hoping my two brothers and dad were okay. Suddenly, she remembered the young man that lived upstairs. He was home from school due to a broken leg. We rushed up to see if he was okay and brought him down with us until his mother got home.

Vincent Hunn and Alice Donnelly

The three of us found our way to the front of the house and we looked outside to find the street covered with debris. Cars were piled on top of each other, several ambulances with flashing lights at the corner, and people were being carried out of the bank building. It looked like a war zone.

Mom screamed, "Here they come; dad and the boys are okay!"

They were jumping over the cars and running for the house. Dad said, "Thank God you and Dorothy are okay. I dashed to the school to get the boys, and we prayed all the way home hoping you were alright." The wind had come and gone; we were all together again.

It was very strange that the tornado hit one part of St. Louis, an isolated area. Talk about Dorothy in the Wizard of Oz! All we needed was Toto, the red shoes (which would come later), and Auntie Em to make the scene complete.

After the tornado, we could no longer live in our sunshine apartment. At the time it was just a move, but little did I know that would be the beginning of my lifelong love of dance and show business. My career was being shaped in the early stages of my life.

*My Mom Alice and my
Aunt Mame, 1913*

We moved to a nice duplex on Union Ave. At the corner, there was a large, two story house. Mom and I passed it every day, going and coming from my kindergarten class at St. Theresa's School. One day, as my mom passed the house, she saw a sign "Ford Dancing School: Register for Fall Classes." It must have been fate! I was three, and loved to do the Charleston, which was the big rage at the time. I have no idea how I came to learn it, but I was dancing the Charleston all over the house. I'm sure mom thought, "This kid has talent," but at the time, it was debatable. That's just being a mother. I guess she thought maybe it would be good for me to take dance class. At least, that's how the story goes.

So my mother took me to the big house on the corner and asked me, "Dorothy, would you like to take dancing class?" I guess I said "yes." A lady met us at the door and told my mom about the dance classes, which would be starting in September. Two sisters owned the house, and decided to turn the living room into a studio. I can vaguely remember the classes, but I do remember the recital because, you see, costumes were involved! I always loved pomp and ceremony, even at the age of three.

John and Vincent Hunn,
ten and seven years old, 1923

Guess Who?, at 2!

My first dance recital was at the Masonic temple. I was Mary, as in "Mary had a Little Lamb." Not much dancing, but they said I pulled that lamb on wheels across the stage "like a pro." My second routine was a song and dance number. I wore white pants and a striped jacket, and sang and danced to a college song: "Collegiates, Collegiates, Yes We are Collegiates." That was more my style. Although, if I had it to do over again, I would have preferred a tutu. But if you're three, and have no say, you're stuck with white pants and a jacket. You

9

have to work the personality. As I was performing, I had my hands raised, palms facing front, a la Eddie Cantor, swinging them from side to side. John and Vincent thought it was quite funny and for years, they would kid me about my window washing choreography.

Many performers say the first time they hit the stage, they knew what they wanted to do for the rest of their lives. Not me. I had no idea why I was there, but something must have clicked.

The Ford Dancing School became a prominent dance studio in the years to come. To think I was the Ford Dancing School's first student! But within a year, I would be living in Chicago. Years later, I was in St. Louis performing at the Jefferson Hotel. I decided to take a trip down "memory lane." I found Union Ave., and the big house at the corner was still there. They built a beautiful new studio behind the big house. I was invited to view a class with many students. Through the years, not only did the Ford School give me my first love of the stage, I'm sure many more talented youngsters went on to fame and fortune. Among them was Ginger Rogers, also from St. Louis.

My smiling Dad, 1918

Dad was still trying to make life better for us. He was offered a job in Atlanta, Georgia, at the racetrack. So, we hit the road with great expectations. It was not a good trip. Vincent was car sick all the way to Georgia, going through the red clay mountains. But we arrived in one piece and ready to pursue our new venture. We were always an optimistic group, but it was short-lived.

When dad reported for work at the track, he was told to report to the man at the finish line. "They will tell you what to do," he was told. His job was to wave the flag at the start and finish of each race. What a great career! Dad came home and told mom to pack: "We're going home. I'm not a flag waver." Mom started packing and before we could say "finish," the job was finished. My one regret, I could have grown up a Southern Belle.

We returned to St. Louis, but the Georgia trip and the racetrack were a promise of things to come for my brother Vincent in later years.

My grandfather Hunn was a stern old guy, and had a sign shop in the downtown area of St. Louis. His three sons, Eddy, Vincent and Arthur, "toed the mark." I remember dad telling the story how my grandfather bought my dad a banjo, and because dad didn't practice every night, he threw it out. That's dad's story. Maybe he just played lousy banjo.

Grandma Mary Donnelly, née Grady, in her later years, 1938
Born in Tipperary, Ireland

Grandpa had married my Grandma Hunn (Anastasia Sheehan), when she was 16 and he was 21. Eddy was the first of their children, followed by Vincent, my father, and Arthur, the youngest. She also had a baby girl named Genevieve. Every time grandma would get pregnant, grandpa would leave town, and she would be on her own. Gee, what a guy! I guess that was his way of dealing with it. She would have the baby, and have to work as a wet nurse (give milk to mothers who could not produce enough for their own). Sadly, she didn't have enough for her own baby, and Genevieve died.

Grandma, Anastastia Hunn, née Sheehan, County of Kildare, Ireland 1884

The most amazing thing to me is that she raised three talented and nice men that had to make it on their own because grandpa didn't give them much help. But what do you think? Maybe that's the reason they did make it later in life.

Grandpa did like my mother, and was very generous to me up until the day he died in his eighties. He would send me gifts as a little girl, and when I would visit him in later years, he always wanted me to stay a little longer. He wasn't fond of the other family members, and would let them know it in a flash. When mom would take me to see him, he would yell down from the second floor, "Who's there?"

Mom would call back, "It's Alice and Dorothy, grandpa!"

And he would say, "Come on up Alice." But if he didn't like you, he would yell, "There's no one home." He was full of charm. My Grandma Hunn was a sweet, easy-going woman who I regret not knowing better. She died of cancer very young.

It must have been hard on my dad with three kids to support, but he was always full of fun and optimistic about the future. He had the gift of gab and a nice singing voice. And he was a great storyteller to boot. Every Saturday afternoon, all the sign painters would congregate at grandpa Hunn's shop. He had "drinks and eats," as they use to say, and the afternoon was spent talking about whatever they talked about. They always said that my dad was never at a loss for words and could keep them entertained for hours. If there had been a talking contest, he would have been the winner, hands-down. Mom said, it rubbed off on her three children. I'm glad it did because it has been a great asset to my career!!

My mother was a Donnelly, with four brothers, and a sister Mary, or "Mae" as we called her. They were as Irish as "Paddy's pig." My grandma, Mary Donnelly (née Grady), was born in Tipperary, Ireland, in 1861 and passed in 1933 when I was ten. I didn't really know her. She was very quiet and reserved, and I never remember a hug, but she was a kind person. She lived in St. Louis and I lived in Chicago; not a short commute. I remember her once asking me if there was "something special" I would like to have. That was the wrong thing to ask me, because I had several things on my list! But before I could tell her, and that was good thinking on her part, she said, "Dorothy, I heard you would like a red coat." I was always the "clothes horse," even at ten. She motioned for me to come over to her, handed me money for the coat, and said, "Be sure it's red." I still love red and have several red coats in my closet to this day.

My grandfather, Mathew Donnelly, died in 1917. He died on the same day my brother was born. The Irish had a saying, "When one leaves this world a new life enters." And that was Vincent, named after my father. I never got to know Grandpa Donnelly as I was still "waiting in the wings" for my turn to join my family six years later. Grandpa was a hod carrier. They carried the bricks and mortar to wherever they were building. He worked on the steeple of the Rock Catholic Church in St. Louis, Missouri. That was one of my Aunt Mae's favorite stories. She had many of them, and mostly exaggerated. You would think he built the whole church. But what the heck, we enjoyed them.

After I got into show business, the "steeple story" took second place. When people would ask her where Dorothy got her talent, she would elaborate, telling them it came from "the Donnelly side of the family."

She would tell everyone how every Saturday night, when they were young, our family would roll up the carpet and dance the night away. And grandpa would do the Irish jig. My mother would look at her, shake her head and say to me, "We didn't even have a carpet." The Donnelly clan was Mary, Peter, Alice (my mother), Mathew, John and Phil. All the brothers were named after the twelve apostles.

My grandpa was a stubborn Irishman, and named all the children. Grandma had nothing to say about it. Grandma had always hoped to name one of her children, but each time a new child arrived, grandpa would dash off to the church to baptize the new baby. He would return and tell her the name.

With the birth of her last son, grandma got her chance. Grandpa was not too quick this time around. It was a weekday, and he had to go to work. The baby was on the bed, and he rolled off on to the floor and hit his head. Now remember — they had no carpet. Being Catholic, if a baby died before being baptized, he would go to limbo. Grandma picked him up and dashed to the church to tell the priest about the accident. He immediately took him to the baptismal fountain, blessed him with the holy water, and asked her the name of this child. She quickly said, "Phillip." She finally got her wish. I guess one out of five is not bad. I don't know if I believe he hit his head; he always seemed perfectly normal to me. I think it was her one chance to name him before grandpa came home. The deed was done, and what could he do? Grandmas have come a long way; face lifts, designer clothing, and working until they're ninety. I'm glad I'm one of them.

Chapter 2: Losing the Blues in Chicago

Dad's brother Eddy lived in Chicago with his wife Peggy. He called dad and convinced him to move to Chicago because there were more opportunities for work there. So dad talked it over with mom, and the decision was made. Dad didn't sit on it long, and mom was all for it. We packed one more time and hit Route 66. Our new apartment was on the north side of Chicago, Lawrence and Lincoln Ave. It was across the street from Sears, the public school, and most importantly, the ice cream shop was just around the corner.

When I was three or four, it was a different world. We had play clothes while we made castles in our sand box. In the afternoon, we had our bath and were all clean and happy when "the dads" came home for dinner. Around two o'clock mom would say, "Dorothy, should we have an ice cream cone?" I'm sure she wanted the ice cream treat before my nap and bath. Mom would give me six cents, and let me go down to the ice cream store. In those days, you didn't have to worry about someone grabbing your child off the street.

I would skip down to the ice cream shop with my money, and give the man my six cents for two cones. One day as I was making my way back, I dropped one of the cones. "Oh, what should I do?" I thought quickly, "Whose cone did I drop?" I walked in to our apartment and immediately said "Oh, mom I dropped your cone."

She just laughed, and I'm sure she thought, "Dorothy will always be able to take care of herself." And, of course, I have.

We did "lose the blues in Chicago." Dad opened a sign shop on Broadway, not far from The 51 Hundred Club, where Danny Thomas got his big break. It was just a neighborhood club, but Danny made it famous.

He was down and out back in those days, and hoping for a break in show business. Danny was married and needed a job, so he made a promise to St. Jude: if the saint could help him get work, Danny would try to do something "wonderful" for him. He made a promise to help children if he could find a way to support his family. The next day he got a call for the job at The 51 Hundred Club. He was such a hit that the club became famous, and Danny went on to big things like, *The Danny Thomas Show* on TV. He also kept his promise to St. Jude, and built the St. Jude hospital for children, one of my favorite charities.

Vincent, John and I were enrolled in Our Lady of Lourdes School. I was in first grade and became Vincent's responsibility. We lived several blocks from the school, and he was given the chore of walking me home every evening. If he had a basketball game, I would have to sit and watch him until it was time to go home. So we became a team for the next 70 years. He was still looking out for me when he passed away at age 84.

When we were young, I'm sure he must have been tired of looking after me all the time. One day after school, I was waiting at the corner for Vincent to walk me home, and it seemed like a lifetime. Everyone had left, and the crossing guard asked me if I was all right. I told her that my brother would arrive any minute. As it turns out, Vincent had come out of school and ran home, forgetting me. I stood on the corner waiting and waiting, and finally decided to chance it on my own.

When Vincent got home, my dad happened to be home and asked him, "Where is Dorothy?"

Vincent said, "Oh, gosh I forgot her!"

My father was so angry. He said, "You did what?" Well, all hell broke loose, and just as they were running out the door, I came walking in all excited to tell dad that I made it home on my own. Dad still didn't let Vincent off the hook. He was grounded for a couple weeks, and he never forgot me again. Lucky me.

Dad and mom decided to move our family closer to school. They would both feel better. Mom found a nice apartment at 4842 N. Ashland Ave. It was three blocks from the school, and Chase Park, where I played most of the time. I was able to come home alone, and stop at the park to swing on the rings and attend free dance classes. There must have been 50 kids in the class, but in those days your parents knew where you were. My neighborhood was magic: the people, the sounds, the weather. Well, maybe not the weather. Everything was close. I could walk to the Uptown and Rivera Theatres, where I watched all the movie musicals that inspired me to dance like Betty Grable, Ann Miller, and my favorite, Eleanor Powell. I'm still trying to be her today in my eighties.

Chase Park was great for the young set. Besides the rings I loved so much, they had a swimming pool, and as I said before, dance classes. The teacher was very nice and said to me, "Dorothy, we will be having a recital in June, and I would like to give you a solo." She explained what she had in mind. I was all excited telling mom that I would be "little black Sambo."

Mom gave me a look and said, "Why would you want to be 'little black Sambo'…he's black?"

I never gave it a thought. "Does that mean I have to have a black face?" I asked.

"Well, yes," Mom explained.

I'm sure Mom thought it was funny. She didn't want to rain on my

"Goofus" routine, 1933

parade. She helped me with the costume and the black face, and got me a straw hat. I was the hit of the show. So there!!

Every Saturday, and during the summer after school closed, I would go to the movies. It was ten cents. Imagine! My friend Shirley lived in our building, and her mom would let her go with me. On the way to the theatre we had to walk from Ashland to Broadway, about eight blocks. We walked along the St. Bonaventure Cemetery, with a high concrete wall. Shirley and I liked to climb up on top and see how far we could walk without falling off. We never gave it a thought we might break our necks. At the end of the wall, we jumped off and headed for the theatre to see the movie. If it

Dorothy on Point, 1933

was a double feature, Shirley and I would go to the lobby, where we played king and queen on the gold leaf chairs. They looked like they could have come from a palace. Shirley use to say to me, "Dorothy, can I be the queen today?"

And I would say in my regal way, "No! I'm the queen." I guess I could have let her be the queen for a day, but it's too late now. Didn't that become a TV show? Hmm.

The uptown district was wonderful, and it had everything within walking distance: Goldblatt's department store, the Uptown and Riviera Theatres, the Uptown Bank and the Aragon Ballroom, where all the big bands played. I was not yet old enough for the Aragon, but little did I know, not too far in the future, I would be doing my own act and working with most of the bands that played there, including Eddy Howard, Lawrence Welk, and Dick Jergens.

Across from the Aragon was Madame Ludwig's Dancing School. The "L" train (the elevated train used as public transportation in the Chicago area) ran alongside the windows of the studio, but no one seemed to mind; we were too busy dancing. Mom signed me up for ballet and tap classes. It was only 50 cents a lesson, and I loved going to class. My first tap teacher, Cassie, was young and pretty. She taught me "the Irish washer woman," and believe it or not, I still use in my teaching classes. I was really sad when she left to get married, but then Bobby Rivers came in to teach tap, and I had a big crush on him.

Bobby was one of the people in my life that I wanted to emulate. Not only did I love his class, but I thought he was a kind young man. He had a big heart. After my dad died a year later and mom was struggling to pay the rent, I was given a scholarship.

I was able to attend dance class, but I had outgrown my tap shoes and mom could not afford to get me a new pair. I didn't care, as long as I was dancing. Then one day after class, Bobby called me over and said, "You know Dorothy, I was going through my taps and found a pair that are too small for my shoes. I bet they will fit your shoes!" And guess what, they did. Now that was magic! And that was kindness. He touched my life more than he ever knew.

My family started living a normal life. Dad had several contracts he was working on — the layouts for the Uptown Bank billboards and gold leaf work on their office doors and windows. He also had a big billboard contract with the Lincoln Tavern Night Club where big acts worked. Dad would paint their picture on the billboard. I can remember him driving mom and me out to see the one he did of Cab Calloway.

John was in high school at DePaul. He had a scholarship for track, and worked with my dad after school. John was a good artist, and it became his profession. In later years, he worked for the city of Chicago in their art department. Mayor Daley had a summer home where there was a tree that he thought would be a great totem pole. He asked John to come out to his home and design a Native American image for the pole. John did a beautiful job, and the mayor was quite pleased. Even with all the security around, the mayor let John take photos of his work.

Things tend to come in threes, and for the second time, a "tornado" hit home. But this "tornado" was of a different kind. It was 1929, and that was the year the depression hit Chicago with a bang. Everyone was affected by it, rich and poor. Dad was under a lot of pressure, and it caught up with him.

When Grandma Donnelly died in 1933, mom took Vincent and me to St. Louis for the funeral. John stayed home with Dad. They took a walk down Lawrence Ave. to the shop, and Dad collapsed on the way. There were no cell phones in those days, and John must have been in shock. He was able to stop a car, and they called an ambulance and rushed him to the hospital. He had a stroke, and would never be the same again. It was a sad time for Mom. She didn't know what to do, but then there is always an angel on your shoulder, and Mom had her angel.

When we arrived home, we went right to the Edgewater Hospital, where dad remained for a week or so. Then the doctor told mom to take him home with a nurse, and see how he did.

Mom could tell that he was unable to focus. Sometimes he knew her, and other times not. She must have been frantic not knowing if she could pay the nurse, pay the rent, and feed us! John was in the sign shop, trying to take over a "man's job," and finish the work that dad had started. As time went on, things got worse, and the shop had to go. Dad would wake up in the middle of the night and have no idea where he was. The beginning of the end came the night he got up and dove out the bedroom window and ran down the street. Thank God we were on the first floor, and the nurse was still with us. But not for long.

When Mom and Dad got married, Dad's best man was Red Smith. He was with the Cardinal baseball team in St. Louis. Red's brother, Gus, and his wife, Nonie, were friends of Mom and Dad's. They came to visit my dad, and could see he had to be in a hospital. So when the "window incident" happened, Mom called Gus. He told Mom that he would use his influence and see what he could do. Gus had a job with the state; he knew who to contact. He called Mom a few days later, and Dad was moved to a state hospital. Thank goodness for Gus. It gave Mom the freedom to find a job and get her life together. I was not allowed in the hospital, but when Mom would go to visit, I would go with her and he would wave to me from the window.

After three years in the hospital, Dad passed away in 1935 at the age of 42. I never really got to know my father, but I do know I have his "gift of gab," and his smile. And I'm so glad, because I thought he had a great smile.

Chapter 3: The Beauty Shop

During the three years dad was ill, mom had to figure out how she was going to make a living. Everything stopped for us except our hearts, and thank goodness we were all in good health.

Mom had to figure out how to pay the rent and all the other bills that kept arriving in our mailbox. She went to the Catholic charities for help, but they turned her down because dad had left her a $7oo insurance policy, out of which she had to pay for taking my dad to St. Louis to be buried. But it didn't matter; they told her when the $700 was depleted, she could come back. She never did, but instead went to the relief department, which gave us a small pittance. After all, this was the depression, and everyone was on relief. They delivered a box of groceries to many houses every week. John was doing any job he could get, but the pickings were small. John had to quit DePaul and go to Senn High School in our district. Actually, Harvey Korman and Shecky Green went to Senn. Both became big television stars.

Mom decided to call her brother John in St. Louis and ask him to loan her $300 so she could register at a Beauty School located downtown. John was a crap dealer at the Mounds Country Club across the river from St. Louis. He had not been affected by the depression and was happy to send the money. Mom registered at the school in June. I was out of school for the summer, so she decided to send me to St. Louis to stay with my Aunt Mae and her two brothers John and Phil. She needed to be alone so she could study for the state board she would have to take to get a license. Both John and Aunt Mae had jobs, but Phil was out of work so he was home. Aunt Mae worked at the shoe factory as a pattern cutter. They were really good to me and I had a great summer.

When I first arrived in St. Louis, Aunt Mae was really glad to see me. "Our first weekend venture will be shopping and lunch downtown? How about that?" she asked me.

"Aunt Mae, can I get my hair cut? I want that new style called the Wind Blowin.' It's so cute." I replied.

She asked if my mom would approve and I lied, "Oh she won't care."

I talked to mom and she said, "Do not get your hair cut! It will be standing on ends." You see, I have no curl in my hair but I wanted to look like a girl I saw in a picture. So off we went to the beauty shop. I was adorable when we left the shop, or at least I thought so. I figured it would grow out by the time I went back home in August. Starting the next morning after the cut, it was standing on ends, but I had to live with it. I guess the old saying is true: mother knows best. At the end of the summer I arrived back in Chicago, and Mom met me at the train station. She took one look and just shook her head. She said, "I hope you're happy. You look like a porcupine."

In Aunt Mae's bedroom, there was an old sewing machine that belonged to my Grandma Donnelly. On the side of the machine, there were three drawers referred to as "the money drawers." When Aunt Mae would be leaving for work she would say, "Darlin'," if you need anything just take it out of the money drawer." It was like I had my own bank. I had made many friends with the kids on the block, and I had my money drawer, so everything was coming up roses. The kids in the neighborhood were rehearsing for a big festival at the stadium about five miles from the house and they invited me to join them. I was having a grand old time, especially with my money drawer.

The first time we left for rehearsal I said, "So how far is this?"

They replied, "Not far." Well, it was five miles one way. The next day, I told the kids that I was treating them to a ride on the streetcar. The fare was only three cents per kid or 18 cents for six kids. They thought it was swell. We walked one way, and then hopped on the streetcar after rehearsal.

When Aunt Mae came home that night she said, "How was your day darlin'?" I was thrilled to tell her how I treated all the kids to a streetcar ride. She said, "You did what? So now you're the big shot of the neighborhood, let the kids pay their own way."

I could not believe this was coming from my sweet Aunt Mae. I said, "Aunt Mae, that's a long walk and we're really tired after the rehearsal."

She replied, "If you want to walk with the kids, fine; if you want to take the streetcar, fine. You have your three cents, but I'm not paying for the neighborhood."

Well I really wanted to be with the kids, so we all walked both ways from then on. I still had the money drawer but my big shot days were over. I could get anything out of Aunt Mae, not that I wanted to take advantage. But she was so good hearted; you just couldn't help but get what you wanted. Gosh that sounds awful, but I do remember her with fondness and love. She was one of a kind and I'm so glad to have had her in my life.

The Donnelly household was a house of laughter. Aunt Mae, Phil and John were born with fun in their bones, so I was in a happy place most of the time.

One evening, Aunt Mae and I were sitting in the kitchen talking when the phone rang. I heard Aunt Mae say, "Oh fine Jean, no problem. I'll see you later." She turned to me and said, "We're going out for a drink when Jean finishes her shift at the hospital, so honey, her boyfriend will be coming over. When you hear the bell, bring him into the living room and give him a glass of lemonade, OK? I'll be in the basement doing the laundry."

About 15 minutes passed and the bell rang. I said, "Hi, come on in! Would you like some lemonade?"

He seemed puzzled and asked, "Where is everybody? Where is Jean?"

I replied, "Oh, she'll be along as soon as she finishes her job."

Whereupon he said, "I didn't know she had a job."

I responded, "Oh yes, didn't you know she's a nurse?" I left to get the lemonade, and just then Aunt Mae came upstairs. I said, "He's here already. I'm getting him the lemonade."

We walked into the living room and Aunt Mae looked at me oddly and asked, "Who is he, Dorothy?"

I said, "Well, you should know — he's your friend."

The young man stood up and asked, "Is Jean home? I have a date with her at 7 pm and it's now almost 8. I asked Dorothy where everybody was and she said in the basement." Aunt Mae decided to cross-examine him.

Just to interject for a moment, there was a lovely family who lived three houses down from us and they had three daughters, two my age. I had become good friends with them. They were part of the walking group. Another sister, about eighteen, also had the name Jean. Well you got it… he was in the wrong house waiting for the wrong Jean and an hour late for his date. Aunt Mae sent him on his way and I said to her after he left, "I thought he was too young for our Jean."

She just looked at me and said, "Dorothy, you are one of a kind."

The next day I saw Jean, who thought she had been stood up. She laughed and said, "You were trying to steal my boyfriend." Could this happen in a million years: two boyfriends and two Jeans!

We didn't see much of Uncle John. He would sleep most of the day since he worked most of the night, but sometimes he would get up early and say, "Come on Dorothy. Let's take a drive." He had a car with a rumble seat and I thought he was so classy. He looked like Bing Crosby. We would have lunch and I loved that. We would go to one of the restaurants where he hung out and knew everybody, and tell them I was his niece. He would say, "Okay kiddo, is there anything you need?"

And I usually would say, "No." And he would hand me a couple dollars and tell me that a lady should never be without money so I should buy myself something.

Uncle John had been in World War I and had seen action, but he never talked about it. He married a nice gal and her name was Dorothy. I was the junior bridesmaid at their wedding and wore my first long dress. When I was about 19 years old, John died of leukemia, much too young.

Dorothy in her new coat, with muff, 1930

Uncle Phil was fun. He would say, "What would you like for lunch?"

And I would respond, "I suppose spaghetti." I loved his spaghetti. He made it with tomato soup and onions. It was not too Italian, but it was Italian enough for me.

After dinner, it was time for a beer or ice cream soda. As you know, St. Louis is hot in the summer. They said you could fry an egg on the sidewalk. To stay cool, Uncle Phil would say, "Dorothy, take the bucket and go down to the saloon on the corner and get me a ticket of beer." I would take the money out of my favorite drawer, pick up the chrome bucket that would hold about four glasses of beer, and take off to have it filled.

There were no questions asked if I was 21 or ten. I would give it to the bartender and he would fill it up and tell me to say "hi" to Phil. I would carefully carry it home to Uncle Phil and Aunt Mae and I would have an ice cream soda — vanilla ice cream and cream soda, those were the days, my dear! We would sit on the back screened-in porch and talk the night away, no television. Aunt Mae would talk about how her mother came over from Ireland in a sailboat. I'm still trying to figure that one out, and how grandpa, who was a hod carrier, would complain about all the foreigners. He forgot he was a foreigner! But then, I love the fact he loved America so much that he didn't think he was a foreigner.

At the end of the summer, it was time for me to go home and back to school. Aunt Mae decided we should make one last Saturday jaunt downtown, have lunch, and shop for my school clothes. I was delighted, and so we took the bus, had lunch, and were off to Famous Barr, the big department store. We made our way to my section, only because I knew the way from being there many times before. Let's face it — it was all about me.

The first purchase was a new winter coat, and I found this dream coat that (as usual) I couldn't live without. It had a fur collar with a hat and muff. Well, the muff did it for me. And it was mine along with several other items. Just as we were about to leave, I saw this navy blue taffeta dress with a v-neck and puff sleeves. So I started my campaign, and Aunt Mae said, "No, it's too old for you."

I begged, "Aunt Mae, I love it!"

She replied, "You're not getting another thing."

She stuck to her guns, and I thought to myself, "You've lost this one."

Then Aunt Mae said, "Come on, Dorothy, we have to catch the bus." But I continued to talk about the dress right up until we got to the bus. "All right," Aunt Mae relented. We turned around, walked back into the store, and I got my dress. I think she was feeling sad that I was leaving, but on the other hand, I think she really enjoyed me. I hope so, because I loved her a lot. And I hope she knew that, and if not, she knows it now.

When it was time to leave, she took me to the train and gave me money so I could go into the dining car for lunch, no packing a sandwich for me. It was five hours to Chicago. I had on my new dress with the v-neck. Aunt Mae had said to me, "Don't you think that's a little much for the train?" I told her that I wanted to look nice in the dining car. I gave her a big hug and told her that I would miss her and be back soon. She was probably thinking, "I hope not for awhile." I took myself into the dining car, sat next to the window, and watched the world go by as the nice waiter with the white jacket took my order. I informed him I had a tip for him, and he just smiled. The big shot was returning.

When I arrived in Chicago, mom was waiting for me. Now this was August, and I had my beautiful dress on, carrying my new winter coat and muff and a shopping bag full of things like roller skates. She said, "What happened to my little girl?"

I said, "I'm just fine. I had a great time! How do you like my dress?!" By the next day, I was back to normal and glad to be home with my family. We never mentioned the haircut. I didn't have my money drawer, but I was home.

While I was enjoying myself in St. Louis and having the run of the house, my mom was struggling to overcome her fears. Mom had started her beauty course. She was very creative with her hands, so learning to cut and shape hair, finger way and marcel was no problem, but the theory part of the course was hard. Since mom did not go beyond the 7th grade, she found it difficult. That is when Jean Gillespy came into her life and pulled her through to get her license. Jean was also taking the course, but unlike my mom, who could do anything with her hands, Jean was a smart gal and the theory came easy to her. She would take mom aside and work with her. Years later, I had a chance to pay Jean back for what she did for my mom … but that will come later.

Mom took the exam and got her license. It was time to get a job. She was worried about me being alone after school, but you have to do what you have to do! She had always taught us to be responsible. She took a job in a department store beauty shop. It was a good beginning for her, but she was not making much money. So, she decided to turn our bedroom into a shop. We moved everything out, John made a sign for the front window, and we blocked off the living room with a screen. Fortunately, we were in the front apartment, so everyone coming down the street could see the sign and we were in business. It wasn't Elizabeth Arden's, and we didn't have a red door, but it was Alice's Beauty Shop. The boys had gone out and found a hair dryer, shampoo board and a small table for manicures.

All our neighbors and friends came to Alice. A finger wave was 25 cents, a marcel was 35 cents, because you had to use electricity for the curling iron, and a manicure was 35 cents, but then our rent was only $27.00 a month. I do believe the shop was the beginning of my love of people. We knew everyone in the neighborhood and they use to call me their Dorothy. They would say, "So Alice, how is our Dorothy?" And years later, they followed my career and would send me homemade fudge because I told one lady her fudge was the best in the world (and I meant it!). Another gave me an evening gown to take with me to South America. Kindness was the name of the game in those days, and they are etched in my mind forever.

Chapter 4: You Can Choose Your Friends, But Not Your Relatives!

Let me just say, I really loved most of my relatives. Most of them were full of life, had a zest for living, and never seemed too run down. It must be in the genes. When I look back on my childhood and teenage years, my family was always on the move.

Everyone during the prohibition days were making their own homebrew, or going to a speakeasy to satisfy their desire for a drink. When I look back, I wonder how freedom had been taken away from most of the people, and the nondrinkers ruled. As I always say, "A little vodka couldn't hurt." Once more, the majority lost. There was lots of money to be made, so let freedom ring for the few.

My dad's cousin, Lill Sadler Amorosa, and her brother Johnny Sadler, had a natural talent. Lill played the ukulele and guitar, and her voice wasn't bad either. Johnny played piano by ear. He could sit down and knock off any tune in a minute. The two of them were a great team, but they didn't know it.

Lill's first husband was one of the boys in the rackets. I can remember as a kid, looking at the beautiful diamonds Lill wore, especially when she was playing the ukulele. She made the instrument come to life. She had that Mae West approach, and when she came into a room, she made an entrance. Remember, "Sophie Tucker"?

Life with the diamond man became a little too much for Aunt Lill, as I called her, and they divorced. She took her diamonds, cashed some of them in, and had enough left over to make her happy. With her brother

Johnny and her new husband Jimmy Amorosa, they opened the Florentine Gardens in Niles Center, a suburb just outside of Chicago. The Florentine Gardens was a combination restaurant, bar and nightclub. There was not much out there at that time. It was mostly farmland. Niles was an unincorporated area and if you dug up the soil, you would find many Indian artifacts. Niles was close to Skokie, Illinois, where later in life, I lived with my husband. The name would give you a hint that the Indians had inhabited the area many years ago, but when I moved there in 1953, it was mostly Germans, Irish and Italians.

When Aunt Lill, Johnny, and Jimmy decided to open the Gardens, it was off a highway. With not much going on, it was a good choice at the time. About a mile down the road was Lill and Jimmy's house. They built it to be close to the Gardens. It was really beautiful, and I used to love to go there.

In the center of town was the Catholic church which had been there for a hundred years, and was the focal point of the town. As I remember, the town was made up of the church and the Florentine Gardens; not much else. I guess people went to church and then headed for the Gardens to have that drink they needed.

People have asked me where I got my talent from and I've always said, "I don't know." But now, I wonder if my talent didn't come from Lill and Johnny. They should have been in show business, but I don't think it ever dawned on them. I remember the story they told about how Johnny had written a song called "Drifting Back to Dreamland" and it was stolen from him. But who would know in those days. It wasn't a perfect world. Unfortunately, it still isn't.

Mom and Dad would take us out to the Gardens for a spaghetti dinner, what else? Lill was married to an Italian man. They had a large dance floor in the center of the restaurant, with tables and chairs and booths on the side. They always had a full crowd. They would perform, and take requests, and the audience loved them.

Aunt Lill would come over to our table, take my hand, and announce, "My little cousin Dorothy is going to dance for you. When she grows up she's going to be a star. But right now she is my little star. Give her a big hand." Everyone would applaud. Johnny would play whatever he thought was a good tune for my number, and I would tap in the middle of the dance floor. When I finished, the crowd would throw me money. It was something right out of a 1930s movie. I thought this was a grand idea, and I always hoped my mom and dad would bring me back many times, and let me tap. After the first time, when I knew we were going to the Gardens, I asked if I could bring my tap shoes.

I said, "You know, let's give them the real thing." My dad gave me a look, but I put them in the car just in case.

One night we went to dinner, and I was looking forward to entertaining. But this night was a special one. There were two brothers known as the Touhy Brothers in the restaurant. They were bank robbers on the run. Aunt Lill knew who they were, but she just took their order, and hoped this was not a stickup. She wanted to keep things lively so no one would notice. She said, "Guess who is here tonight — my little star Dorothy." Oh, did I forget to tell you, I was only about eight or nine? She continued, "She would like to do a number for you, and she brought her tap shoes." Johnny sat down at the piano and started the music, and I tapped away. I guess Lill thought the bank robbers wouldn't hurt a kid. When I finished, the brothers threw several coins out on the floor. I wonder if they were from the banks they robbed. My family knew that Dorothy saved the day. At the time, I just thought they liked my performance.

Aunt Lill had one son, Jackie, who was the apple of her eye. When he was in high school, he was six feet tall, and a good-looking kid. He and I were close in age, just six months apart. We had our graduation party from grammar school together at the Gardens. Jackie and I really liked each other and had fun together. By this time, my dad had died and Aunt Lill was still counting on me being a star. Once I was in show business, and doing my own act in the Empire Room of the Palmer House, in Chicago, she was so proud of me.

Jackie and I would double date with our respective escorts. Jackie had a convertible, and why not with a mother that was crazy about you? Sixteen was the legal age to drive. We were only sixteen, going on thirty, or so we thought. I can always remember the four of us driving along singing with the songs on the radio "I don't want to set the world on fire, I just want to start a flame in your heart." Gosh, what happened to those good old days??

Jackie had some of Lill and Johnny's talent, but not enough to make it. He went to New York, and money was no object, but it didn't work out. He eventually came back to Chicago, and married a great gal named Sylvia. They moved to California, had one daughter, Mary, and four sons. The last I heard, they had a hotel on Catalina Island called the Glenmore Plaza Hotel. I think Jackie passed away a few years ago, but they were a big part of my growing up, and I'm glad I had them to grow up with.

Aunt Lill had to make a trip to St. Louis. She called my mom, knowing she had relatives there, and asked if she would like to drive with her. Mom said that she would love to, if she could take Dorothy and Vincent. Lill said that would be fine, since Jackie would be along as well. She picked us up early one morning, and told us kids to get in the back seat, but don't jump around back there.

We thought that was a strange request, but we did as we were told. Still, we had a good time laughing, and playing word games, and watching for the Burma shaving cream signs. Remember those? We had a song sheet with all the popular songs of the day, and sang all the way. We started hearing clicking every time we went over a bump, but then this was not exactly a super highway.

Finally, Lill said, "Kids, are you hungry? Let's stop for lunch. Watch for a restaurant." As we were all looking, she said, "I found one. See over there, it's the 'Go Me In' restaurant."

My mom looked at her, and said, "Lill, it's not the 'Go Me In.' It says 'Come In.'" We laughed all the way. After lunch, we returned to the car and noticed the back seat had moved. Something was rattling when we opened the car door. Aunt Lill got very serious, and told us: "Sit down easy. I don't want those bottles to break."

Mom said, "Lill, have you got booze under the seat?"

Lill replied, "Well yes, Alice. I just didn't want to alarm you. I'm taking it to a friend in need." My mother held her breath the rest of the way, and she was so glad when we passed over the Chain of Rocks Bridge into St. Louis. Lill made her delivery and all was well. The trip back was a lot more comfortable, and we were glad to be home. I guess Lill didn't have a return shipment.

Many years later, I was working at the Queen Mary in Long Beach, California. Jackie called, and asked if he could stop by with his sons and take me to lunch. It just so happened that I had the privilege of comps for VIPs, so I decided he was a VIP in my book and we went to the Sir Winston restaurant on the top deck. We had a lovely lunch and I got to know his sons. It is a nice memory to have.

Chapter 5: The Neighborhood Gossip

Mr. Eich was the son of the owner of our apartment building. The first of every month, he came to collect the rent. One month, he arrived at the door and said, "Alice, I see you have gone into business. I noticed the sign in the window: "Alice's Beauty Shop."

Without taking a breath, my mother said, "Bill, it's a good thing this apartment is in the front of the building, so people will know I'm here. You know, I have my beauty license, and I'm ready to go. I have to make a living for myself, and my three children. You see, Bill, I'm sure once everyone knows I'm here, they will come to me to have their hair done. They can see the sign in the front through the window, and in no time at all, I'm sure I will have a flourishing business. I won't have to worry about the rent or feeding the kids."

I do believe Bill was in shock, as he said, "Alice, you know this apartment is not zoned for business. I don't think you can have a business here."

What was her next move? She quickly retorted, "If I can't have my business here, then I won't be able to pay the rent, and we will be on the street. So it's your move, Bill."

Bill was young, and very sympathetic. He knew the depression had caused many people to be displaced, with no jobs and living on relief. He didn't want to add to mom's grief, so he took the rent and said, "OK Alice, I do hope your business flourishes." I wonder if that would happen today. I think we know the answer to that.

The bedroom was now known as "Alice's Beauty Shop," and it was open for business. She had one dryer, a table for manicures, a dresser and chair, a shampoo board in the bathroom, and chintz curtains on the window to make it look bright and cheerful.

The closet in the room was a two way closet. If you opened it from the shop, you could walk around the pull-up or pull-down bed, open the other door, and be in the living room. Mom and I slept on the pull-up. Every night, we pulled it down, hopped in, and had a good night's sleep. In the morning, we jumped up, straightened the sheets, flipped the bed into the closet, moved the furniture back into place, and the living room was back in order. As the saying goes, "If you build it, they will come." Indeed they did. Mom's appointment book was full, and we were all so grateful.

The only thing lacking was a permanent waving machine. One day from out of heaven, a man called and said he had a new cold wave machine, as he called it. It had just come on the market. He gave mom a demo, and told her to keep it until he returned in a few weeks. She could try it, and if she liked it, she could purchase it. Well, he never came back, and mom was the proud owner of the cold wave machine. Somehow, it was kind of strange, but we didn't ask. Mom had another angel on her shoulder, and was very busy giving everyone in town a cold wave permanent.

John and Vincent slept in the dining room on a daybed, with a screen around them, just in case some of the ladies wandered into the living room. We all had sweet dreams, but I vowed that someday, I would have a lovely bedroom. That day did come, but those fond memories will always be about almost sleeping in a closet.

Mom should have put out a newsletter. All the ladies came in to talk and exchange the happenings of the week. Unlike today, no one was malicious. It was all fun and jokes. One of the ladies was Viola Carter, better known as "Carter," for reasons I will relate presently. Carter was a looker, as we used to say, and had great wit. She was full of fun, and she and my mother became great friends. She came into the shop one day out of the blue for an appointment, and after that, she had a weekly appointment for a shampoo and finger wave. Carter always gave a big tip, which made mom very happy. She would say, "Alice let's have a highball." And since this was our apartment, Carter assumed we must have a bottle of whiskey some place in the kitchen.

Mom would tell her, "It's for medicinal purposes. Not a good idea. Carter, you're under the dryer, and the heat will get you."

Carter would laugh and come back with, "If you knew the heat I've had in my life, this heat is just a breeze."

Carter had two adopted daughters, Viola "Jr." and Patsy. The girls also went to Our Lady of Lourdes. I knew them, but not well. Viola, Jr. was three years younger, and Patsy was in first grade. Carter didn't work, had a lovely apartment, and didn't seem to have any financial problems. She enjoyed men, and was on her fourth husband when we got to know her. His name was Wally. She did marry him – twice! When she decided a relationship was over, she would call the locksmith, and have the locks changed. On her next hair appointment, she would say, "Alice, another one is gone. I think I'll go back to the church." And go back she did. They always had open arms for her, and she was forgiven for making another mistake.

*Chicago Sunday Brunch
with Viola Carter, the widow of
Dean O'Banion, 1970*

As each divorce was final, and the Monsignor would welcome her and say how nice it was to have her back. Money really counts when you're having fun!

Carter didn't have many lady friends. She was a man's woman, but she liked my mother. She invited mom out to dinner one night and told mom a little about her life in the fast lane. She and her sister Vivian were twins. They were raised in Canada. When they were 17, their mother passed away. Their father sent them to boarding school, but it was not to their liking, and they asked their father if they could move to Chicago where they had relatives. He gave his consent, and the two of them were off for fun and adventure. They found a little of both.

In her wild days, Carter met and fell in love with an Irish waiter, who was full of charm, by the name of Dean O'Banion. She married him, and the rest is history. Books that mention him always refer to his young days as an altar boy at Holy Name Cathedral in Chicago. Later on, they were probably saying, "another Catholic gone wrong." And now I'll tell you how he went wrong.

*Viola Carter, with her two adopted
daughters, Viola Marie and Patsy
Viola Marie married my
brother Vincent.*

33

When prohibition came into law, buying and selling alcohol became a crime. But that didn't stop most people. So everyone went underground. People still wanted to drink, and so the speakeasy was born. It was a large or small nightclub behind closed doors. Some even had a password to get in. This, of course, meant big business!

Dean was already a waiter, so he knew the "in and outs" of the business, and the right people. He went into business for himself, and found the source to supply his willing customers that would pay big bucks. Dean had the north side of Chicago tied up. Unfortunately, on the south side, the notorious Al Capone was the other supplier. The two gangs started fighting over territory, and it got nasty. At first, one or the other gang would lie in wait and hijack a truck, or break into a warehouse and steal the contents or smash the bottles.

Not everyone went to speakeasies. They made their own homebrew in their bathtub, better known as "bathtub gin." As the gangs got more powerful, each gang wanted to take over the other gang's business, and that's when the killing started. It was a sad time. Police would raid the speakeasies and arrest everyone, then haul them off to the station. Usually, the place would reopen the next night. They did keep the police busy, but then the police were being paid off, and waiting for the next raid.

Dean O'Banion was not only an altar boy, but he loved flowers. So what's wrong with that? I'm sure, every time there was a murder, he sent flowers. He would have had many orders; it was a profitable business.

He opened a floral shop across from the cathedral, which turned out to be his undoing. He was in the shop one day tending his flowers, when three men walked in. They had a chat, then pulled out their guns, and shot Dean in the back of the head.

Carter, being so young at 19, was in shock, but she did survive and got through it. Dean had told her if anything happened to him, to get to the safe deposit box immediately. Thank goodness she was good at taking directions. She didn't walk, she ran, and what surprises she found I do not know, but we all remained friends and relatives all our lives. She adopted her girls, changed her name to Carter, and got on with her life.

When the war came, she got a job in a defense plant, continued getting married, and continued changing the locks. Viola, Jr. married my brother Vincent, and in 1966, they moved to Las Vegas. Carter decided she might like a change since she was getting older. She had no more locks to change, and the desert weather might be beneficial for her. As it happens, sometimes, daughters with snappy mothers have a few problems. Vi, Jr. could not deal with all the fathers in her life as she was growing up, although her sister Patsy had no problem with it. They had different personalities, and there was conflict between Vi and Carter all the time. It was a love/hate relationship. Patsy and her family were also living in Vegas.

Carter moved into an apartment in Vegas, but after a while there was a problem. Carter didn't drive, and didn't have a car, so she was confined to the apartment. This was very hard on such an active, independent woman.

Public transportation was out of the question. The 120-degree heat would be too much for her to wait for a bus to go anywhere. And so it was decided she should move in with Viola and Vincent. Bad move.

Before long, Viola and Carter where hitting heads. The next I heard, Viola had put Carter out on the front lawn in the heat, and told her to go back to Chicago. Carter called Patsy to come and get her, and she packed for her trip back to Chicago. At the time, I was still in Chicago. Carter was living in an assistant living home on the north side, and would frequently call me. She would say, "So Dot, are you taking me to brunch Sunday?" I would say okay, and when I picked her up, she would tell everyone I was her daughter. She was a colorful, fun person, and I'm glad to have known her.

After the war, Vincent opened a restaurant and bar on Lawrence and Ashland Avenue, just a couple blocks from where we lived, called the Steeplechase. It was a great place and everyone loved Vincent, due to his wit and fun-loving ways. He always had music playing, and hired a blind piano player named Sykes. Sykes had a big following, and so the place was a great success.

Sykes would sit at the piano and several of the regular customers would yell out a request. Sykes would say, "Is that you, Charlie?"

One night, Charlie yelled back, "You know Sykes, I think you're peeking." Of course, everyone howled.

Another night, Vincent wanted to be sure Sykes got home okay. He lived two blocks from the restaurant, but going home at 2 a.m. was tricky for him. The gas station across the street had an oil pit. Unlike today, the pit was cement and about ten feet below the ground. The mechanic would get under the car to change the oil. But the pit was not covered. So this night, Vincent said to Sunny, our cousin who was working for him, "Take Sykes home."

Well, you guessed it, Sunny decided to take a short cut. He didn't know about the pit, and the two of them fell smack into it. Can you imagine, it's pitch dark with one blind man, and one not playing with a full deck, trying to find each other and get out. It was kind of like Indiana Jones, and the lost tribe. Thank goodness they were okay.

The next night, when it came time to go home, Sykes said, "Vince, it's okay, I'll get home on my own."

I truly believe Vincent was my mother's favorite. I know you're not supposed to have a favorite, but he used to con her and she loved it.

This was before his marriage, and both he and I were still living at home. In the 1940s, that's the way it was. You didn't dash out and get an apartment when you were eighteen. He would come into our bedroom around 2 or 3 a.m., now that it was a bedroom again, and wake mom and me. Mom would say, "Vincent, what do you want?" He would then relate several happenings of the night, and we would laugh for the next hour with him. Even losing his leg in the war didn't bring him down. What a guy!!

Upstairs, over the Steeplechase, was a bookie. During the day, you could hear them calling the races. It was run by some of our "finest" politicians, who were in the 47th ward. They were friends of Vincent. They knew he had lost a leg in the war, so they decided he should run for alderman. Well, the man he was running against had been in politics for years, as was his father. So it was a fight to the finish, and there wasn't a "chance in hell" Vincent would win against that group. Just as well, Vincent was too honest. He would be for the "little guy," and as you know, the "little guy" doesn't count.

Chapter 6: Childhood Antics

After my dad took sick, I was still at Madame Ludwig's dancing studio every Saturday. She was my first dancing teacher in Chicago. I loved my ballet and tap classes. I had my first experience performing. Madame came into the studio, and told us we would be dancing at the 1933 World's Fair, on fair day. Sally Rand, the famous fan dancer, would also be performing, and trying to keep her fans in the right place. That year, we danced at the Knights of Columbus, and the Knickerbocker Hotel as well (big doings for me)! I was so thrilled not only to perform, but also get paid. I took that money home to my mom, and I was so pleased with myself. I just knew that this was what I had to do for the rest of my life. Mom put the money in the "kitty," and I don't mean the animal kind! Our family was big on money kitties. This experience really taught me not to live in fear of going on stage. It was

Scholarship letter from Madame Ludwig, 1933

so natural for me. I kept thinking, "Come on world, here I am."

I was back with Madame due to her scholarship. She sent mom a letter, offering me a scholarship so I could continue with the classes. Mom talked to her, and asked if there was anything she could offer her for this

37

kindness. Madame said, "Well, Mrs. Hunn, I know your husband passed away. He had a sign shop, and your son was working with him. Would it be possible for him to touch up my sign on the side of the building?"

Now this is the side of the building where the train (the "L," as we called it) whizzed by every five minutes. So Mom said, "I think the boys can manage that." And so the comedy of errors began. Very reluctantly, Vincent, who was only interested in playing cards, hopped on the scaffold. John ordered him to take it up to the second floor, with the paint buckets, and brushes and a prayer in his heart. Up he went, pulling one side, then the other, not too sure what he was doing. But, he decided not to look down.

John was yelling at him, "Now lower the scaffold!" So he did, and nearly fell off, but he made it. He was happy to be on the ground again, but as soon as he hit the

Dot tapping, 1933

Ice Skating Tap Number with Mary Alice Brewer, 1935

ground, John gave another command. "Okay Vin, time to head up again." Poor Vincent. Up he went again, but this time he forgot to take John with him. By now he had the hang of it, took it down, and both took the ride up ready to go to work painting. John, being the older brother, told Vincent how to accomplish their task. John had already worked with my father on high jobs, so this was a joy ride for him. But Vincent kept telling John, "Don't rock the scaffold! There's nothing to hang on to!"

38

Just then the "L" train whizzed by, and everything rattled and rocked, including the paint. Vincent finally got the hang of it, and that's not a pun. The sign was done. Vincent told Mom, "John can be the artist, this is not for me." Madame was pleased with their work and did give the boys something extra.

In the musical *A Chorus Line*, the cast sings a song, "What I Did for Love." In this case, from Vincent's point of view, it was "What I did for my Sister." Growing up with John and Vincent was fun never a problem or a dull moment. They always looked after me, and I could never imagine life without them. But then, that time does come in life, and all you have are memories. But they are great ones for me!

My dad was much harder on the boys than he was on me. I guess it's because he had been their age once upon a time. I always remember mom saying, "Dad could cuss with the best of them, but the boys better not utter a word."

Once, Vincent asked for a bike. And my dad said, "No, you're not riding on the street and getting yourself killed." But then I asked, and my wish was granted. I was only seven or eight, and I got a small two-wheeler. One day, mom asked me to go to the store for a package of jell-o. So I hopped on my bike and decided to take a short cut through the back alley. A young man in a truck came along and didn't see me. The next thing I remember, I was in the hospital. I flew off the bike and landed on my back. Thank goodness I was okay. My back was bruised and sore for weeks, but I lived. My bike days were over.

Here's another "save my little sister" from Vincent. There was a girl named Wendy, and not from Peter Pan. She tried to send me flying off my bike several times. When I first got my bike, I was only allowed to ride past Mr. Thompson's grocery store, not far from my house. Wendy was always in front of the store, waiting to make trouble. She was older than me. She would be waiting until I got to the turn around, and bang, she would hit the bike and I would fall off. I asked her to stop, but it fell on deaf ears. One day, I came home with bloody knees and hands. Wendy didn't know it, but it was over for her.

Vincent took one look at me and said, "What happened to you?" He grabbed me, and down the street we went. He took Wendy by the arm and held her against the store wall. Then he turned to me and said, "Punch her now."

I said, "I can't."

And he said, "Yes you can — now!"

So I did. He looked at her and told her to keep her hands off of me or the next time, he would be the one punching. After that, when she would see me coming, she would disappear.

Madame Ludwig eventually decided to give up the school, and my heart was broken. Why? She had a new sign, and all seemed right with the world. We never found out why. She was just gone after the summer, and my scholarship was — gone!

When mom and I would take the bus to the loop, it would go down Michigan Avenue. Mom looked up at a second floor window, and observed the sign saying, "Gladys Heidt School of Dance." Mom said, "Should we?" And I said, "Yes."

We got off the bus, crossed the street, and walked to the second floor. I often wondered why I was always on the second floor. A lovely lady greeted us. Could she be the teacher?? No, she had teachers. She gave us a tour of the studio. It was beautiful, with big plate glass windows across the front looking down on Michigan Avenue. My first thought was, "We can't afford this, especially since my last school was free." Then I was thinking to myself while mom was talking to Miss Heidt, "Gosh, I would be taking the bus and coming to the loop all by myself." And – well, I rather liked the idea.

I heard mom say, "Alright, Dorothy will see you on Saturday." So once again I clicked my heels, and I was on my way.

After a few weeks, Miss Heidt invited me to take four classes a week, and I nearly burst with joy. One day after class, Miss Heidt called me into her office and asked if I would like to take piano lessons.

"Would I?" I said. "You bet!"

Her mother was a piano teacher, and Gladys thought her mother could have her hair done for the lessons. What a deal. We had an old upright piano. And so, once a week, Mrs. Heidt would appear, and we would "c-d-e-f-g" for an hour. I loved her, even though I was like a barter kid. You know, ten chickens for ten apples. But it all paid off.

Just for a moment, let's go back to my transportation to the loop for these great classes. With dance bag in hand, I would walk to Wilson Avenue, which was about five blocks from our apartment, to catch the bus. On my first day going it alone, I was all excited and thought, "I will ride on the top deck, what fun! At the bus stop, I will sit down and wait for the double deck bus." Every other bus had a double deck and I could hardly wait to take the steps to the top deck.

I was all set to leave the house when mom had a few words of wisdom for me. "Dorothy, this is your first time going to the loop alone and I know you will be fine but if you take the double deck bus do not go up to the

State and Lake Theatre, 1936
My big moment, 4th from right!

second deck. I don't feel safe with you up there." I was crushed, but didn't go up.

In all of my many years taking trains, planes and busses, I could never bring myself to go to the top deck of a bus.

Then Ken, I'll tell you about him later and I were in London a few years ago, and we jumped on one of their fabulous two-deck busses. I followed Ken to the top

without even thinking about it. Suddenly Mom's words came back to me, but it was too late. I was on top of the world and it was wonderful.

Then came the most exciting thing of my unknown career. Gladys announced that a group of us would be performing at the State Lake Theatre, across from the Chicago Theatre, on a real stage. We had white ties, tails, and top hats. I guess you know what the routine was. I'm "Puttin' on My Top Hat." The big day came, and when I hit that stage, it was magical.

After a year, Gladys closed her studio. Talk about closing a show? I kept closing studios.

I was twelve, and mom heard about a studio on Ashland and Montrose, on the second floor, what else? The Chicago Academy of Theatre Arts! A long name, for such a small studio, with a mirror, dance barre, and a piano.

Marguerite Comerford was the teacher, and Fred Weaver, the director of what? I never knew! But I loved Ms.

Chicago Academy
of Theatre Arts, 1938

41

Comerford. She was a great tap teacher. I can truthfully say that she was my best teacher at the time. She gave me the kind of advanced tap I had never had before, and I could not get enough of her classes. She took an interest in me. She took me to my first ballet, the Ballets Russes. I was mesmerized! And suddenly, I was going to be a ballerina. Unfortunately, in the 1940s, the ballet was not appreciated, and the theatre was only half full.

Then one day, she asked me if I would like to train as a teacher. I said "yes" to everything in those days. So the training started and one day, I had my first teaching class. Two young boys were in the class, Charles Grass and Bob Fosse. Bob was about ten or eleven; I was thirteen going on fourteen. Mr. Weaver took Charles and Bob under his wing, and worked with them so they could perform. So all three of us did shows at the Elks Club, and Knights of Columbus. I remember my brother, John, getting us a booking at the Lincoln Tavern, a nightclub in a suburb of Chicago. We thought we were big stuff. I was just getting the hang of it when Ms. Comerford left to get married, or so the story goes. I did continue to teach after she left, but I was not a happy camper working with Mr. Weaver. So one day, I just told him that I had to move on. And move on I did, to the Merriel Abbott School, in the loop. How many people can say they taught Bob Fosse when he was just a little guy? And how wonderful to watch him become the famous choreographer.

I graduated from grammar school, and what a year. I had this mean nun who disliked me, mostly because I loved to dance. And let me say, a little dancing in her life might have helped her small mind. Second, I was not one of the rich kids in the class. The seating in the class went from smart, to average, to dumb! I was in the second to the last row. Right then and there a child would say to oneself, "I guess I'm not smart, or even average!?!?" and become intimidated. But my mom thought I was darn smart, and encouraged me to ignore all the pettiness. It's so amazing the things that stick in your mind about your youth.

Valentine's Day arrived that year, and all the girls were giddy, wondering if they would be receiving any valentines. I didn't give it a thought. All I wanted to do was go to the studio, and dance! After lunch, the priest came in holding a box and said to the nun, "Sister, I have just come from the eighth grade boys' room, with some valentines for the girls. Would you mind if I pass them out?" She gave him a nod, and he started calling out names. Lo and behold, the first name he called was "Dorothy." Being the only Dorothy in the room, I assumed it was me.

So, remember, I'm in the second to the last row. I walked up, took my valentine, and before I started back, he said, "Don't go away. I have several for you." The nun just glared at me, and I knew I was in trouble. The priest left, and the nun immediately called me to the blackboard, and gave me a problem that I would never be able to figure out.

And then, with her small-minded, malicious way, she took me down. "If you were not so interested in the boys, you would be able to do your school work," she said.

I saw red! Me, who was always on my way to dancing school. I answered her back, which of course is not the Catholic thing to do. I said, "I'm not interested in the boys. The boys are interested in me."

Then all hell really broke loose. She said, "Don't you talk back to me." At that point, I set the chalk down, walked into the cloakroom, put on my coat, and walked out the door. I arrived home, and interrupted my mothers work schedule. I told her my story.

She said, "You go back after lunch, and inform her that I will see her after school." Mom "took care of it." It was over. But as you can see, at my age now, not forgotten. I did vow it would never happen to any of my children if I ever had any. And of course I did (my son Craig)! I had a few battles, but as I always say, "I won the war."

At this time in life, I was very religious. But then, that was only natural, when you attend Catholic school. I guess every girl in class wanted to be a nun — except me!! I just wanted to be Catholic, but I will say, those statues got to me. I loved all the pomp and ceremony, singing the lovely hymns at children's mass on Sunday, and being part of something beautiful. I loved looking at the statues of the Blessed Mother, St. Anthony, St. Therese and St. Jude. Every year there was the crowning of the Blessed Mother. I so wanted to be chosen for this special tribute to our lady.

I had watched the procession for seven years. But they were looking for a passive girl, with a "holy" appearance. I don't mean the Blessed Mother was passive, but that's the way they perceived her. I didn't fit the image. I was just as loving and holy as the next girl, but I wanted to look like Lana Turner. I'm sure the Blessed Mother knew I would have given her a crowning they would never have forgotten. I was meant to be a dancer, not a "crowner."

Mr. Finnegan was our gym teacher, and he was giving a gym exhibition before graduation. The eighth grade would be performing a jump rope tap number. This was my cup of tea, and Mr. Finnegan had me center front. My "favorite" nun came in and spoke to Mr. Finnegan, and the next thing I knew, I was in the back line. She told him my uniform was too short. Not true!! After the exhibition, the Monsignor came to the school to congratulate us on our performance. He then asked, "Why was Dorothy in the back line? I could see her, and she was very good." The nun didn't know where to go, but I spoke up and told him what she had said to Mr. Finnegan. He just looked at her, and then told me what an excellent job I did. "You see," he said, "you will always be found, even though you are in the back line! Just remember to find an opening, between the people in front of you, and go for it!" Well I've been "going for it" ever since. How am I doing, Monsignor?

The beauty shop was doing well. John was trying as hard as he could to make a dollar, and every dollar he did make, he gave to mom. Vincent was hanging out on the corner of Lawrence and Clark Street, with his buddies, Izzy and Sallie. They ran the newspaper stand for their dad. All the kids would meet there and pitch pennies. There was no money, and no jobs. The news stand was right in front of a saloon, and down the block was "The Rainbow Gardens," where many events were held. One was the dance marathon. Remember those? It was my favorite, and mom and I would go every chance we could to watch them dance around in couples. Most of the time, one of the couples would be holding on for dear life. Everyone was so tired but did not want to get disqualified from the competition, so they didn't want to give up.

As a group, they had an exercise time, and would walk around the block from the front of the Rainbow Gardens, from Clark St. to Ashland Avenue, and back to Clark Street. I could see them from our front window, sprinting along. Some of the contestants would perform in the evening if they had a talent.

Mom and I would sit in the bleachers. As time went by, the couples would be eliminated, until the last couple was left on the floor, and they won the cash prize. Red Skelton used to MC these events, before he got his break and became the great Red Skelton.

Years later, when I was working in the Empire Room of the Palmer House, a date and I went to see Gypsy Rose Lee at the Rainbow Gardens. Mike Todd, the famous producer, opened the Rainbow Gardens as a nightclub. Gypsy Rose Lee was a great entertainer, and I had the good fortune to see her there. I still remember her coming out as a southern bell, and slowly removing her gloves one at a time. She was a sexy lady. She played to the audience with such charm and savoir-faire. She was an extraordinary performer. As my friend, George Gobel, used to say, "They don't make them like that anymore!"

Chapter 7: The Abbott School

My mother's friend, Jean Gillespie, had helped mom get her beauty license. She had a daughter, Jean, who became Jean Horvath. But for now, Jean was just a little girl who also wanted to dance. Her mom enrolled her in the Chicago Academy of Theatre Arts, where I was taking class and teaching with Miss Comerford. Jean, Jr. was a few years younger than me, so she was not in the same class. But Jean, Bob Fosse, Charlie Grass and I were all in the dance recital together in 1938.

Twenty years later, Jean, Jr.'s son Jim studied tap with me in Chicago. Jean, Jr. and her family lived in Maywood, a suburb outside of Chicago. I was teaching a master tap class in the area, and it was advertised in the newspaper. Jean, Jr. saw the ad and called the studio. She inquired if I was Dorothy Dale. She went on to say she had seen me perform at the Chicago theatre. Her mother reminded her that Dorothy Dale is really Dorothy Hunn. I was so glad to hear from her and just thought she was calling to say hello, but then she went on to tell me about her son Jimmy, and his ambition to be in show business. Would I meet with him, she inquired. Suddenly my mind thought back to Jim's grandmother, Jean, and how she had helped my mom get her beauty license. I said, "Absolutely, have him meet me next week before my class."

He came and studied with me for two years. One day, I told him, "I've taught you everything I know. You need to move on." I sent him to a school in the loop where he would be taking class with professional dancers. He did move on, and eventually auditioned for Bob Fosse's production of *Dancin'*. When it opened at the Shubert in Los Angeles, my son Craig and I had front row seats. After the show, Jim arranged for us to attend the opening night party. You see how life works?

I am still in touch with Jim. Every time Ken and I go to New York, we get together with him. I'm very proud of all his accomplishments and so glad I was there in the beginning.

One day, my Miss Comerford was gone. She had taught me so much and I didn't even get to say goodbye. I'm sure she was tired of being the bread winner, as Mr. Weaver sat and told stories of his past. In Fosse's book, it does mention how he influenced Bob as a kid. But I never really knew what he was doing during the studio hours, except collecting the money.

Mr. Weaver did book us in small engagements. It was all wonderful, but we were not going to Broadway in those days. I'm sure he did see something special in Bob, and decided to capitalize on his talent. This is not to say Charlie Grass did not have a special talent as well. And he did go on to do many wonderful things. I just don't think Charlie had the same drive Bobby had. I also don't know why Mr. Weaver exposed Bob and Charlie to the Silver Cloud, a sleazy strip joint in Chicago, at the age of sixteen.

I did see Bob a few times after I left the academy when we were older. He was teaching at a dance studio in the loop, and good old Weaver was there too. We talked, and I learned that he was still plugging away. Bob was a nice kid and I really liked him. The next time I saw him was several years later, in a drug store around the corner from the Blackstone Theatre. I believe my date and I were going to see *Call Me Mister*. Since we were a little early for the performance, we decided to get a Coke. When we walked into the drugstore, I heard my name called out. "Dorothy Dale! Hey kids," Bob said to some of the chorus kids sitting at a table, "You want to see a great tap dancer? Here she is, Dorothy Dale!"

I asked him what he was doing in the show, and he said, "Oh, I have a little number." Well, that little number was sensational, and he was a sensation.

After Bob became famous, I always remembered how generous that statement was about me to the dancers that evening. When I moved on from being a student, and became a professional dancer, Ashland Avenue, and the Academy of Theatre Arts, was in the past, I never looked back.

Now, I'm fourteen and starting high school at Amundsen High (the same school Bob attended). It was time for me to get on with my dancing. I told Mr. Weaver that there was a lot I needed to accomplish, and so I had to find a new school with advanced teaching. He said okay, and I was on my way. The last time I saw Mr. Weaver was at his wake. I was happy to see Charlie Grass there as well. Charlie had married, had children and was still dancing. Ken and Charlie knew each other from working dance conventions, and one day, about ten years ago, Ken and I found his phone number and called him. He was in shock.

Back to Bob. He was working and couldn't make it to the wake. When I walked in, there were about eight of us. It was sad, but I realized Mr. Weaver did recognize Bobby's talent, and moved him in the right direction. You know the song "Everybody Needs Somebody Sometime."

Every Saturday in the Chicago newspapers was the nightclub section, with photos and coming attractions at the nightclubs, theatres and hotel show rooms. All the big bands like Tommy Dorsey, Jimmy Dorsey, Eddy Duchin, Ray Noble, and Chico Marx would be at one of the venues. At that time, Chicago was truly a toddling town. The Chez Parée would headline with Lena Horne, the Empire Room featured Hildegarde and the Merriel Abbott Dancers. I would always watch for the photos of the Abbott Dancers, with beautiful costumes. I wanted to be one of them.

I knew there was an Abbott Dancing School in the loop in the building next to the Palmer House Hotel. I told mom, and she told me to check it out. So I took the bus to the loop, found the address, and took the elevator up to the second floor. Another second floor! This would be a lucky second floor for me.

The lady at the reception desk was very nice. A woman greeted me, and she showed me the studio, where a class was in session, and boy, I was impressed. I thought to myself, "This is where I want to be! Like, now!"

She told me about the classes and the price. She said, "You take five classes a week: two ballet classes, tap, acrobatics, and high kick classes. This is the weekly schedule." The price was $15.00 a month. Wow, and of course, the price is unbelievable by today's standards.

I rushed home and gave mom all the information. And as usual, she said, "I think we can get that together, at least for three months. And then, we will take it from there." I dashed back to the studio, paid the first month, and signed up for the September session. It was the beginning of my career as a performer.

The school was run by, Merriel Abbott. She had been a gym teacher, with dancing experience in her youth. And by the time I met her, she was in her fifties. She hired wonderful teachers. She would bring them in from New York. She was very aware of everything going on in the studio. She had great style, and a sense of show business like I had never known. She was married to Dr. Lewin, who was a very prominent doctor. They didn't have children, and so I believe the Abbott girls became her children.

"Teacher," as she was called, or "Teach," was approached in 1933 to train a group of girls to perform in the Empire Room of the Palmer House Hotel in Chicago. She recruited twelve girls, and the Merriel Abbott dancers were born. They were not your usual chorus girls. Every girl had excellent training in all types of dance and acrobatics. They did aerials (cartwheels without hands), back and front flips, spotting walkovers, high kicks and splits. Teacher hired top choreographers. The costumes were designed for each girl, who was fitted right in the sewing room on the 2nd floor. Mariah was the head costumer and she was wonderful. Her costumes were outstanding.

When I started in the Empire Room, Dick Barstow was the choreographer. He later went on to become a world-renowned choreographer and the man who changed the look of the failing Barnum and Bailey Circus. He developed a new and glamorous look to it: the new sensational Barnum and Bailey.

Replacing Dick Barstow in the New Ray Noble Show

When he took over the Abbott dancers, his routines were sensational. The chorus line did aerials with tennis rackets, and trays that were painted to resemble 78 records. They would hold them in two hands, run, handspring, turn around and repeat. To watch eight girls do this at once in 1940 was really something. Just remember this was before *Cirque du Soleil.*

Circus director, choreographer Richard Barstow is dead at 73

New York Times News Service

NEW YORK—Richard Barstow, who began a theatrical career as a child dancer and for 29 years served as director and choreographer of the Ringling Bros. and Barnum & Bailey Circus, died here Saturday after a series of heart attacks. He was 73.

Barstow, a youthful-looking man with a full head of white hair and a lightning-like wit, left the circus four years ago.

His last major work was as director of the Jones Beach theater presentation of "Annie Get Your Gun," starring Lucie Arnaz in 1978.

Barstow never really retired. At his death he was working on his autobiography, "Fools Rush In."

Barstow, who never married, leaves no immediate survivors.

Dick Barstow Death Notice

"The Hunt Ball" was another memorable routine. The stage was set up with small privets about 8 feet apart in a circle. Each girl was costumed in a red equestrian jacket, riding boots and cap. One of the girls was small, and so she was the fox. The hunters were in a chase and the fox would do back flips, and cartwheels in and out of the hunters. But the acrobatics stayed mostly in the center, as the hunt girls would grand jeté over the privets. It was wonderful! 1-2-3-leap-1-2-3-leap – wow!!

Teacher also booked all the acts for the room, like Lena Horne and Jimmy Durante. Jimmy was a kick, and he loved to kid teacher. She had a thing about her girls going out with musicians — and acts!! She wanted her girls to marry out of the business, and have a normal life. In other words, doctor, lawyer — well maybe not an Indian chief, but someone to watch over us. She didn't think "show business people" were dependable. But then, I married a doctor, and it was the most boring time of my life. So who's to know what is right for someone.

But I digress. Jimmy Durante would say to teacher, "You have great looking girls!" And she would look at Jimmy and say, "If I catch you with one of my girls, you're through!"

He would come back with, "You know, you're da cutest one of all!" And of course, she would just laugh.

Besides Jimmy, every headliner wanted to play the Empire Room. Hildegarde, Liberace, Peter Marshall, and all the big society bands like Ray Noble, and Eddy Duchin. So now you can see why I wanted to be part of all this, and I will tell you how it came about.

Ray Noble

The first day of class, I arrived full of enthusiasm, not knowing what to expect. But I was ready for whatever came my way. It was a ballet class taught by Elvera, who had been with Teacher for many years. She was an excellent teacher. I was so inspired, and could not wait for the next class. The next day was the tap class, and I could hardly wait for the teacher to come into the room. Eddy Shavers was a young black man, and I liked him immediately. He was low-key and easy to dance with. My prayers were answered.

Then came the kick and character class. Acrobatics were very important, but so far, so good. No class was mentioned. You see, I was not an acrobat. So I was safe for the time being, but not for long. Teacher also brought in guest teachers from New York and Philly. One of my favorites was Dorothy Littlefield, who I just adored. She and her sister had the Philadelphia Ballet Company, and I understand they also choreographed the *Ice Capades.*

After a few weeks, I heard the rumor that Teacher would be returning from Hollywood, where the Abbott dancers (the line of girls) had just made a movie with Jack Benny. There would be a tryout for replacements in the line for the Empire Room. The girls in the replacement line were known as "scrubwomen." Every so often, Teacher would hold these auditions, and if something happened to one of the girls in the Empire Room, you could be the next one in line for her spot. Wow!

Eddy Shavers
Merriel Abbott Tap Teacher

But I was not a great acrobat, and had not yet had a class with Mr. Rozanas, who was a fabulous acrobatic teacher. Now, I could do a backbend and handsprings, but aerials? Oh, please! I needed two hands for every trick. So I was in panic. I knew that I wouldn't make it, and then a miracle happened. And it happened just in time, because I was on my last $15.00 for tuition. Eddy Shavers came to me and said, "Dorothy, you're a good tapper. And there's a tap contest in your future, when Teacher returns from Hollywood. I know you can win it. I want you to look good, put on a big smile and hit every tap!"

I ran home and told Mom, and she said, "Well, we have to make you a new rehearsal outfit." And the sewing machine came out. She made me pink shorts and a top, and I had white oxford tap shoes. I looked good. So, I knew I could tap great, and guess what? I did! But before that happened, I had the ballet, kick and character, and my one week of acrobatics. That turned out to be the only thing I didn't pass.

So now the big day arrived! I put on my tap shoes and walked into the dance room. The music started, and I could see Teacher watching me. I gave the performance everything I had. Then, it was over. It was time for the verdict.

"And the winner is...Dorothy Hunn!" Wow!! Teacher called me over, and said, "Come into my office, I want to talk to you." I was so nervous, I could hardly speak, but the hard part was over.

She said, "I know you're not an acrobat, but that can be fixed. You will start with Mr. Rozanas next week. He will make an acrobat out of you. But in the meantime, I am very impressed with your tap, and the way you handle yourself. So I am going to call Georgie Tapps, who is the headliner in the Empire Room in the present show. I'm going to ask Georgie to give you a routine for the next show. You will be in the 10 o'clock "little show." If you do okay, and the audience likes you, I will move you to the big shows."

The big show was with the headliner, the Abbott Dancers, and the big band with another act of some kind. The big show was at 8 p.m. and 11:30 p.m. The 10 p.m.

My first choreographer in the Empire Room of the Palmer House, 1940

"little show" was with the band, the featured vocalist with the band, and me. I could not *believe* what I was hearing, but I *liked* what I was hearing, and could hardly wait to get home and tell Mom and the boys. Two days later, I was in the rehearsal room with Georgie. He was a wonderful tap artist and so easy to work with. This man was a star. And here he was, working with this kid that, until a couple months ago, didn't know what the Empire Room was. He did work me hard. We tapped every day from 10 a.m. to 3 p.m. until the show opened.

Georgie wanted every tap clear. They call it tap dancing so hit the tap loud and clear. And believe me, that took a lot of energy. But it was worth it, 'cause even today, I want to hear clear taps coming from my taps. No air taps for me (air taps are what happens when the tap dancer doesn't hit the floor). I worked so hard that the calves of my legs locked. I had what you would call a Charlie Horse, and Teacher had to send me for a massage.

Show people are generous with their talent, and Georgie was one of them. He wanted me to succeed. He did two shows a night, and then the next morning was working out with me. Quite generous, sharing his talent with a new kid who had never done anything except the Elks Club.

My lesson from Georgie, I would always try to do the same for other dance students. Now I'm in my eighties and still dancing. When fans from the audience come up to me and ask, "Where do you get your energy?" I tell them I had many great choreographers in my life. Guess I wanted to be like Georgie, full of energy. He went on to other engagements, and I opened in the new show. I will never forget him and the knowledge I gained from this wonderful man.

Chapter 8: A New Name, and Several Encores!

Georgie went on his way to other engagements, and I opened in "The Merriel Abbott Review" with the Charlie Baum Orchestra, Singing Marines, Blanche Bradley, the DuPond Jugglers, and Dorothy Dale (me). It also featured the Abbott Dancers and Gary Stone was the master of ceremonies.

The next big surprise was the name change — mine!!

Teach called me in her office and handed me the entertainment section in the newspaper. She showed me the Palmer House/Empire Room advertisement for the new show. "Here you are," she pointed out, "Dorothy Hunn or should I say, 'Dorothy Dale,' your new name? Do you like it? I think it fits you." I was speechless, but there I was, big as life. This time, I was kicking my heels with the big time. True, I was in the ten o'clock little show, but you have to start somewhere. And I knew in my heart that I would make it to the "big shows." The wardrobe department was called in. They found me a short yellow lace costume that fit like it was made for me. So I was ready to tap my heart out. And by the way, I loved my new name. I guess she knew what she was doing.

The Empire Room was considered one of the most elegant dining rooms in the city. Victor Fritz Hagner was the long time *maître d'*. He wore tails and established the high standards of the room. There would be no talking during the show, or serving drinks, out of respect for the performers. The waiters were a class act and most had been there for years.

There was a secret door that led into the "backstage" of the Empire Room. The outside of the door was covered with mirrors. When it closed, it became part of the rest of the mirrored wall in the Empire Room. Behind that door was the dressing room for the Abbotts. We would come down from our rooms on the 23rd floor, get into our costumes, freshen up our makeup, and wait for our cue to go on.

That's where all the acts and the Abbotts would make their entrance through that door. We would run through the tables to the dance floor, which of course, when the lights went out and the spotlight hit, it became the stage for the show.

The Abbotts had a tradition before they headed for the stage. They would throw a kiss to the gold goat head at the top of the stairs.

I had a new name I didn't even know about, and it was already on the program, advertised in the news-paper, and I didn't know it was me! It was a lucky name for me. I was part of something that would be part of my life forever!!

Charlie Baum, Merriel Abbott, 1940

It was an opening night to remember, at least for me. The consequences that followed were very

Empire Room, Checking on the "Good Luck Goat" we'd kissed in the 1940s before going on stage for good luck, 1998

unexpected. I went through the mirrored door, gave the goat a kiss, and flew down the stairs as Charlie Baum announced, "Ladies and gentlemen, a newcomer to the Empire Room, Dorothy Dale!" Charlie gave the downbeat, and in that moment, I was a performer. When that spotlight hit me, I had this feeling that I made it. The first part of my routine was a soft shoe to "A Pretty Girl is Like a Melody." One chorus, then a tacit (no music)! Then I would beat off 1-2-3-4, the music would start up again, and I would start tapping to a very fast "rhythm beat" to the end. When I finished the applause was very good and I dashed off to find the goat.

But the applause continued (I guess the applause was better than I thought!) and Charlie called me back. Now understand, I did not have an encore prepared. I guess they thought I wouldn't need one. But when he called me back, he said, "Come on Dorothy, the audience would like to see a little more." Well, how could I let the audience down?

So I forgot the goat and headed back to the stage. What to do, hmm! So I said, "Okay, take it from the tacit." I beat out 1-2-3-4, and I repeated the "rhythm tap" again to the finish. I took a bow, and I knew I was in show business! And thought to myself, "So, they didn't think I would need an encore!"

Most people knew June Taylor who, for many years, was the choreographer for the Jackie Gleason Show on television. June had been an Abbott dancer, but had contacted tuberculosis. She was a good dancer, and one of Teacher's favorites, until she decided to go on her own several years later. She had been with Teach for many years and worked in the Empire Room. After she was in remission, Teach decided to keep her busy

Dressing Room! Notice photo hanging above the dresser on the side of the wall!
Sophie Tucker, 1998

while she recuperated. She hired her for the switchboard in the Empire Room, taking reservations.

She was also there to keep an eye on the girls. Hmm! To watch the routines, and be sure they were up to par. Then she would "report" to Teach. If the girls were reported a bit "ragged," of course, that would be reason for a rehearsal. She had her eye on me opening night, and had a lot to say to Teacher about my performance the next day. I thought I had really done well, and I knew Teacher was in the audience. Why did Teacher want to see me the next day? After all, the audience did want an encore!

When Teach called me in, she said, "Why are you doing an encore, when you don't have one?! You do not repeat the same number over!"

Trying to defend myself, I told her how Charlie had called me back. She said, "Okay, but don't do it again."

The next night, the same thing happened; applause, encore and all. And I was in her office again! She shook her head. "I know what happened. You did do a good cover up! And handled yourself like a pro, so…I'm putting you in the big shows!!" They made me a beautiful new costume. Red, white, and blue, solid sequins. And I got my encore, just in case!

Now to digress, In the 1980s, I was living in California. I saw in the entertainment section of the newspaper, an ad for a one-man show at the Westwood Theatre, "Whatever happened to Georgie Tapps?" I called and got my ticket, drove to Westwood, and watched this master of tap that had given me my first professional routine. He was in his eighties and I thought, "Will I be able to dance like him when I'm 80?" Guess we know the answer to that!

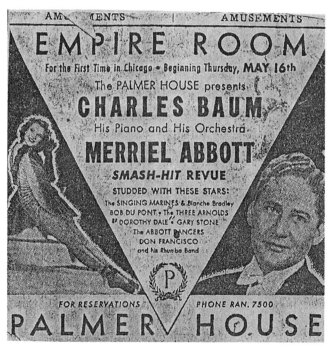

My first show in The Empire Room!

I went backstage, and a line of friends, were waiting, so I joined the line. When it was my turn, I said "Georgie, you probably don't remember when you were performing in the Palmer House — Ms. Abbott asked you to give a kid a routine. Well, I'm that kid 40 years later."

He said, "Oh, yes I do. And I'm so glad to see you, Dorothy!" He never knew until then what a great gift he had given me. I sent him a note the next day. I said I wanted him to know, even though it was late in coming, how much I appreciated what he had done for me. Thank you, thank you, Georgie – I know you are up there watching me!

Now that I was in the big show and everything was going great, I decided to change schools. Not dancing schools — high schools. Most of the Abbotts were going to YMCA College. They also had a high school.

It was in the loop, and very convenient to the Palmer House. You also had short hours, since you were exempt from gym and swimming.

Off I went to Amundsen for my transfer. I went to each class to say goodbye to the teachers. I really liked Miss Staple, the Spanish teacher. She was an ex-nun who came out of the convent, due to her mother's illness. When I came into her classroom, I told her that I was trans-ferring to the YMCA in the loop due to my job.

She said, "And what kind of a job, Dorothy?" When I told her that I was opening in the Empire Room, she was very surprised, but said, "How wonderful!" Then she announced it to the class and wished me good luck. She didn't know you should never wish a performer good luck, just break a leg. But her luck must have been with me anyhow.

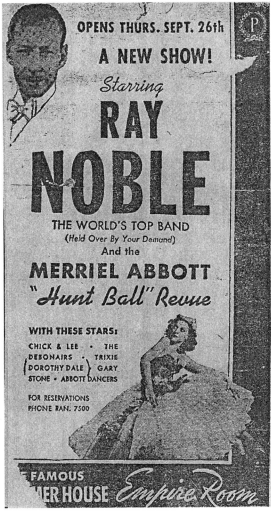

Dorothy Dale, Ray Noble Ad

I was settled into my new school and the Charlie Baum Show closed. I was in rehearsal for the new show with the Ray Noble Orchestra. The choreographer was Dick Barstow, and what a joy he was to work with. Dick was in *Ripley's Believe It or Not* as the "iron-toed boy." He was credited with standing supported by one toe wedged into the neck of a Coca-Cola bottle. And he could also jump to a height of eight feet. This is beside the point, but I thought it was interesting.

He was a great dancer. Dick was a British immigrant and at the tender age of seven, he performed with his family who formed "The Five Barstows." In 1949, he worked for Barnum and Bailey's circus as choreographer and director for 29 years. In 1979, he retired from the circus, but continued to choreograph Broadway musicals. He directed and choreographed the movie *A Star is Born*. How wonderful for me to have had this kind of experience and to work with this man.

The first day of rehearsal, Dick said, "Come on kid, let's get started. You will be doing 'Take the A Train.'" We worked on it for a few weeks and when it was finished Dick said, "I want to start you on another routine." This surprised me, but he didn't explain. I thought I was only allowed one routine, but lo and behold, this was the greatest compliment of my life so far.

"Dorothy, as you know," Dick said, "I have been rehearsing with the girls for *The Dude Ranch Review*, our new show. I am featured in the big cowboy/girl number.

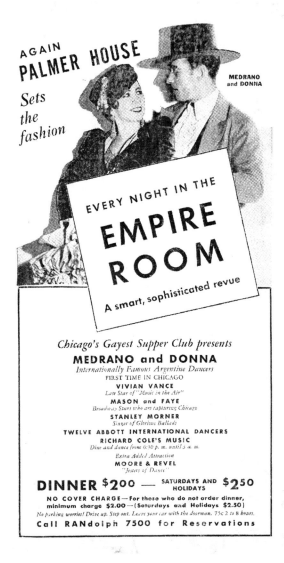

Empire Room, Palmer House, 1933

It's a difficult routine, but I told Teach you could do it. I'll explain...the girls will be dancing with and around me. I will solo at one point in center. You will be doing jumps and leaps and spins. After a few weeks with the show, I will be leaving for Hollywood with the Abbott traveling group to choreograph the new Jack Benny movie and Teach is happy with my choice to replace myself — you!"

Boy, I was going to click my heels in the air this time around!! I loved it; what a challenge! So the new show opened, and I did take the "A Train." And when Dick left, his last words to me were "Don't miss a tap, and get those jumps up — and keep spotting." (Spotting is a dance term to focus while turning and keeps the dancer from getting dizzy). When an announcement came out in the newspaper that I was replacing Dick Barstow in the new show, I loved it. I was replacing this master of dance.

The movie was completed, and he returned to choreograph the new show with Eddy Duchin, and what a show! I was given another solo, and this would be the one. It was with me until I "retired" from show business (or so I thought I was retired).

"Zing Went the Strings of My Heart" was the tune. It was a great number, and I loved doing it. Then came the next adventure. I was joining the traveling group of the Merriel Abbott dancers, and we were going on tour. We played all the big theatres across the United States. This was the time of the five-a-day. You performed five shows a day, seven days a week. It would be a set show with Eddy Duchin, the Abbott Dancers, Billy de Wolf (who later would be part of Doris Day's TV show), Bob Evans, a ventriloquist, Marilynn, Dolly Thon, and me. When the tour was finished, we would be going to Rio de Janeiro, South America. What an adventure this would prove to be. "South America — take it away!"

Chapter 9: Abbott Weigh Day, the Scale of Justice

Abbott loved her girls for many different reasons. She always found the best in each, and every girl, and would help them find the best in their talent. Some she liked better than others, but she always looked for the talent first, then determination and chutzpah. If you came in and told her that you had just learned a new trick, she would stop doing whatever she was doing, and want to see it. So you had to be ready for her. Her reaction was, "You said you could do it, so do it."

Being an Abbott girl was not only about performing, but also learning to deal with the world: the good and the not so good. She wanted her girls to be proper young ladies; to dress well, be polite and thoughtful, and to be socially acceptable. She would give us advice on fashion and always tell us, "When you finish dressing, take one more look in the mirror, and whatever jewelry you have on, take one piece off. Never over-do anything."

Well, I must say, I did abide by that for awhile. But as I got older and acquired more jewelry, that advice went out the window. Why leave it in a box? You either have it or you don't. Or as Mamma Rose said in the musical *Gypsy*, "Ya either got it or ya ain't!"

We also learned to be responsible. "Don't be late, and always consider other people's time," In show business, you learn to be on time, or you'll miss the show. That could cost you a job and your reputation.

We had a weigh day every Thursday. Each girl had a set weight, and you had to maintain it, or you were fined $5.00 out of your salary — not a good thing when you were making $27.00 a week. Teacher's husband, as I mentioned, was a doctor, and the $5.00 was donated to the interns at the hospital (or so we were told)!

61

On Monday, we would start to cut down on the sugar. No more trips to "Fanny May" for chocolate, or your $5.00 would belong to that intern. Preparing for the big ,weigh day, we would weigh ourselves in at the kitchen in the Palmer House. They had the meat scale on the third floor, as I recall, and we all hoped for the best.

That was a ritual on Tuesday and Wednesday. If the scale came up with that pound or two over, then we dashed to the 23rd floor, where our rooms were located. We would get the Epsom salts, fill the bathtub with hot water, jump in, and try to lose the pounds. The girls with big boobs would complain that it wasn't fair the way the weight was set. One gal always said, "Each one of my boobs weighs five pounds." Fortunately, I never had that problem. My weight gain came from ice cream sodas.

As soon as we weighed in on Thursday, down we would go to Landers restaurant and have a date crunch and be happy for another five days. It certainly kept us alert and conscious of our looks. To this day, I try to look my best at all times. You not only owe it to your fans and audience, but also to yourself.

Teacher was good to us. Every opening night there would be an expensive bottle of perfume on our dresser with a little note. Then one day, she would take you shopping and buy you a wonderful hat, dress and shoes from the shops on Michigan Avenue. Boy, I had moved up from my days at Goldblatt's, (that was a very popular department store in the heart of Chicago). I still remember when she bought me a black braided dress, and it truly was very elegant. I thought I was miss "rich bitch" when I wore it.

Show business, is a pretend world most of the time (it's a wonderful world) as in the real world (which I have never considered my favorite place), sometimes life will toss you a curve when you least expect. Some of the Abbotts experienced the unexpected.

Marilyn Dyer and I went into the Empire Room at the same time, and we were both the same age. I got to know her from class, and then she made it to the "scrubwomen," which was the Abbott group that you auditioned for before you made it into the Empire Room. If you remember from an earlier mention, if one of the girls in the Empire Room dropped out to get married, or for some other reason, you had a chance to fill the spot. I loved Marilyn. She was a kick, and we became best friends, and stayed that way until she passed away.

Marilyn was the first one to nickname me Dale. She would say things like, "It was just stunning Dale," and before I knew it, Dorothy went "out the window." And everyone called me Dale for many years. Marilyn and I enrolled in the YMCA College, along with several other Abbotts.

Most of the girls married and settled into a normal life after their Abbott experience. But Marilyn and I, at this time, were more interested in being an Abbott. We would double date often. She married one of "our" double dates, a really nice young man, Eddy Conrad. But the other half of the "double dates," my escort, another nice young man Nick Lombardie, just didn't do it for me. I just wanted to dance.

When Nick introduced me to his family at his sister's wedding he told them, "This is the girl I'm going to marry," I knew it was time to move on, or I would be making pasta the rest of my life.

When I was living in Las Vegas several years later, I got a call from Marilyn telling me that her son, the apple of her eye, who had just passed the bar exam, was killed in an automobile accident. He was leaving for California, for a position with a law firm. The night before he left, his friend gave him a going away party, and on the way home, it happened. A couple years later, Marilyn died of cancer, much too young. I think it was a broken heart. She did have a daughter, Linda, to help fill the void, but she somehow couldn't get over that tragedy.

Dorothy Dale is one of the Merriel Abbott dancers appearing with Eddie Duchin and his orchestra on the stage at the Riverside

Dorothy Dale, Riverside Theatre, Milwaukee, Wisconsin on Theatre Tour, 1941.

Another Abbott that went on the theatre tour was Jeanne Guest, a nice gal, older than me. She married and had triplets. After a few years, I heard she had committed suicide. How tragic for one so young.

Rita Roper was a great acrobat, and very cute. She reminded me of June Allyson. We were good friends and always kept in touch. She married Earl, a dentist, who had his office in Skokie, where I lived after I got married. Rita would stop off at my house on a Friday night, and wait for her husband to finish his appointments. My husband Chris would be home and we would have a drink, a little conversation, and then they would be off to ski for the weekend. Then the curve struck.

They had a darling little girl, Wendy, about five. She had a brain hemorrhage and passed away. Life is not all dancing. It's dancing as fast as you can. I am so grateful!

Merriel Abbott reunion, June Taylor center with "Teacher," 1970

The Abbotts had a reunion at the Palmer House in 1970. It was a lovely luncheon in the Empire Room. Ms. Abbott was there, as was June Taylor, and her Sister Marilyn, who married Jackie Gleason a few years later. It was one of the last times I saw Marilyn Dyer Conrad. About fifty girls attended the luncheon. They had worked in the Empire Room through the years. It was really great, and brought back such wonderful memories.

Hessie Smith was the rehearsal pianist for the Abbotts, and also wrote special material and lyrics for the group. She was wonderful, and had been with Teacher for many years. The day of the reunion, she was introduced, and this is what she had to say to all of us:

Teacher — and All the Girls I Saw Grow Up

By Hessie Smith

I've been given a difficult assignment
Pertaining to this occasion
I've been asked to discuss
"What an Abbott Dancer is"
And it took a bit of persuasion,
For my department is music and lyrics
I've never really danced,
Except underneath the keyboard
Where fifth position was slightly cramped,
But in forty years of exposure
To Teacher and her rules.
I think we have all been molded
And if not, we were the fools.
She laid down the laws, and believe me
They kept us all in line,
For example, take off half that makeup,
If you're overweight, pay a fine.
Remember, no dates with musicians,
Continue on at school,
Acrobatics won't hurt you
Deodorants are the rule.
Bathe each day before show time,
Don't mingle with the guests,
A prize for your first back aerial,
A prize for an "E" on a test.
If you make a mistake, make a good one,
At least get out and try,
Fall on your face, but smile girls,
Style is what makes you get by.
If you want a trip to Europe,
Here's what you have to do,
Acrobatics, toe, tap and ballet,
And be a lady too.
Perhaps you won't make a dancer,
Who passes the test,

65

But if you're only a scrubwoman,
Be your absolute best.
Don't smoke, or drink, or flirt, girls,
Study French instead,
You'll travel with a chaperone
And, she'll be more than a figurehead.
Remember I've got second sight
There's nothing you can do
That I won't learn about sometime
Maybe as quickly as you.
But you'll see the world
You'll have a ball,
You'll be in the movies
You'll thrill to it all.
You'll come out smarter
You'll marry well,
You'll send your kids to Miss Abbott's,
And be sure to tell them
Of the good old days
When you went to her school
And learned P.D.Q.
About all of her rules.
They seemed tough at the time,
But look what you got,
Culture and character,
With your entrechat quatre.
Kidding aside, since we've all had our fun,
Let's be serious for a moment
And pay tribute to one
Of the world's greatest teachers,
We're all in her debt.
Miss Abbott, we love you
And we'll never forget.

We did learn a lot from Teacher, and most of us took that knowledge with us after we went out on our own. I'm sure along life's way, we all made it work for us, without realizing from whence it came. It is such a lesson for all of us to realize how important our teachers are, and I was so fortunate to have many of the best!

Let me introduce you to Frank Lewin.

As I was winding down *I'm Not In Kansas Anymore,* a thought came to mind. I started to read the chapter on the Merriel Abbott Dancers.

I remembered, Teacher and her husband Dr. Lewin had adopted a son Frankie. I knew he attended Hardey Prep, the same school my son attended.

Frank knew I was in the Follies. And that I had been with the Abbotts way before he arrived in the Lewins' life. He called me regarding a book he was thinking about writing. He didn't have much information on the older Abbott dancers from 1940. I'm one of the last still dancing. I told him I would be happy to help.

As I was checking my chapter on the Abbott dancers I thought I would contact Frank. I told him about my book and would he be interested in writing something about his mom. To my delight and joy, I received the following.

Dorothy,

Thank you for giving me the opportunity to say a few words about Mom.

I was adopted by Merriel and her husband Phil Lewin. Dad was a renowned Orthopedic Surgeon and Mom was at the time Director of Entertainment for the Hilton Hotels worldwide. Her home base was The Palmer House where she directed the floor shows in the Empire Room. Most of my early memories of her were all about her office, the phones that never stopped ringing and all these people jumping at orders from "Miss Abbott." Needless to say Dad and I were no exception, even at home.

Home was in Highland Park, Il, where Mom kept a beautiful and elegant show-biz community. Most of the celebrities were house guests at some time during their engagements. As any Abbott Dancer will tell you, "Teacher" ran a tight ship. She demanded excellence from everyone. She could be tough and demanding, but her ability to combine this with generosity, compassion and plain thoughtfulness made her unique. On her daily rounds of the hotel, she encountered guests from all walks of life. She was an ardent conversationalist and if there was something to make a stay more memorable, she would see that it was done. If it was a Serviceman on a layover she saw to it that he or she got a good meal and enjoyed a good show.

Dad passed away in 1960 and shortly after we moved into Chicago. In the 1960s Mom was seeing her world changing rapidly. She retired from the Hilton, but kept the office at The

Palmer House. She would ask me, "Frankie, who are the kids listening to, who do they want to see?" Needless to say I don't think that The Rolling Stones ever made it to the Empire Room. Nevertheless, she continued to book and sell out shows consistently. She even found time to manage my own band. "The Foggy Notions' into clubs and even 1968 "Love-in" at North Avenue Beach (she is in her seventies and managing a rock band.

But alas things finally changed too much. The supper-club era passed and The Empire Room finally threw in the napkin. It closed its doors in 1977. Mom would not go to the last night and sent me in her place. I can't remember now who closed the room. It was either Phyllis Diller or Carol Channing, but stars called in to share memories from all over the world. In her name I took the bow for her, for all her accomplishments, for she was truly a legend and an exceptional parent. "Teacher" passed on November 9, 1978 at the age of 84. The last person she spoke with that night was Hildegarde, calling from a cruise ship she was working, "Just to talk."

Thank you, Frank, I'm sure you brought as much joy into Teacher's life, as she did in yours.

Chapter 10: The Best is Yet to Come

The time came for us to pack for the theatre tour before leaving for South America. At each theatre we played, we did five shows a day. A current movie, *Pathé News* and the stage show with a big band. In our case, it was Eddy Duchin. It was hard work, but we loved it. The theatre was usually filled to capacity, and to be working for this big of an audience was a thrill for little old me. When we played the Chicago Theatre, one of my mother's customers from the beauty shop came to see me.

She told mom, "What a great show, and to think our Dorothy is on the Chicago Theatre stage!" They did have a few comments.

For example, when I was getting ready to go to Rio, one lady said to mom, "Alice, do you think it's a good idea to let her go that far away? You don't know what could happen to her."

Mom, always the positive one, said, "It could happen to her right down the block, right here on Ashland Ave. I don't want her to miss this opportunity to see the world."

Carolyn Truax, Marilyn Marsh,
Dorothy Dale, Fox Theatre, 1940

We played all the big theatres, but the one that stands out in my mind was the Fox in St. Louis, Missouri. Not only had I taken my first dance lesson in this town, I was born there. I was really giving it my all for the old hometown when I heard something crack. It was in my rib area. It was a matinee, and I was doing spotting walkovers. All of a sudden, I felt something click, and it wasn't my heels. I was in pain. I had twisted the wrong way, and I had a feeling I cracked a rib. I finished the routine and got off the stage. Mr. Duchin was so kind and concerned. As soon as he got off the stage, he called the theatre doctor and rushed me to his office. He bandaged me up, and I returned to do the next show. The bandage remained on for about a week and I was back to normal.

Billy De Wolfe, 1940

Every closing night, we would all be packing and usually catching a train, so it was a tense time. You're "getting it all together," so to speak. Without thinking one night, some of us thought it would be great fun if we snuck into Billy de Wolfe's dressing room, and tied the laces of his street shoes together. We forgot he had a train to catch, the same as we did, only his was earlier. The difference: we just packed for ourselves. And the rest was taken care of by our dear man Randolph and his wife.

We passed Billy's dressing room and he was frantically trying to get the shoelaces untied. We could hear him saying, "If I catch who did this, I will wring their necks. And I'm pretty sure I know who they are!" We got out of his sight. It took him several weeks to talk to us again even though we apologized. Show business was full of funny happenings. We did love Billy, and he was fun to work with. I would stand backstage and watch his act. After five shows a day, I could do it verbatim. I loved it. Gosh, how I hate not being able to connect to a person.

We did an early morning show around 11 a.m., so we were not exactly awake. Some of the other acts in town, working at other venues, would come to the early show and sit in the front row. When you made your entrance, they would all pull out the morning newspaper, open it, and start to read like they weren't interested in our act. We would crack up and just laugh. It was all done in good fun. Of course at the end of our performance, they would all stand up and cheer us off.

In Columbus, Ohio, the fire department came out to meet us and took us for a ride around town on the fire engine.

Fire Engine, Columbus, Ohio, 1940

I don't know what would have happened if there had been a fire. It would have been our first experience as a firefighter.

After about eight weeks on the road, we hit Cleveland. One of the girls didn't feel well and her neck was swollen. Leah, our chaperone, called Teacher with her symptoms. Teacher talked to her husband, the doctor, and he said, "She has the mumps." Oh gosh, panic set in. Here goes the show!

Well, not so fast! Teacher got a hold of the hotel manager, and told him the problem. Would it be possible for him to give us a large room away from everyone, she asked. He was very understanding, his concern was with the hotel guests. He moved twin beds, one for each girl, into the ballroom. He closed the door, and we waited for further instructions, which came quickly. It was after the last show that this all came about. We were saved by the bell, Dr. Lewin told Teacher to give each girl a bottle of citrus magnesia. Need I say more! It was definitely a night of "movement." But it worked like a charm.

The next morning, we were all fine, and the show went on as scheduled. The girl that had caused the almost outbreak was Marilyn Marsh. And from that day forward, she was known as "Mumps."

Another time, we had finished the last show, and Eddy took us out. We would always go to the variety club in the town we were visiting, and that was fun. One evening, Eddy had taken us to the variety club in town, and we were hungry as usual.

So he said, "Let's go to the White Castle!" Now for those of you who don't remember the White Castle, it was all white, with a counter and stools, and it had great fast food.

We all ordered, and I said, "Oh gosh, we were in such a hurry, I forgot to call my mom!" Well like a flash, Eddy said, "What's the number, Dorothy?" So, I gave it to him.

And the next thing, I hear him on the wall phone saying, "This is Eddy Duchin, Alice, and Dorothy wants to talk to you." He did those kind of nice things all the time!

One night at the variety club, we were all singing and laughing. I sat down at the piano and started to fool around with my "C" chord. Who, sits down next to me, but Eddy. And he was cracking up.

He said, "I didn't know you could almost play the piano?" Then he said, "I bet you know Chop Sticks!"

I said, "Yes!"

And he said, "Okay, hit it!" I actually played a duet with Eddy Duchin. I didn't say how good I was...I just said I played with him.

Dorothy Dale and Marilyn Marsh
Fox Theatre, St. Louis, Mo. 1940

Chapter 11: Life in the
Fast Track; Knitting!

We were living "life in the fast track," being on the theatre tour. It was fun, but we had to hit those trains in record time, to get to the next town; Chicago, St. Louis, Omaha, Milwaukee, and more. Then, we hit New York City, and heard the call, "all aboard." We made our way to the pier, to board the S.S. *Argentinean* (Moore McCormick line), on our way to South America. I had never been on a large liner before, and, as they say, "It was awesome." We were in first class, and that was exciting. The staterooms were very nice, so our adventure began on a high note. Did I ever think I would be going to Rio de Janeiro?

A bon voyage party was going on in several of the staterooms. We were invited to join in, and we paid a visit to everyone. I don't know if it was my undoing, but at the time, I did not drink alcoholic beverages. Someone gave me a rum and Coke, and I was feeling

Bob Evans, 1941

On our way to Rio, 1941

quite good. We set sail at midnight. We all went up on the top deck to wave goodbye to New York, the USA, and the Statue of Liberty. She was beautiful. Then it was time for sweet dreams.

Sleep was not on my mind, but I was wrong. I was exhausted, and soon went off. I didn't know what the next morning would bring, but I soon found out.

I awoke feeling squeamish. I started to get dressed, my head spinning. I made it to the dining room for breakfast. The first person I saw was Bob Evans, who was going with us to Rio to perform in the show. He beckoned for me to join him at his table. One look at me up close, and he knew I was fading quickly.

His great sense of humor did prevail. He delighted in saying without malice, "So Dorothy, have some eggs and bacon; really delicious." One look at his plate, and it was all over! I headed for the ship railing, and the blue Atlantic had suddenly turned green. Me too! I composed myself long enough to reach the stateroom, and hit the bed. It seemed that everyone on board had a cure for me, but nothing helped. My misery lasted three days. In the end, I made up for lost time. My appetite returned, and I hit every buffet, tea and snack bar on the ship.

Everyone called us "Abbott's Rabbits." During this trip, we were velcro'ed together, especially the younger girls. "Teach" thought it might be a good idea to dress us alike when we went out as a group, so we would be easy to spot. I know it sounds like kindergarten, but we did have a tendency to wander. She outfitted us in green and white print skirts, and white blouses.

Our first port was Barbados. We went down the gangplank looking like a school group laughing, and thinking how foolish we looked. The other passengers followed us off the ship and I must say, they told us we were adorable.

As soon as we hit land, the natives were waiting for us, calling out "money lady, money lady."

We replied, "No money, Sonny, we're school girls." It was a lovely island, untouched by highrise hotels and fancy restaurants. Remember this was 1941. We strolled along the streets until we came across a small department store. It was more like a general store, with the needs of the villagers. As soon as we entered, I had a strange experience. Something came over me; I knew I had been there before. Today, they would call it déjà vu. That was way before Shirley MacLaine's "belief of another life." I somehow knew where every department was located, and able to tell the girls which way to go to get what they were looking for; perfume, yarn or other articles. They thought it was odd, but didn't pay much attention. I just went on my way, and didn't think much about it. But I couldn't shake the feeling.

I'm not sure what I was doing there in a previous life, but I hope it wasn't catching fish. I would much prefer being married to the rich plantation owner. I guess I'll never know...or will I?

We took a head count to be sure we didn't leave anyone on the island, 'cause we didn't know if the ship would turn back for them.

Soon, we were back on the ship and waved goodbye to Barbados. The girls unpacked their knitting needles, and by the time we set sail, they were giving me my first knitting lesson. They had made me buy yarn on the island. It was very cheap, and it's a good thing. I'm glad I didn't invest a lot of money, 'cause knitting was not my big need in life. They came away with skeins in every color.

I decided, since I was just beginning to knit, a nice tan cashmere and a blue angora sweater would be a good start, just in case it didn't work out. And as it happened, I must have had a vision. The cashmere was intended for Vincent. I would start with his sweater first, and work up to the angora. I had two projects to keep me busy, and so I started with great confidence.

Over the next two days, I was concentrating on my "knit one, purl two," and thought to myself, "Heck, there's nothing to this!" But just as I was gaining ground, Carolyn (one of the girls) came by to check on my progress.

She looked and said, "Oh, we have to do some ripping. You dropped several stitches.

I said, "Where did I drop them? And will anybody know?"

She said, "Get serious." I was horrified. My confidence went right down the drain.

I was ready to give the whole thing up, but I had already written to Vincent and told him about his cashmere sweater. So I plugged away, and pretended I was enjoying it. This is where my bright idea comes into play. Nine months later we arrived back in New York. I dashed to Macy's, and bought him a cashmere sweater. I hoped I could pass it off as an original "cashmere by Dorothy," but the label inside said "made in London."

It was the first time performing on the ship, and what an experience that was. The line of girls did a routine with trays, which were supposed to be old 78 records. The trays were painted black to resemble a record. Great routine. They did back flips and aerial cartwheels, but the movement of the ship left a lot to be desired. As soon as they started to dance, the trays went flying in all directions. The sound of the tin trays could be heard all the way to China. The audience loved it, as long as they didn't get hit with a tray. Now, I was ready to hit the stage with a lot of apprehension. I managed to stay on my feet, but it was not my finest moment. I thought I would be seasick again. I was sliding all over the stage, but nothing hurt except my ego.

There were many fun things to do on the ship and the most challenging one was the costume party. You had to create your own costume from something you found on the ship. I set out to find one of the crew, and borrow his sailor hat. I guess you know what I went as. On board were several celebrities. There was Igor Cassini, the second journalist to write under the byline

Sugarloaf Mountain,
Rio De Janiero, Brazil, 1941

Cholly Knickerbocker, pseudonym, as society editor and writer of a syndicated gossip column and brother of the famous fashion designer, Oleg Cassini.

We arrived in Rio, and the view from the ship was magnificent. You could see Sugarloaf Mountain and the beautiful sprawling beach. When we were ready to leave the ship, and say our farewells, this nice young man who took a liking to me, named Blue, came to say goodbye. He told me he would come to see the show opening night. He did come, and I

Copacabana Palace swimming pool with Teacher, Leah (our chaperone), Jean Guest, Dorothy Dale, and far right, Jane McNulty.

received a lovely box of long stemmed red roses from him on opening night. I had never received roses in a box with a big ribbon, and card. It was something wonderful for this little girl from Chicago.

We waited for the limo to pick us up and take us to our new home away from home. It was a lovely two-story house, within walking distance to the ocean. A lovely lady greeted us at the door named Felicia. I liked her right away, and knew I would love her cooking. I could smell something wonderful coming from the kitchen.

She took us on a tour of the house and showed us our rooms upstairs. "When you're ready," she said, "visit me in the kitchen. I have some chocolate chip cookies and brownies for you." We also had a nice little maid, she didn't speak English, so we didn't get to know her very well. She took care of our personal needs.

The kitchen being our favorite place was a problem, since we still had weigh day to consider every Thursday. We did use the same old formula, though. Thursday, through Sunday pig-out days. Then Monday, Tuesday and Wednesday: starvation.

The following morning, the car picked us up to drive us to the Copacabana Palace Hotel, where we would meet our French teacher at the swimming pool. "Teach" had arranged for us to take French, whether we wanted to or not. She did not believe in wasting time. We had to always be busy learning, or accomplishing something. I guess her teaching stayed with me; now I'm in my eighties, and I still can't stop trying to accomplishment new things.

The order of the day was to put on our snappy bathing suits and bathing hats. In those days, you did not get your hair wet. The diving and swim coach arrived and we all hit the pool. A few days later, he started to teach a few of us to dive, and I loved it. But I was not looking forward to exhibiting my new found accomplishment.

One morning, Teach appeared, and after sitting and watching us, I heard my name mentioned. Fear came into my bones. "Dorothy," Teach said, "I hear you're doing very well and I would like to see you dive."

"Oh," I said, "Right now? I mean, I've only been at this a short time."

She said, "Now!" So I went to the side of the pool and dove in.

When I came up, I heard her say, "Oh, I know you can dive off the side of the pool. I want to see you dive off the ten foot board."

I said, "You know, that's kind of high, don't you think, for a beginner?"

"You can do it." she insisted. It was always a challenge. She then gave me an incentive. "If you do it," she enticed, "I'll give you a gold charm of South America!"

We all had gold charm bracelets, and everywhere we would go, we would buy or receive a charm as a gift. I have a piano from Eddy Duchin, and a bullfighter from Cantinflas, the famous comedian from Mexico who was the star of "Around the World in 80 Days."

So I headed for the ten-foot board, climbed to the top, took a deep breath, and dove into the water. A perfect dive! I came up and could not believe it. I was so glad I survived the dive and the charm was mine.

"Not so fast, lady," she said. She wanted to see it again! After just yelling bravo! I wished she would just let me go. I took the steps again, took a deep breath, and belly flopped. I hit that water, and for the next couple of days, I was black and blue. I cherish that map of Rio, but needless to say, I have never gone off a ten-foot diving board again! It did teach me a lifelong lesson: never live in fear and always try new things in life.

The Copacabana Palace was an exquisite hotel and the show room was lovely. It had a glass floor with lights under the glass. Not an easy floor to dance on, but you always survive any floor in show business.

This was a dream come true for me. To be dancing on the same floor that the wonderful Paul Draper danced on just a week before was a thrill. Paul was a great ballet tap artist. All the famous people came to see Eddy Duchin, and the show was wonderful. One evening, the president came, and the press took pictures of everybody including the Abbotts. And they were in *Look* and *Life* magazines. The headline, "The Good Neighbor Policy." We were close to World War Two, but at our age, we had no idea what it all meant. Unfortunately, within months we found out.

This was definitely the Eddy Duchin show: Eddy sitting at the grand

"AMBASSADOR" DUCHIN, relaxing from his routine of appearances in Rio de Janeiro, emerges dripping from the surf at Copacabana beach, surrounded by several decorative members of his troupe. Eddy launched his South American engagement by playing at a ball given by U. S. Ambassador Jefferson Caffery.

THE MAESTRO does a bit of alfresco rug cutting while the girls gather 'round. Eddy's musical entourage got a big hand from Rio de Janeiro's fun-loving public; musicians and entertainers were feted wherever they went

LOOK MAGAZINE, "Day In The Sun."
Eddy Duchin, Carolyn, and Dorothy, 1941

piano, looking handsome, with the most wonderful, enchanting smile. His orchestra was ready for the downbeat, and then the Abbotts in white gowns, with black notes on the skirt, roll out miniature white pianos on to the stage. That picture alone was magnificent. Each girl sat at her piano, and when Eddy started to play, the girls joined in.

Eddy's distinctive style brought the house down, especially when he raised his hands a foot high off the keys. And when he started to play "Music Maestro Please," and then accompanied me on my routine to "Zing Went the Strings of My Heart," it was magic.

Blackie's Island, Carolyn Truax, Jimmy Drum, Dorothy Dale, and Jane McNulty, 1941.

We had several routines, but the hardest one was the toe number on stairs. It was a disaster. Six steps up and down on point. I use to think sometimes, "Can't we make this easier?" But no, "Get on those toe shoes." Lucky for me, I had strong feet and legs. But I had very weak arms, and I really worked at keeping my elbows straight doing back flips. After I fell on my head a number of times, it sunk in. "Keep your elbows straight!"

We were in Rio for eight months and had fun, fun, fun, along with a few happenings. The Brazilians were very hospitable and we were entertained royally. One weekend, we were invited to Blackies Island. A very nice gentleman owned the whole island. We spent most of the day on his sailboat swimming and water skiing off his impressive boat. After the ten-foot

Sailing with Dorothy, Mailynn, Leah, Marilyn, and the President of Brazil's Son, Vargas, Alberto, Bob Evans, and Dolly, 1941

dive, I was up for anything. So I put the water skis on, and before I knew what happened, I was holding on for dear life at the rear of the boat. Off I went with the wind blowing in my hair, and fear in my heart, but I had such fun!!

On the ship, coming over to Rio, were several college boys. They were on board returning for their summer vacation. All the girls were ecstatic and hoping to meet one of them as soon as possible. One of the young men was Jimmy Drum. Jimmy was tall, with a wonderful smile. He was returning from Dartmouth College to visit his parents, who had a house in Rio, but also resided in New York. His father was involved in international banking. I met Jimmy and we laughed a lot. We played shuffleboard, and that was all I was interested in!

But Carolyn had her eye on him, and she got him! Actually, when we returned to

Eddy and Me, Rio, 1941

Chicago, they had already become engaged. Unfortunately, after they married, Jimmy was drafted and went off to war. While he was gone, Carolyn met Jimmy's cousin, divorced Jimmy, married the cousin, and moved to the Philippines and Manila. From all accounts, they lived happily ever after. When her husband passed away, Carolyn ran into Jimmy. His wife had died, so the two of them remarried. Jimmy also passed away a few years later.

I do remember, I was working at the Chez Parée, the famous nightclub in Chicago, in the early 1940s. And one evening I received a note backstage from Jimmy. He asked me to join him. He looked like the same old Jimmy, except he had a patch on his eye. He was still in uniform and out of the hospital. I was so glad to see him, and to know he made it back from the war. Life has many twists and turns. But I do have such fond memories.

Last day in Rio with the gang, 1941

Chapter 12: Back To the USA
(Keep an Eye On the Girls)

Performing at the Copacabana Palace was magical. The Eddy Duchin Orchestra sitting on the stand with the beautiful girl vocalist, June Robbins, in her lovely gown, waiting her chance to sing. and Eddy playing his theme song. I was very lucky to have Dick Barstow choreograph my routines. And except for my first show in the Empire Room, which was choreographed by Georgie Tapps, Dick was the one for me. I found Dick very easy to work with and full of enthusiasm for whatever he was doing. His attitude, of course, gave me such inspiration and I was mesmerized by everything he did. My favorite number, as I mentioned, was "Zing Went the Strings of my Heart." When I left the Abbotts and went on my own as a single act, Teacher allowed me to perform all the routines I had done while working for her, lucky me.

Our Rio engagement was coming to an end, and as much as we were looking forward to our return trip to New York, and then home, it was going to be hard to say goodbye. We would miss all of the wonderful friends we made. And we would miss looking out at Sugarloaf Mountain, strolling on the beautiful beach, going to the Catholic Church where Jayne and I would go to Mass on Sunday, and then stop at the little ice cream shop on our way home. The ice cream had a different taste. It wasn't like our American ice cream, but it was a treat, and we looked up at Coronado the Christ overlooking Rio, it was so beautiful.

We came home with many lovely gifts from the people in South America who came to know us; one gentleman gave me a beautiful topaz and diamond ring. Rio is known for their beautiful stones, and I was so glad to come home with several. I had a beautiful bracelet with precious stones that I broke up, and gave several of the stones to family and friends. What a dumb move, but I was young.

Once again we were on the high seas. We did miss Felice's brownies, but not for long. Every time you took a breath, there was a plate full of goodies to make us happy, and forget about the scale waiting for us on Thursday, our Weigh Day! Talk about tipping the scale! Well, some did and some didn't.

And once again, I could feel that dizzy feeling and for three days I was seasick. But as soon as I returned to normal, I started enjoying myself as usual, and the trip back was just a continuation of fun and games. Our chaperone could be very annoying, but most of the time she was okay. She kept an eagle eye on the younger girls, of which I was one, along with Jayne, Carolyn and Marilyn. The other girls were between 21 and 25.

One of Leah's favorites was Dolly Thon, who had been unofficially adopted by Teacher when she was quite young. Dolly was a lovely looking child and very talented. She came from a middle class Polish family, but without much future due to finances. She did have a sister who was much older than her, and she took an interest in Dolly. She took her to the Abbott School for training and Teacher fell in love with her. She became a good dancer and fabulous acrobat. Teacher put all her energy into making a star out of Dolly. At one point, when the traveling group went to Hollywood to do a movie, she had the chance to make a screen test and while there, became engaged to Mickey Rooney, or so the story goes.

The engagement and the screen test didn't work out. Dolly (being the chosen one) had the best of everything in her wardrobe. On the other hand I had just enough to get by and was perfectly happy. As you know, there are many activities on board, and one day I met this young man who was on his way back to the University of Wisconsin. His name was Carl and he seemed to be around a lot.

One day he approached me and said "Hi!" He was tall, blond and very handsome, he was on his way back to school from Sao Paolo, Brazil. I said "Hi" back, and he sat down.

His opening line, "You were the one that was seasick. I kept waiting for you to get better and just heard you are all well…would you like to play shuffleboard?"

Well of course I did, so off we went, and after several days of fun and conversation, he asked me if he could take me to the ship formal. Wow! I was so excited, and I told Dolly and the other girls.

About an hour later, Dolly came on deck and said, "Dorothy, come with me, I have something I want you to see." So off we went to her stateroom, and there was Leah and this beautiful black strapless gown on the bed.

"So what do you think? Would you like to wear it to the formal?" Dolly looked at me with anticipation.

I was speechless, but only for a moment. I said, "Gosh yes, but I'm 34A and you're 36D."

"Not to worry," Dolly said in a flash, "Leah said she could take it in!" And so she did, and I was Cinderella for a night. All those times that Leah had yelled at me vanished, I forgave her forever. Thank you, Dolly, wherever you are.

I was ready for the ball! Carl picked me up, and the Prince and Cinderella danced the night away. Afterward, we took a walk around the deck, and stopped to look at the moon over some part of the ocean. Carl kissed me, and my first big romance started with a college man, can you believe?

We did keep in touch, and he came to Chicago on weekends to see me perform. He even took me to a lovely dance at the Stevens Hotel, but those long distance romances never seem to work. He was a college man working for a degree, and I was a tap dancer, I had my own dreams ahead of me. It was a nice interlude in my young life.

I really loved swimming, and spent a lot of time at the pool with Carl. My thought was to buy a white dress and against my "perfect tan," I would be the talk of the town. Well, not to be. After the first day at the pool, I returned to my stateroom, and the lovely tan was a blistering red. I could hardly move, and everyone got very excited and finally called the ship doctor. I was banned from the pool for the remainder of the trip, but I made up for it with the wonderful desserts, and when the bell rang for brunch, lunch, or dinner, Carl and I were the first in line. I'm glad it didn't happen before the Cinderella Ball.

I thought I would be all healed by the time we arrived in New York, but I was still as red as a berry, and when Teacher laid eyes on me she was not happy. "What happened to you?" she barked.

I had no answer, but she was furious, not only with me, but with Leah. "You are the chaperone and responsible," she continued on her rampage. "You didn't check on her? My gosh, woman, you must have seen her sitting in the sun with her skin, and known she would bake."

Poor Leah was so upset she just apologized, and said, "I'll take care of it." We had two weeks before we opened at the Strand Theatre in New York, and by that time, I would be healed…or so I thought. I did heal, but I was full of freckles that remain with me to this day. Now they're old freckles. I look at them, and I think about the time and the place I acquired them, and it was worth it. It was the most exciting time of my young life.

Before we left South America, I had written to my mom and asked her to come to New York. Her answer back, "Yes! I already have my ticket on the Greyhound bus," Mom excitedly said. I hadn't seen her in nine months, and I really missed her. She was still busy doing finger waves for $.25, but she was just as anxious to see me, as I was to see her. She took the Greyhound bus from Chicago, and arrived a few days after we docked in New York. The whole cast stayed at the Paramount Hotel.

This was my first trip to New York, and I've never gotten over it. It seemed to me that everyone in the world lived in New York. The theaters, shops and hotels were all lit up, and I thought I was in Never, Never Land. Mom and I shopped at Macy's, and I bought a plaid taffeta dress. I can still see it today.

The Dorsey Orchestra was at the Paramount Theatre, with Frank Sinatra, who was the big sensation of the day. All the young girls were waiting in line to buy tickets to see him. One of our girls, Marilyn, knew Buddy Rich, the famous drummer. She took herself over to the Paramount to see Buddy. He made a date with her for a couple of nights later, and she was thrilled. Unfortunately, we were not allowed to go out alone at night, and so Marilyn asked my mother if she would chaperone. Mom agreed, and it was okay with Leah.

Off we went to Lindy's, a New York restaurant, known for their famous cheesecake. Marilyn said to my mother, "I'll just meet Buddy and see you later!" She jumped up, and left the restaurant before we knew she was gone. We were dumbfounded, but then you see life's little disappointments shake their ugly head, and she was left without a date. She arrived at the theater, and waited and waited and waited for Buddy; he was a no-show. I guess you could say honesty is the best policy.

Mom and I had two great weeks. One day, Teacher had scheduled us to meet Eddie Cantor, the great comedienne with the big rolling eyes. One of his famous songs was "Makin' Whoopee." Mr. Cantor was producing a new show on Broadway, "Banjo Eyes." Teacher thought we would be great in the show, so she made an appointment with Mr. Cantor to audition the girls at the Waldorf Astoria Hotel, in the ballroom. I was so excited that I was fidgeting while waiting to start my number. The girls had finished their routine, and then Mr. Cantor said to me, "I can tell you're eager to do your number for me!" "Yes sir," I blurted out, "I can't wait!"

And he said, "Well then let's go." I flew out on that floor and danced my heart out. Teacher, in the mean time, sitting next to Mr. Cantor, was in deep conversation. He told her, "I really think your girls are terrific, but they're not right for this show. But I'll take the little blonde tap dancer, Dorothy."

Teacher came back as quick as a rabbit, "Well you can't have her. She's under contract to me!"

And there went my big dream of Broadway. But I was so young and inexperienced; I didn't even realize that I didn't have a contract with teacher. It really would have been a big chance for me, but then what you don't have, you don't miss. It was nice to know he wanted me for his show. You win some, and you lose some.

It was time for Mom to return home. After she saw the show, she hopped on the Greyhound bus and headed for Chicago. We opened the

Strand Theatre Marquee, New York, 1941

show at the Strand Theatre. We did five shows a day. Besides the regular acts that had been with us on the theatre tour, The Warner Brothers Navy Blues Sextet, Kay Aldridge, Georgia Carol, Peggy Diggins, Marguerite Chapman, Lorraine Gettman, and Alice Talton joined us. They had just appeared in the film *Navy Blues* with Ann Sheridan and Jack Oakie. One gal, Georgia Carol, in later years married Kay Kyser, the orchestra leader. They were all great and we had a lot of fun.

Another evening, while still in New York, Eddy took us to the Astor Roof, and who was there but Frank Sinatra. He came over to our table to say "Hello" to Eddy, and he introduced us to Frank, my mother was introduced simply as "Alice." After some conversation, he must have seen us watching his every move, and decided to have a little fun with us.

He walked over to my mom, and said, " Alice, may I have the next dance?" Well I can tell you, Alice was in shock. She picked herself up, and waltzed off with

On Stage, Strand Theatre, New York, 1941.

Mr. Sinatra, while all the glamour girls sat there in utter disappointment. I'm sure that was the biggest story ever told in Alice's Beauty Shop back in Chicago.

After our engagement at the Strand, we packed and headed for the train station and back to Chicago. It was good to be home, but it was not for long. After a couple of weeks, we had to hit the studio again, to restage and rehearse the show. Our next booking was in Mexico City working at the Follies Bergère. It was a big review with Cantinflas, the Latin American Star and Comedian, who later on starred with David Niven in "Around the World in 80 Days."

I packed my trunk again, and with a few misgivings, was ready to say goodbye to Mom, Vincent and John. I had no idea what the future had in store for me, or the United States. Flying was not very popular at the time, so we were back on the train again off to Mexico City. We had bedroom compartments, which were quite snazzy.

I didn't know at the time how much time I would be spending in that compartment. Everything was fine until we hit Laredo, Texas, which was on the border of the United States and Mexico. We had to

Mexico City, "The Folies Bergère," 1941.

go through customs, with our luggage, and all the trunks which held our costumes. I only remember starting to cross a bridge back to the hotel, where we were staying overnight, and suddenly I passed out. The next thing I knew, I was back on the train in my lovely compartment, and very ill. When we arrived in Mexico City, the press was waiting for us; but not little old me. The cast got off the train, and the press was shooting pictures and welcoming us to Mexico City.

Unfortunately, I was carried off the train and taken to our apartment, where eventually the doctor showed up. He said, "It's nothing drastic, you're in Mexico. It's the altitude. She'll be okay in a couple of weeks. She just has to get used to the climate and she'll be good as new."

The phrase "couple of weeks" did not go over big with Teacher. The cast started rehearsals at the theater, and then finally one day I was feeling better, and Teacher decided I should come to rehearsal. So I packed my dance bag and headed for the theater.

I thought, "I'll be okay," and so I hit the stage. But when "I hit the stage," that's what I mean. I went for a back flip, and my elbows buckled and I fell flat on my head. It didn't seem to bother Teacher, but then it wasn't her head.

She just said, "Get up and try again, you'll get used to it." I tried to tell her that my balance was still a little off, but she would have none of it. Her philosophy was "Get up and do it, you'll be fine!" But this time, it didn't work. I still needed a little time to "come back," but in her threatening way she said, "I guess I'll have to send for Carol to replace you."

I didn't even flinch. I looked at her and said, "Well I guess that's what you'll have to do. It's okay with me."

With that, she looked at me, and with a slight wave of her hand dismissed me. I do believe she realized I really didn't have my balance back, so she told me to be back tomorrow and work on it.

"We only have a couple of weeks before we open," she warned, "And keep those elbows straight!"

I did get my balance back, and the altitude didn't bother me anymore. It was one of the most wonderful times of my life in Mexico, with the lovely Mexican people. But we did have problems. It was not a show without injury. Poor Jayne had bleeding

Mexico City, 1941

toes from the point number, and a couple of the girl's got hurt doing "over the back" flips, but we all survived.

Once I got my balance back, I kept my elbows straight and didn't hit my head anymore. Working with Cantinflas was a pleasure. All of South America and Mexico loved him. We did two shows at the Follies, and after the last show, we hopped in our bus and drove to the "El Patio" nightclub, where we did a late show. The "Patio" was the very popular and "in" club, and all the movie stars would take their vacations in Mexico from Hollywood. They would all come to see the show, and it was awesome to see Charlie Chaplin, Paulette Goddard, Clark Gable and many stars sitting in the audience and applauding us. The routines we were doing were outstanding.

The El Patio Night Club, Mexico City, 1941

One number was "Au Claire de la Lune." Rita Roper took the part of Pierot, the famous clown. She did back flips, while the other girls in ballerina skirts carried masks.

Then there was another fun number, "Got a Date with an Angel." The girls were dressed in red tights and devil ears, holding the Devil's pitchfork. There was a blackout, and the girls would run and hide beneath a table close to the dance floor. When the lights came up, a beautiful white angel would be dancing on point and the Devils would fly out and dance around her, doing flips and other acrobatic tricks. It was a spectacular number.

I had an unusual experience. I loved to perform "Zing Went the Strings of my Heart." I had performed this number at least 500 times, but one show I came out, and lost the whole thing in a second. I guess I was having early Alzheimers. So what do you do? Start to fake it. I brought back every step I had ever known, and of course as the saying goes, "When in doubt, keep turning!" I did every turn I knew until I was dizzy, and took my bow like Eleanor Powell. After three shows, it suddenly came back like it had never left, and I was back to normal.

We settled in, and we all loved our time in Mexico, particularly going to Xochimilco, the floating gardens, thirteen miles from Mexico City. We arrived, and stepped onto one of the beautiful wooden boats called Trajineas. The Mariachis were playing as we came along side other Trajineas, with floating kitchens. You could order wonderful Mexican food while you cruised up and down the canal. We also loved going to Sandbourns American Restaurant, and Cantinflas taking us to the bullfights on the day he was fighting the bull. He was very funny. He would enter the ring and acknowledge the crowd as if he were the greatest matador in the world. The crowd would applaud and yell as the bull entered the ring. Cantinflas would dance around with all his great moves, and then his pants would start to fall down, and the crowd would roar and rock the stands. He would come over to the stand where we were sitting, and dedicate the bull to us, and that's no bull. Of course, that was an honor.

Marilyn Marsh, our Buddy Rich girl, was taken with one of the matadors. We were invited back to meet them after the bull fights. We had the privilege of meeting several of the young handsome men. She asked the one she had her eye on if she could have a souvenir and he gave her his sword with which he had killed the bull. Marilyn accepted the bloody gift and took it back to our apartment. We never thought any more about it until we arrived back in Chicago. Marilyn's Mother opened her trunk and the stench almost gagged her. Marilyn was our problem child, but fun, and I do have fond memories of her.

Her Royal Highness, Grace of Monaco, was a roommate of Marilyn's when they were both starting out in New York. Marilyn loved to impress you. She was a name dropper. Years later she would say, "I really need to call Grace."

I said back to Marilyn, "I would have called her, but I didn't have her number."

After a few weeks in Mexico, the stage door "Johnnies" or I guess you would say, stage door, "Josés" started arriving. They had to pass Leah's inspection.

I met Fofo, a real charmer. He did charm Leah right into allowing little old me to go out with him. He came from a very prominent family that supposedly owned a big Mexican cigarette factory. He took me to lunch one day and said, "I'd like to show you my office."

I wondered why, but what could

DOROTHY DALE, L/
"VENUS DE ORO"

Dorothy Dale, "LA VENUS DE ORO," Mexico City, 1941

happen in a cigarette factory, so trusty me said "Okay." I knew it would be all right with Leah, 'cause she seemed to like him.

FOLIES BERGÈRE, Mexico City, Dorothy waiting to "hit the stage"! Carolyn, Jayne, Marilyn, sitting Betty Olds

I thought, "That's an old line, but I'll take a chance," since he knew that I knew that Leah knew, so off we went. We went into his office, and posters of me that were posted throughout Mexico advertising the show covered one wall. Dorothy Dale "La Venus De Oro." I must say I was impressed. And he became my favorite date in Mexico.

Most of our time was spent doing shows, but we did find time for fun until December 7th, 1941. We were in our dressing room when a news bulletin came on, and some of the staff in the theatre came running to tell us that Pearl Harbor had been bombed. The announcement didn't mean a thing to us. We had no idea what or where Pearl Harbor was, or why we should care, until the next day when we heard that the Japanese had bombed our ships and we had lost many, many young men that were stationed there. It was a surprise attack. Now we began to wonder how this would affect us, being in another country. We continued in our normal way, until our contract was up and then we started packing to return home. One of the ex-Abbott Dancers was Betty Lou Michleberry, she was married to a serviceman who was stationed there and was killed.

Christmas Card from Cantinflas, 1942

92

When it was time to leave, Fofo came over to say how much he would miss me and hoped I would come back to Mexico some day. He gave me all these wonderful gifts to take with me: Mexican records, music that I loved, perfume, linens, a lovely watch, etc. Our stay in Mexico City will never be forgotten.

We arrived at the train station with our gifts and luggage and it all had to go through customs. Now that there was a war on, it was a nightmare.

The agent confiscated my records and when I asked why, he said, "There might be a message on them!"

I believe he just wanted the records, 'cause he told me they would test them and send them to me. I'm still waiting. I was able to bring a leader of the Tabu cologne home. Though some people snub their nose at Tabu, I still have it on my dressing table. It brings back fond memories.

I had a feeling I was going to click my heels again, and life would never be the same. There would be new happenings, new places, and new people would enter my life. I was looking forward to whatever came along. We had some time off and since the show in the Empire Room was already set. I was rather restless. I was working out and taking dance class every day.

Eddy Shavers was the young black tap teacher who had urged me to try out for the tap contest, and once more Eddy was there for me.

We were talking after class one day and he said, "Dorothy, I think it's time you go on your own, get an act together. You need an agent!" He told me how to go about it, but I really didn't understand what it would entail. He continued, "There's a war going on out there, and there's lots of work. You have to take the first step and release yourself from Teacher. I heard what she did to you in New York when Eddy Cantor wanted you. If you don't get out now, you never will."

Here I was at seventeen, and a virgin in the business, and many other ways. I would be going into a world I only half knew. I had been protected as long as I was with the Abbotts, but now I would be responsible for myself and make my own decisions.

I thought about the hard decisions my mom had to make, and said to myself, "You can do it." I knew I had to make peace with Ms. Abbott, because she had done a lot for me. So I clicked my heels and made an appointment to see her. I walked in and said "Hello" and she asked me to sit down.

"Dorothy do you have a problem?" she inquired.

I started. "No Teacher, it's not a problem, it's a decision. I've come to tell you something and I want to be honest with you about what I have in mind. I've decided to get an act together, and go out on my own. But it's

U.S. Naval Training Station,
Great Lakes, 1942

kind of like a young man asking for the hand of your daughter. I would like you to say it's okay and let me go with your blessings."

She studied me for a moment and then asked, "Well Dorothy, what makes you think you're sprinkled with stardust?"

Quick as a flash I said, "You did!"

I saw a twinkle in her eye, and then I went on, I was on a roll. "I wondered if you would sell me my costumes, orchestrations, and tap shoes, 'cause you see, I have no money to get new wardrobe."

I am sure she was amused. "Well Dorothy, is there anything else you would like?"

I said, "No!"

She picked up the phone and called the wardrobe lady. She said, "Get together Dorothy Dale's costumes, music and tap shoes. She will be over to pick them up!" And then she said, "Good luck!" I guess she was my first "angel" in show business...

Teach did ask me for one last favor. She said, "Eddy Duchin called today, and asked if you would join him at Great Lakes Naval Station for a show."

I said I would be happy to, especially now that I had my costumes, music and tap shoes. She just laughed. I met the band bus on the appointed night, and we took off for Great Lakes with Eddy and the band. It was an enormous crowd of "navy blue and bell bottoms." Eddy Peabody, the great banjo man, was head of special services. When the show ended and the deafening applause subsided, I was

Eddy Duchin 1942

in total shock. Eddy turned to me to take another bow, and also asked the band to do the same. We thought it was the end of the show, but then out of the blue we heard a voice.

Eddy Peabody made the announcement. This would be the last night the Eddy Duchin band would be together until after the war. Eddy Duchin would be commissioned as an officer in the navy. We all said goodbye. It was an honor to have been the last act to perform with The Eddy Duchin Orchestra. So now I would be on my own, doing it alone.

I did know the choreographer Fred Evans at the "Chez Paree" and some of the "Chez Paree Adorables," the line of beautiful girls who backed up the acts at the Chez!

The Chez Paree was in an old warehouse, not far from Lake Michigan on North Fairbanks Ct., the two owners were Mike Fritzel and Joe Jacobson. It was on the second floor. At the entrance, the doorman would greet you. You would never suspect what was beyond the elevator door. When it opened, and you stepped into this lavish setting, it took your breath away. It was blue

Seventy years after Eddy Duchin was inducted into the service at Great Lakes Naval Station, Peter Duchin and I met again, at the Marriott Hotel, Palm Desert, Ca, 2001

and gold, with this humongous dance floor, and tables and chairs surrounding the dance floor. To perform on this stage would be awesome.

All the great stars of the 40s and 1950s played this room, and so to be part of this would be a miracle. Jimmy Durante, Lena Horne, Helen Morgan, Harry Richman, Danny Kaye and Milton Berle, graced its stage, just to name a few. So after my talk with Eddy Shavers, this was my goal: to work the Chez.

"Now let's see," I thought, "How would I go about it?" I guess I would call the choreographer and ask to see him. He set up an appointment for me. I was excited, I could hardly contain myself. The bewitching day

The last of the Abbott dancers from the forties, fifty years later!
Marilyn Ruckberg, Jayne McNulty, Dorothy Dale and Carolyn Truax,
2000.

"The Glory Days," The Chez Paree, the 40s

arrived, and I put on my best hat, took my resume and tap shoes, and headed for the train to the loop, to the unknown. I got off the elevator, and heard talking. I followed the voices to the dining room where the choreographer was rehearsing some girls. I said "Hi!"

He said, "Let's chat!" I gave him my resume, and he said, "Oh, I've seen you in the Empire Room! So now you want to move on?"

"Yes," I said. "And I would like to work here."

In the blink of an eye he said, "Well get out those tap shoes, and let's see what you have put together." My first reaction was, "don't blow this," and I went into my act.

He said, "Very nice," and excused himself. He came back in about ten minutes, and said the magic words, "How would you like to be in the new show with Phil Regan, the singing policeman from New York?" And so my dream had come true.

We did three shows a night. The dinner show and late show were the same, and the middle show was different. You had to have enough material to cover both shows. I had a few weeks before the opening, so I was very busy working on my act. Opening night arrived, and I was very

The Big Time, 1942

excited and nervous at the same time, but it went really well. The headliners were Phil Reagan, Jackie Miles, the comedian, Mata and Hari, the famous dance team, and Dorothy Dale, ME!! It was really a thrill for me to be working with these people, and they were all terrific and nice to the "new kid on the block."

Now the mystery began. All the agents in town wondered who this kid was, and how did she get the job? Who booked her in this famous club without an agent? I was approached several times by agents asking. But the only one I liked was Ray Lite from the O'Malley Office. He didn't come on like, "Who are you and how could this happen?"

He introduced himself, told me who he was representing, and how much he liked my act. No hardball; just nice. Then he said, "You know, you have to have an agent. They get you the work, and I would really like to represent you."

I said, "I think I would like that!" He gave me his card, and told me to come and see him, which I did. And I had my first agent.

When the Phil Regan show closed, I stayed on. Harry Richman came in as the headliner. He was a lovely man. I didn't know it at the time, but I quickly found out. This is one of my favorite stories about Harry. I was not too savvy about things at that time, not as bright as the young people of today. One day, this woman came knocking on my dressing room door and introduced herself as the hat lady. I was bewildered and wondered what she wanted.

Back in the 1940s and 1950s, everyone wore hats. She was a real hustler and started to take hats out of a box for me to try on. "You know Mr. Richman sent me down to see you," she explained. "He would like to buy you a hat!"

I said, "Why would he want to do that? I can buy my own hats. I would thank you to tell him no, but thank you very much."

She was persistent, I said "No, now please leave." A little while later, as I was going into the dining room, I had to pass Harry's dressing room. As I did, a hand came out and grabbed my arm.

Richman to Chez Paree May 22

Mike Fritzel and Joe Jacobson are shrewd enough to sign stellar attractions to appear during the Summer months at their Chez Paree on N. Fairbanks ct.

The first of the new stage presentations, opening May 22, will be headed by Harry Richman. Comedy will keynote the revue with a comical lad, a newcomer, Alan Carney in the lineup. Carney has confined his talents to clubs and stages in the East and South. Mike Fritzel returned from a recent talent hunt in the South and reports that another clever entertainer is Danny Kaye.

Following the show starring Richman, will be Milton Berle . . . providing motion picture commitments do not interfere.

Messrs. Fritzel and Jacobson plan to do some more serious searching for new acts to build around the stars scheduled to appear at Chez Paree in the near future. Many well known acts today gained their recognition because of the opportunity to appear at the famous Chicago night club.

The current Fred Evans production at Chez Paree features Phil Regan, singing star, plus Jackie Miles, comedian. Mata and Hari, international dance satirists, the Murphy Sisters, Dorothy Dale, Buddy Franklin and his orchestra and the Chez Paree Adorables complete the show cast, with Lucio Garcia and the Chez Paree Rhumba Band appearing as alternate musicians.

DAILY TIMES, CHICAGO

Navy Pier show dispels gloom of boys in blue

(Pictures on page 14)

Gorgeous gals, uproarious comedy, and plenty of sweet and swingy music!

Those were the weapons utilized last night by the Chez Paree crew of merrymakers in a blitzkrieg on the blues staged for the entertainment of more than 3,000 sailors and marines stationed at Navy Pier.

There was no need to ask if the mission was successful. Absorbed attention paid by the boys in blue to the smooth singing of radio and screen star Phil Regan and their uproarious shouts of laughter at the antics of emcee Jackie Miles gave ample evidence of direct hits by all the gloom dispellers launched by the Chez Paree company.

GIRLS GET MANY ENCORES

The Murphy Sisters, an easy-to look-at trio, scored instantaneous popularity with their rendition of some of the songs which their recordings have made famous. They were recalled for encore after encore, as were Dorothy Dale, who demonstrated heel and toe dexterity in a fast-moving tap ballet number, and Mata and Hari, a clever comedy acrobatic team.

One of the high spots of the show was the intricate precision routine staged by the eye-filling Chez Paree Adorables. They went through their paces to the music of Buddy Franklin's orchestra, which supplied the musical background for the entire show.

Scrapbook Memories, 1942

Harry said, "So you don't want a hat?" I went on to explain that the hat lady was only trying to make a sale, and she was using him. He said, "I've been used before my darling!" And then he laughed and said, "I wanted to be used. She's just trying to make a living. I really would like to buy you a hat. Come on now, be nice, then I can take you to dinner and you can wear it!"

What a night, with Harry Richman, (Puttin' On The Ritz Man). Just saw the show at the Empire Room, and stopped for a coke.

It was the beginning of a really nice friendship, and for the run of the show, he took me everywhere and I met all his fabulous friends. When the show closed, he gave a great party at his suite in the Hotel Seneca. He moved on to his next engagement and so did I, but I have wonderful memories of Harry.

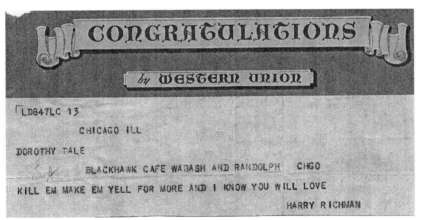

Opening night at The Blackhawk, Chicago, 1942

Chapter 13: On the Road Again

When my next engagement at the Blackhawk (the famous night club in Chicago) ended, the O'Malley office immediately signed me on and I started playing nightclubs, theatres and hotel showrooms across the USA. I did get butterflies every time I started to pack and catch a train to where ever the agent sent me. Just another adventure – "ON THE ROAD AGAIN!"

A new theatre opened in Chicago in the downtown area known as the Downtown Theatre, now that's original. Honestly! The movie showing was *Swing Hostess,* staring Martha Tilton. On stage The Mills Brothers, The Carl Ravazza Orchestra with vocalist Jackie Van, Ladd Lyon and, "yours truly," Dorothy Dale. What is so amazing is that we did four shows a day, 12:30, 3:30, 6:30 and 9:00 p.m.

Remember, this was in 1942 and things were very different for black acts. The Mills Brothers were the headliners, but they

Opening Show at The Blackhawk, 1942

The Blackhawk, 1942.

ALL BRACED and ready to soar on the Flying Scooters at Riverview Park are Dorothy Dale and Art Jarrett, dancer and band leader of the Blackhawk Cafe.

*Return to
The Blackhawk, 1942*

Porky Dankers, 1942

had to dress in the basement of the theatre, and yet they stopped every show with their wonderful harmony. They had hit records, and many awards, but no matter, that was the way it was and they lived with it.

In 2000, I was in the Follies. The Mills Brothers, were the headliners, only this time it was one of the original Brothers, Donald, and his son John. I brought in the original newspaper with the theatre section advertising the Downtown Theater in 1942, I asked Donald to sign it for me. What a treasure for my memory book.

My sad return in 1988 to the Blackhawk. All the Big Bands played there in the 1940s.

This time working together, they were upstairs in a lovely dressing room and I was downstairs in the basement with the cast of the Follies. What was amazing about working movie theatres was that you usually did four to five shows a day, six days a week. If the patrons made the matinee before 1p.m., the cost was 37 cents, and then 50 cents after that, plus tax. Now to see a movie for two, it's $25.00. With popcorn and two cokes, forget it!

How things have changed. The Chicago Theatre was another wonderful theatre right on State and Randolph. I loved working the Chicago Theatre with Eddy Duchin and Billy De Wolfe, the funniest man alive. Several years later, Billy worked on the "Doris Day Show" on television. I used to stand in the wings and watch Billy do his act, and after a hundred shows, you can do most everyone's act.

If you can, picture this. The theatre is dark, and from the side Billy makes his entrance as Frankenstein. A green light hits him, and he starts to walk down the aisle. The audience is screaming, and then he turns around and heads up the side steps to the stage. The lights flicker, and suddenly, he is standing in his coat and tie to great applause. My favorite was when he did Mrs. Murgatroyd, the lady who stopped off for a little nip after shopping. Billy had a lady's hat on with a flower on the front. He kept having another nip until he could hardly get up and then staggered off.

One of his great lines when he was doing an impression of a chorus girl, looking up at the light man, and saying with a twinkle in his eye, "See you after the show honey!" Of course he was in drag, and no one cared, it was just a character he was playing. That was before computer lighting.

Now, I always say, the light man use to follow me, but now I have to follow the light man. It's all computerized. The lights are set for every move you make, and you better hit your mark, or you're out of the light. God forbid an act would be out of the spotlight. My, how things have changed! But in those days, I loved talking to the light man and asking his advice on which light would be best for me. It was a kinder time. It was not the fast pace we live in now.

I find it very hard as a dancer who likes to cover the whole stage. In a recent production I was in, if you went too far, a memo would come back that you were out of the light. I feel it takes a lot of your freedom of movement away, but that's today's technology. You have a zero for center stage. Left Stage and Right Stage are numbered 0 to 12 on both sides.

Downtown Theatre

We had a gentleman named Don McCardle in the cast of the Follies. He was my favorite, I guess because he loved to talk. So we would sit in the green room and discuss world events, and many other happenings. One day, he came in during rehearsal and told me he just couldn't get to sleep last night. Between looking for the spotlight and how far he could go, and the number he should hit on the stage, he couldn't remember the routine. So you see, dancing in a group is not just a "walk in the park."

Don was a great tap dancer, and taught in his own school in Stow, Ohio for years. He was always a jolly fellow who would do anything for you. One day, I came into the green room for my break expecting the news of the day from Don, but he seemed down.

I asked, "Is anything wrong?" He said, "Yes, but I don't know what to do about it." "Well, Don, tell me about it," I had a sincere interest. He said, "I'm too embarrassed!" But I told him, in my usual manner, "Spit it out."

"I don't know how the whole thing

Downtown Theatre,
Newspaper article.

got started," he continued, "except human resources called me into his office." He told me that he had gotten a complaint from the manager of "See's Candies," which was down the block from the theatre. See's gave out a free sample of chocolate to anyone that came into the store. Don knew everyone in the store and had made several purchases. I remember at Christmas, he had a five hundred dollar order. The HR person said, "I hear you go to See's every day and get a free piece of chocolate. We don't want you doing that. It's not good for our image."

I said to Don, "What right does the Follies have to tell you what to do outside of the theatre? That's your private life, and your business. I think you should go down to the store and ask the manager if he reported this to the Follies."

So Don took my advice and marched himself to See's, and asked the manager if they had called the Follies about him.

The manager said, "Don, what are you talking about? We would never do that to someone that has spent as much money in this store as you have! We give samples out every day. Do you think we keep track of who is getting a piece of candy?"

The next day, HR was passing through the green room on his way to the theatre. Don and I were sitting on the couch, I said to Don, "Now is your chance, get him." I do believe I pushed Don into it. He jumped up and immediately confronted the HR man. He told him he had talked to the manager and what he said. HR didn't know where to go and admitted it was a hoax.

Don McCardle, Mimi Hines, and Dot

Don asked him why he would do something like that and HR said, "One of the cast members had been talking in the green room and made a statement that you always go into See's for a piece of candy every day. We didn't want you to do that." Is the jury still out? Don quit the show at the end of the year. Too bad, he was an asset to the show. In my day, I don't remember anything so petty and childish. I guess we were too busy worrying about "freedom" for our country.

I was booked into The Shreveport Hotel in Shreveport, Louisiana, with Tommy Lowe's Orchestra in "The Zephyr Room." I loved Shreveport. It was a charming city, and I made many friends, including many service men. They were stationed nearby, and came to see the show when they could get a pass. The girl singer with the band, Karen, and I hit it off immediately. Among our friends was Ellie married to Russ, one of the musicians in the band. It seemed like we had our own fan club with about ten soldiers, who seemed to be at our show more than at the camp. We would have dinner with them, and sometimes if they had a stay over pass, we joined them for breakfast. On their last pass they told us they would be moving out and asked, would we write?

Karen, Ellie and I talked to the band, and decided to give them a send-off after our show. Back in the 1940s, they still had a detective on duty in hotels to be sure no "funny business" was going on. They actually toured the halls of the hotel. If they thought something was going on, they would knock on the door to check it out. We were having the party in Ellie and Russ's room, so there wouldn't be a problem. But with all the noise we were making, we still got the knock on the door.

We opened the door and there was the house "dick." We told the detective that we were giving the boys a send off. Stoically he just said, "Okay, but keep it down." Just before it was time for us to say goodbye, one of the guys asked Karen to sing a song. He said to me, "Dorothy, we would love one last dance from you but the detective might come back." She started to sing this lovely heart-rending song that was very popular at the time:

When you're a long, long way from home
It's nice to know you're not alone
It's nice to have a friend that's true
That you can tell your troubles too, and
When you write a letter home
Your Mother's voice rings in your ear, then you
Cross the T's with kisses what a great world this is
Then you dot the I's with tears
When you're a long, long way from home.
When you're a long, long way from home

As you can imagine, there was not a dry eye in the room. We gave them all a hug, a kiss, and wished them a safe journey.

The Kentucky Hotel and the Brown Hotel in Louisville, KY were two of my favorites. They both had great showrooms. The Brown's showroom was the Bluegrass Room. It was great to play it during the Kentucky Derby. The Kentucky Hotel showroom was the Terrace Room. It was a larger room and had the big bands. I played it with the Bernie Cummins Orchestra.

Stan Kramer and Co. joined me at the Kentucky Hotel. What a joy to count them as my new family. Mom, Pop and

Louisville, KY, Kentucky Hotel, 1943

Stan, who was around my age, comprised the company. We hit it off immediately. Their act was sensational. Pop and Stan worked marionettes or puppets, whichever they chose for each particular act, and they were adorable. They had a mobile home, due to all their baggage, like a sewing machine so Mom could make the costumes for the puppets. What was really fun — they would have the acts from the show over for dinner, and sometimes after the show. I thought it was a hoot to have dinner in their home-away-from-home parked in a trailer park. They adopted me forever more, and we continued to work many places together like the

Stan Kramer and Co., 1943

Judy Blair and Larry Hooper, Riviera Night Club, St. Louis, Mo, 1945. Judy moved on to the Del Courtney Orchestra, and Larry joined Lawrence Welk on TV.

Edgewater Beach Hotel right on Lake Michigan. They also recommended me to WBKB, the first television station in Chicago.

Many years later after the war, Mom and Pop passed away and Stan found a partner to share his life. We lost touch until I was looking at a TV show one day and Stan, who worked at the TV station, was being interviewed. They were showing his beautiful house, and the Christmas Wonderland he and his partner had created. Bob Floury, my friend at the time, called the station and got Stan's phone number. I called him, and after 30 years, we found each other again. The first time he invited us to dinner, we headed for the family room, on the wall behind the bar was the picture I had given him all those years gone by. I loved those people, but then they knew that.

My next best friend was Judy Blair, who sang with several of the big bands; Del Courtney and George Olsen to name a few. I was booked into the Rivera nightclub in St. Louis with the George Olsen Orchestra. The first person I met was this pretty Portuguese and Irish girl who was the singer with the band, Judy. We became friends almost from that first moment. Judy loved to laugh until she cried. I use to kid her and say, "Is this one of those sad or glad moments?" And of course, it was always a glad moment. It was a fun band to work with, and the musicians were great. When Larry Hooper left George Olson, he went with The Lawrence Welk Orchestra. He was the pianist with the low voice.

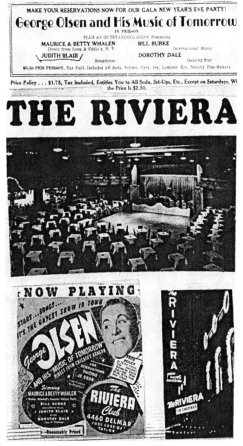

St. Louis, Mo, 1943

George Olsen was also the musical director for several Broadway shows. One was "Sunny" with the famed Marilyn Miller, in 1925. He also made several records. The one I remember was "Sweet Kentucky Babe" and on the other side was Judy singing, " Chickery Chick, Cha La Cha La." It was on all the jukeboxes, and when it came out, the band happened to be in Chicago. My brother Vincent took Judy and I out one evening, and we hit several places with jukeboxes. Judy would say to Vincent, "Oh Vin, play my record." Then Vincent would run over to the juke box, and play every record but hers. Then we all laughed. We remained friends, or I should say "sisters," until she passed about five years ago. I truly miss her, and all the good times we had. I hope she is singing wherever she is.

The New Colosimo's (a famous Chicago Night Spot), as opposed to the old Colosimo's, was at 2126 S. Wabash, not far from the loop, near the south side of Chicago. Let's go back to the prohibition days, the 1920s and

1930s, when Big Jim Colosimo ruled the underworld longer than any other man, including Al Capone. He owned brothels, and dealt in a white slavery ring and a prostitution ring, among his many enterprises (or so I've been told). Colosimo's Café was recognized as a social and political power center. All the Aldermen, vice lords and powerful community leaders would meet there to conduct business. After Jim Colosimo was killed, the restaurant was sold to the manager. He ran it through the 1940s, with acts like Abbott and Costello. In 1945, I was booked in this famous old nightclub with Ted and Dennis Peters, The Nelson Marionettes, Mel Cole's Orchestra, and the Colosimo Beauties. The added attraction was, Miss Detroit of 1945. How about that? To add to this magical evening, a Whole Broiled Lobster Dinner was $2.50. Don't you love it?

NEW Colosimo's

Presents
PAUL MALL
M. C.
TED and DENNIE PETERS
Nelson's Marionettes
DOROTHY DALE
MEL COLE'S ORCHESTRA
COLOSIMO BEAUTIES
WHOLE BROILED $2 50
LOBSTER DINNER

ADDED ATTRACTION
Opening To-night!
MISS DETROIT OF 1945
Limited Engagement!

ALWAYS GOOD FOOD

For Reservations Call PAUL BERGAMINI
VICTORY 9210—2126 S. WABASH

Colosimo's, near South Side of the Loop, Chicago

Every new engagement was a new adventure. You would arrive at your destination and head for your hotel, sign the register, get your room key, and head for your room. Depending on your rehearsal time, you would go to the venue you would be working. You would be prompt for your rehearsal time out of courtesy to the orchestra, and the other acts in the show. You would arrive at your scheduled time, give the orchestra your orchestrations, and work out your tempo and lights. Most of the time, you would bring your costumes, makeup and anything else you needed for the show, be assigned to your dressing room, and be ready to go depending on the time of the first show. I would usually catch a bite to eat at the nearest restaurant, and go back to the hotel to get ready for the show. You were responsible for yourself to be there on time and find your spot in the lineup. It varied from place to place. I guess I am stressing this because today, everyone seems to have such a "cavalier" approach, to show up on the scheduled time.

A new nightclub opened in Chicago; it was called the Latin Quarter. It was on the second floor and had been a Chinese restaurant called the Oriental Gardens. When the Gardens closed, the Latin Quarter took over. It was a great location at Randolph and State Street, across from the Oriental Theatre. Do you think there was a connection? This was the theater that the Gumm sisters played. You might remember one of the sisters, better known as Judy Garland.

The star of the show at the Latin Quarter was Jackie Coogan. He was a child movie star, better known as *The Kid* with Charlie Chaplin. Jackie had been married to Betty Grable, the GI's pinup girl in World War II. Jackie was not a kid anymore, and had many problems with his parents over the money he made as a child performer. They spent most of it, or so the story goes. He decided to work out an act and perform in night clubs across the country. At this time, he was engaged to a lovely young gal, Ann McCormick, and she was part of the act. So was

Jackie Coogan, Latin Quarter, Chicago, Illinois.

his sidekick, Harry Howe, who played Chaplin. They did a revival of *The Kid*, it was one of the first motion pictures when Jackie was five or six. Jackie would sit on the lap of his sidekick, just like he sat on Charlie Chaplin's lap when he was "The Kid"! It was very funny, and the audience loved it. The other acts on the bill, the famous Latin performer Diosa Costello, and once again, "herself," Dorothy Dale.

Jackie was a lovely man. He said to me one evening, "Dorothy, you live right here in Chicago, yes, on the north side?"

I said, "Yes," and then he went on to tell me about his new station wagon and how much he loved driving it. "How do you get home Dorothy?" he inquired.

I said, "Well, I take the 'L' and then when I get to the Wilson Ave. Station, I take a cab."

Diosa Costello, Latin Quarter, Chicago, Illinois.

Jackie paused for a moment, and then said, "I would be happy to drive you home. It would give us a chance to break in the new car." For the duration of our engagement, I was chauffeured home by Jackie Coogan, Ann, and Harry.

No matter if you're in show business or another business, you always run into people taking advantage of you. Someone with Jackie's star quality was ripe for every scheme out there, wanting a piece of the action.

One day, I passed Jackie's dressing room and saw a gentleman discussing something with him, but I went on my way. When I returned, I passed his room again. His door was open, but he was sitting alone. He saw me and waved for me to come in.

"I just had a visit from Billboard Magazine," he said somewhat downheartedly. Billboard was the bible of show business newspapers, along with several others. It was full of information on who's who and where they were playing. They would also critique the shows in town. Everybody read it, and you hoped you would get a good review. He looked over at me and said, "I can tell you right now, our show will not be getting a good review. But that's okay, the audience loves us." It was just an "all right" review when it came out. The rep from Billboard was trying to pressure Jackie to buy the back cover, and when he said "no," that was it for the show.

When you're in show business you have to live and accept criticism; rejection is another word for, "so get over it." But it didn't matter. The show continued with turn-away crowds and we all lived happily ever after.

To close the door on Jackie, I have one funny story. He was going bald. He used to sit in his dressing room with the door open so he knew when to go on. The entrance to the stage was right there, and I would stand waiting for my music to start. Jackie would yell out to me, "Dorothy,

I wish I had your hair. Gosh, you have thick hair and look at me."
enough hair for three people. But with or without hair, he was one
nicest men I ever met.

The O'Malley office was a great agency to work with. All the agents
associated with the office, and Ray Lite my first agent, were great. They
all worked together to get you the best jobs. Doris Herdick, who was a
former dancer, booked a lot of club dates. Tweet Hogan was always after
me to play a club on the North side that he booked called Helsings. It was
a bowling alley with a nightclub. You might not think this was a dream job,
but the club was really lovely with graduated rows of tables and booths.
The only problem was, the stage was not built for a Broadway show. It was
large enough for a five-piece band and a standup comedian. If you took a
step forward, you would be in the bartender's lap. The bar was below the
stage, so you see the problem. Everybody from George Gobel, John Gary
and Mark Fisher played there, and I loved going there on a date. Every
Monday night was agent's night. They would come to catch new acts and
also established acts that might want to try out new material. Everyone
worked there, and it was fun just to go and see the show.

Unfortunately the stage was much too small for a dancer, but Tweet
would pursue me at least once a month, to play Helsings. I would tell him
the same thing every time I went to the office. He would see me from his
office and yell out to me, "How about next week, I can book you."

I would yell back, "I'm not ready to commit suicide, Tweet."

He would laugh and he'd say, "I'll call you next month, but in the
meantime I have a couple dates for you."

I loved working club dates and for those of you who are not familiar
with "club dates," they are mostly for organizations and conventions. The
pay was great and you could stay at home and work three or four nights
a week. They were so easy. You would arrive at your destination, find the
showroom, give the band your music, and wait to go on. Most of the time,
the orchestra would be a relief band; ten or twelve pieces with great
musicians. They would play at the hotels and nightclubs like the Chez
Paree, The Blackhawk and Palmer House on the regular band's night off.
Hence the term "relief band."

Lou Diamond was one of my favorites, and I did many club dates with
him. My favorite, the Tea Dance at the Sherman Hotel, in The Panther
Room, on Saturday afternoon. The couples would dance the afternoon
away. Lou and his band played all the "ballads" and swing music. And
between tea and rum and Coca Cola, we listened to "Give Me Five Minutes
More," "I'll Walk Alone," and if you remember, "Kiss me once and kiss me

twice and kiss me once again, it's been a long, long time," and "'Til We Meet Again." All those songs were great; some made us feel good and some sad, depending if that favorite GI guy was coming home or going overseas.

I remember one club date. Tweet called and said another act would be picking me up. It was a country club and I had no transportation. George Gobel, a country singer on WLS radio and on *The National Barn Dance*, would be picking me up. If you were from my generation, you will remember George on TV in 1954 to 1955, *The George Gobel Show*, which was rated in the Top 10. George picked me up, and while driving to the gig, we talked about how great to be working club dates. He said, "Boy, I love these club dates. It gives me a chance to perform live."

At which point I said, "Is there any other way?" Of course we did run into some dead audiences.

He went on, "You know, you can break in new material and pickup that check every Friday." Not too many years later, club dates were a thing of the past for George. But look what happened to him; he became a big star and a very nice fellow to boot.

So club dates came and went, but one was unforgettable. I had just returned from Cleveland.

Monaco's, 1940s

While there, I had met this charming opera singer, Placida, who was married with two children. She and her husband invited me to dinner several times. When she said she would be coming to Chicago, I said we would get together. Little did I know, she had been exposed to the measles. After they left town, I had a club date. I awoke with red rashes all over my body. It was German measles. I had to call the office, and cancel the date, but they all thought it was funny even though they had to find another act. Tweet gabbed the phone and said, "You're being punished for not playing Helsings." I could not imagine where I caught them until it dawned on me that Placida had told me her children had just gotten over them before she left for Chicago. We stayed friends, but I always checked from then on when and who and where she had been before we made a date.

It was an agent's blunder that almost cost me playing at my favorite nightclub in Cleveland. Monaco's was a lovely dinner club, and I played it several times a year. Mr. Monaco was a wonderful man to work for, and I always had a good working relationship with him. The club had a great house band. That was the band that would remain for each show while the variety acts always changed. I was still performing the Georgie Tapps routine. I was in the lobby, on my way out, when four gentlemen came out of the dining room. The one man eyed me, and with a big smile, started walking toward me. Then he extended his hand, and said, "Dorothy, well done. I enjoyed your performance. Thank you for using my song." Well, of course you know, it was Irving Berlin.

Now getting back to that blundering agent who will remain nameless. Several months after I closed at Monaco's, my agent called to tell me he was booking me in a new club in Cleveland called Lenny's. Enthusiastically, he said, "It's going to be the in-spot and the money is terrific. I want you to play it." I was skeptical, and told him that I did not think it was a good idea, since I always worked for Mr. Monaco, and would feel like a traitor.

He said, "No problem. Acts always play other spots. Not to worry, it will be okay." I signed the contract and was off to Lenny's. I lived to regret my decision. I arrived at Lenny's and everyone

NIGHT CLUB show without trippers of the light fantastic would never do, and here are some of the dancers currently appearing at Cleveland night spots. Dorothy Dale (left) is the tap expert in the floor show at Monaco's Cafe. Lischeron and Adams (right) form the ballroom team at Herman Pirchner's Alpine

Monaco's, 1940s

seemed nice. I rehearsed with the band, checked out the other acts that had arrived, said "hello," and went into shock when the one gal, and her parrot, both said hello.

115

Now I love animals, but I was not ready for this one. I knew right off that she was a stripper and would be dancing with that Macaw during her number. He would be picking off parts of her costume in very private places. Then to make things even worse, the ad came out in the newspaper advertising the new club and the show with me in it! Unfortunately, I had signed the contract and I was stuck. I called the agent, and told him how angry I was, and that I didn't work with strippers or birds of any kind! I could not believe he had booked me in this club. My next move was to see Mr. Monaco and try to explain. He was furious with the agent, not with me. He told me to go do the shows, and he would fix it within the next few days. A week later, the agent called me to say I was out of the contract and would open at Monaco's for six weeks, the following week. So I said "goodbye" to all the acts, and told them to break a leg; but of course not the Macaw.

While I was at Lenny's, one of the owner's had a son. Nat, wanted to be friends, and as you know, I make friends easily. He looked like Rock Hudson and that helped a lot. We hit it off and he was a charmer. I went to dinner with him a couple of times. He asked me out again, and I told him that my mother was in town, to which he said, "Bring her along." That made points with me. Off we went, and had a wonderful time. The owners of the club also owned an after-hours club that was opened from midnight to four or five a.m. We liked to go there after the show to eat and listen to the music.

Right after mom left, Nat invited me to the after hour club for a bite. We finished eating, and I told Nat I was tired and had to go back to the Hotel. He put me in a cab, and I left. And may I say, it was just in time. I do have good timing. I got back to the hotel and got in bed. About an hour later, the phone rang and it was Nat. He sounded very anxious, and said, "Dorothy, there's been a shooting at the club, and I had to get out. Can I come to your room until it calms down?" My Catholic, School girl training came out, and I said, "No Nat, you can't come to my room." I didn't know if I believed him or not about the shooting, or was it a ploy to come to my room. Need I go any further? That romance ended just before dawn. It was true about the shooting, but I never found out if he was involved. I was just happy to leave it there. The incident headlined all the newspapers the next morning.

I headed for Gene Kelly's hometown, Pittsburgh. I have fond memories of the acts in that show. The Southern Sisters and their mother who traveled with them; they had so many stories, and we laughed for the run of the show. They were great friends of the Andrews sisters, and told many funny tales about them. Then there was "Texas Tommy and his horse, Baby Doll." Yes, I said a horse. This was a "night club horse." All he did was bow on cue, but he was adorable, as was Texas Tommy. The horse was very well trained, unlike the parrot, and I had a much better relationship with him. I don't know if Tommy is still around, but I'm sure the horse "hit the dirt." Tommy would sit between shows and carve beautiful pieces out of wood. One day he came in to my dressing room, and handed me an envelope. "Just a little something I thought you would like," he said. He had carved me the most adorable cowboy boot earrings.

Texas Tommy and "Baby Doll"

Pennsylvania had the blue law at this time. No liquor sold after a certain time, which then created the after-hours spots. It was such a foolish law; it just made people want to drink more and break the law. My way of thinking is the "good doers" really were the "bad doers." There was a big after-hour club in town where all the acts would congregate after their last show. A band was on hand, and whatever acts where in town, the MC would announce them, and where they were working. They would ask them to come up on the stage and sing, dance or tell a few jokes. It was fun, and we never got back to the hotel until three or four in the morning. Whatever happened to the good old days?? I live in Palm Springs, everything closes at ten o'clock, but then we have a lot of golfers living here. Probably retired show people. I will NEVER retire.

Back in Chicago, I was walking down State St. and I heard my name. I turned around; it was one of the "Abbott gals." After exchanging news on everyone, she asked me if I knew that Eddy Shavers was back from the war. She said he was having a really tough time, and he needed a job. I was booked solid, but I thought, "Why not get in touch with Eddy? He was after all the one who pushed me to go on my own! And now that he needed help! I should ask him to choreograph a new number for me." He was pleased to hear from me, and so the next week we started work on "Begin the Beguine." I had decided I needed a little Spanish in my act; I became a Blond Senorita. I only had a couple of weeks to work on it, but we got it done, and it was a great routine. I was so happy I could get him going again.

We got the orchestration, and then I had to find the time and place to break it in. There was a nightclub on the south side of Chicago called "The Southside Casino." It was one of my favorite clubs to work. The band was excellent, and it had a raised stage for the show that was lowered after the show for dancing. It was a great place to try out new material, so I got booked for a couple weeks.

I opened there and, everything was going great, the new number seemed to please the audience. I was just rolling along happy as a lark, until one night the lark hit a sour note. I was in my dressing room when I heard a knock at the door. "Dorothy, it's Paul." Paul was the *maître d'*. "I need to discuss something with you!" he called.

So I said, "Come in."

"Dorothy," he forged ahead, "There is someone at the bar that is asking for you and he's black." I figured it was Eddy and I told him Eddy is my choreographer, he just wants to check out the new number. But Paul was adamant, and asked me to speak to him. He said, "Tell him he is not welcome."

I said, "Absolutely not, he is alone and only interested in seeing my routine." I marched down to the bar and sat next to Eddy, and asked him about the number. He gave me a couple of suggestions, had a drink, spoke to me for a few minutes, and left. I'm sure without me saying anything he got the message from Paul's look. I never mentioned my conversation with Paul. It was another time.

The first time I worked the South Side Casino, a young Tommy O'Connell was the singer in the show. He had a lovely Irish tenor voice and nice personality. We took off as a couple

Tommy O'Connell, Mom, and Aunt Mame!
Love that hat!

before the first show was over, and became engaged a few months later. He loved show business. He was from the south side, so he had a great following. Plus he came from this very large Irish Catholic family. He had a little sister that was handicapped in a wheelchair. The family was very devoted to her, and the siblings were expected to share some of the responsibility. That made it difficult for Tommy to be available for out-of-town jobs, and you can't refuse many or the agents will stop calling. I don't know what happened in his life to make the decision he made, but it was one I never expected. We went out one evening and he told me he wanted to break our engagement. He was going into the seminary to study for the priesthood. At least it wasn't another girl. I gave him back his ring and wished him the best. I told him to say a prayer for me. I'm sure he would have had a great career if he could have hung in; I hope it was the right decision for him. As it turned out, it was also the right decision for me.

I met Frank (Doc) Striganic through a friend. He was Polish, loved going to dinner, sports events and anything that was happening in town. He was a newspaper reporter, my kind of guy. We started dating and it seemed every weekend we would attend a Polish wedding. It was great fun doing the Polish dances and by the end of summer I knew them all. He had all these young people working for him. They always invited him to their weddings 'cause they knew he was a generous check writer.

He was also very generous to me. For my birthday, he gave me a lovely fur jacket. When he picked me up for a date, he would tell my mother, "You know Alice, Dorothy could care less about the food; it's all about atmosphere." We dated for about a year and then I broke it off. I can't remember why, well maybe I do, but I'm not sharing it with you.

Shortly after the break-up, I began to worry. He was stalking me in his car. He began parking across the street from where I was teaching and following me home. One night I was going to a novena service at my church, and he was waiting for me when I came out. I was on my way to my sister-in-law's house. He pulled up along the side of the curb, jumped out, and handed me a cigar box. Not a word! That really made me nervous. I dashed over to my sister- in- law's apartment with the box. I told her what happened. I was not sure I wanted to open the box. She said, "Maybe it's a bomb."

I said, "But it's not ticking; maybe it's a snake."

Then she said, "Just drop it on the floor and kick it open."

I did, and then the two of us jumped back getting ready for a getaway. To our surprise, it was filled with money. It also contained a note saying, "This was for your engagement ring, but since that won't happen I want you to buy yourself a ring you would like as a gift from me." Of course now we are laughing, and Vi said, "Let's go to Florida." We didn't go to Florida, but I did go to the bank the next day, and had a money order made out for the amount he sent, and sent it off to him. I asked him to please stop following me. He did.

The Ambassador Hotel in Chicago was famous not only for its elegance and celebrities, but its famous "Pump Room" was the place to meet, greet and be seen. "Kupcinet" was the gossip columnist in the town. His column was in the Chicago Sun Times. He always had booth "number one." Everyone read his column. One day, I received a call from the modeling agency I was with at the time. I had a photo shoot on the roof of the Ambassador for the "Speed Chandler Air Show" that was coming to town. This was exciting!

Jumpin' Jeepers ...AND stronger exclamations might be in order for these female daredevils, Shirlee Jewel (left) and Dorothy Dale. They are the first entrants in the spot parachute landing contest of Maj. Speed Chandler's air show, opening next Friday at the Chicagoland Airport. They're not daring you, but go ahead, get your entry in and your neck out.

Speed Chandler Air Show

I arrived at the hotel, met the other model, and we took the elevator up to the roof for the shoot. We changed into bathing suits and took our places holding a parachute. I was hoping they wouldn't ask us to jump; after all, we were on the roof. I guess that was the easiest way to get it across that this was an air show. In the background was this handsome man talking to Major Chandler and he looked very familiar. We just kept holding the damn parachute that was quite heavy, and we wondered who he was. Before long, we had the pleasure to meet the one and only Clark Gable. Major Chandler had an entourage of friends with him. When we finished the shoot, he invited us to join him for lunch in the Pump Room. We joined the group and were escorted to our table where Mr. Gable was so kind as to pull out my chair, and sit down next to me. The conversation was lively and interesting, and he was cordial and charming. As Judy Garland once sang, "Dear Mr. Gable, I'm too young for boys and too old for toys but either way for me, Dear Mr. Gable, it was lovely meeting you."

Every city or town has its own charm. Some cities like New York and Chicago were wonderful to work, and then there were the smaller places like Panama City, Florida. Right on the gulf, it was a lovely town with an air base close by. So naturally, during the beginning of the war, a very smart gentleman opened a nightclub. It was a great club, and humongous in size, with a wonderful dance floor and band. I had decided to take my mother with me since she had never been to that part of the USA.

We arrived, checked into the hotel, and took a walk around town until it was time to go to the club for rehearsal. The band was really good, and all the musicians were fun, so I knew this would be a good time. One of the musicians started walking with me as I left the club. His name was Sal, and I immediately liked him. He had a great smile, and full of the old "one-two." He asked me, "What are you doing for lunch?" I told him I would be going back to the hotel to pickup my mom. There was dead silence. Rather stunned he inquired, "Your mother is here?"

"Well yes," I said. "Is that a problem? I've only walked two blocks with you, and now you're concerned about my mother?"

"Oh, well I didn't mean that," he hastened. "I was just surprised. Can I take you both to lunch?" From then on, it was breakfast, lunch and dinner with Sal. He was a panic and loved mom. And if I had something else to do, he would take mom.

But Sal could drive you crazy. He would be at our door in the morning yelling, "Come on you two. Get up and shine. It's a beautiful day. Let's have breakfast!"

Then Captain Larson came along. He was tall and very handsome. He came into the club several nights for dinner. Finally he asked me to dance, and then of course it was dinner. Sal was fit to be tied.

He would say, "I don't know what you see in him when you've got me — and I like your mother!" He would sit on the bandstand and glare at Captain Larson dancing with me. I don't understand how he didn't miss several notes while playing the arrangements. At the band break, he would come over and sit with mom, if she came to the club. I would see him laughing and pointing to us and making cracks, but all in good humor.

The Captain was from the South, so that really gave Sal a lot of material to work with. I can still remember one evening, Sal was trying to get my goat and said, "Boy, the Captain is quite the gentleman, but of course you love all that stuff. Being from New York, I'm not use to all this southern jazz; he's too polite. I noticed when he dances with you he takes his handkerchief out and places it on your back so his sweating hand doesn't stain your dress. Now that's a gentleman." That was a little sarcasm, but funny.

I said, "Oh Sal, get off it and let it rest. You're just jealous. You don't own a handkerchief."

One day the phone rang, and it was my brother John. He was going to be discharged from the service; he was in Alabama and would be able to visit and see the show. Of course, we were so excited. It was a lovely reunion. He told us he would be discharged within the next few weeks. I could not believe it was the same date that I would be closing in the show. We decided we would meet him in Dothan, Alabama, and come home together. How ironic, I was there at Fort Sheridan when he was going overseas, and here I was taking him home after four years. I said goodbye to Sal and Captain

Ruff Davis, Battle Creek, Michigan

Little did I know I would be back to see my brother Vincent in 1945.

Larsen. Mom and I took the bus to Dothan to meet John. It was a nightmare on the bus, crawling with cockroaches coming out of the curtains on the windows. Bugs just go with the territory in the South, due to the heat. But I must say, the people are terrific.

Vincent arrived home a year before John. We had received the dreaded telegram from the war department, telling Mom that Vincent was "slightly injured." They would keep us informed on his condition. He had lost his leg in Metz, France.

He was flown back to the Percy Jones Hospital in Battle Creek, Michigan. Just a few weeks before we got the news about Vincent, I was performing at the movie theatre in Battle Creek, with Ruff Davis, who later was on TV in *Petticoat Junction*. The hospital called, and asked if we would do a show for the servicemen who were there. We were delighted. "Maybe we can put a little joy in their life," I thought. "They have risked their lives for us." It was an experience I will never forget. Young men, without arms and legs. I got a firsthand look at the price they paid for our freedom. Little did I know, I would be back there at a later date to see Vincent with my mom and Uncle Matt.

The war was ending, and the servicemen were returning home. It took a long time to get back to normal. John was lucky enough to find a nice apartment for his family. Housing was at a premium, and with all the boys returning, it was hard to find a place. Many of them had gotten married, and had to live with their parents until they could find something. Vincent was released from the hospital, and came home to mom and me. It was also a time to find a job. Some were lucky and able to return to their old jobs, but those who were drafted at 18

Percy Jones Hospital, Dorothy, Vincent and Mom. Our first visit.

had no work experience. But they did have a chance to go back to school on the GI Bill to continue their education.

Vincent's profession was one that you didn't find in the "want ads." For instance, there was no listing for a bookmaker, cards, horses or crap dealer. So he was limited, but it didn't hold him back. He came home one day and told us he was going into business. Mom said, "Vincent, what kind of business?"

"Well mom," Vincent explained. "I hit the jackpot. I found this store right across from Lake Michigan, and I made a deal with the landlord. I got all the fixtures on consignment. I'll be ready to open "Vincent's Hamburgers" in about two weeks."

Mom said, "Are you doing this alone? You can't stand on your feet and flip hamburgers. Remember, you only have the use of one leg."

He laughed and said, "One good leg is better than no legs! The prosthesis is okay. I'll be fine." It was only for a short time. Vincent never planned on this venture being permanent; it was just a beginning. So after about eight months, he was on to "Vinnie's Pizza" on Western Avenue. Each time he made a move, he had something better in mind. He was doing okay. Then he decided to buy "The Coach Light Restaurant," a small place, but quite more upscale than "Vincent's Hamburgers." He was on his way, and what a way as you will see in another chapter.

I did several USO shows on tour. In Kansas, we did twenty-nine "one nighters" at different air and army bases. It was fun. We traveled by an army bus with acts, and the army band. We stayed in army barracks, and usually did two shows; one for the "Non-com," and one for the Officers Club. On the bus we would

Vincent's first outing with Mom and me at the Blackhawk, 1945.

sing and make up words to songs relating to the tour and the army like, "We are the girls of the USO. We joined up and now we know, what it's like to be a girl in the USO." We laughed a lot, and the band guys would be playing cards, or shooting craps, in the aisle of the bus. They would tell the driver not to hit any bumps 'cause the dice would flip. It was a scene out of a 1940s movie. Most of the musicians had worked with one of the big bands before they were drafted, and we would talk about different places we had worked together.

It was all coming to an end, and so was the show business I knew; theatres, stage shows, nightclubs, and hotel show rooms. The business was moving in another direction, and everyone hoped there would be room for us, and our talent. Some moved on to stardom in the new medium television, while others decided to move in another direction. A great era came to an end.

My brother John in uniform, 1943

THE FORT WAYNE JOURNAL-GAZETTE

Dancing Star, Soldier-Singer On Show

DOROTHY DALE   PFC. BILLY GATES

Two more specialists to appear in "Baer Faces," the revue staged next Tuesday night at the Palace theater under the auspices of The Journal-Gazette, are Dorothy Dale, talented and beautiful tap dancing star who will come direct from an engagement in Chicago's Edgewater Beach Marine dining room, and Pfc. Billy Gates, the scat-singing soldier now stationed at Baer Field.

"Baer Faces" combines the talent of soldier and civilian entertainers. Proceeds will go to The Beacon, base publication at Baer Field.

Entertaining the Troops, World War II

Chapter 14: Take the A Train, and Every Other Train

My next engagement was at the Netherland Plaza Hotel in Cincinnati, Ohio. It was a beautiful hotel. They had two show rooms, the ice skating revue and the Patio Room, which had the floorshow. I guess you know which one I was performing in. Ice skating was not my thing at that time, but I became very fond of it soon after I arrived.

After checking in and getting settled, I gathered my orchestrations together and headed for the Patio Room to rehearse with the musical director. Another act was already rehearsing his music, so I sat down until he was finished. His name was Danny Harden and he was a wonderful singer. He was also very handsome. I could tell he would be fun from the kibitzing going on with the band. When he finished I sashayed up to the bandstand and introduced myself to the band and Danny. He said "Hi, see you at show time, okay?"

The show was great, and as I was leaving the dressing room, I saw Danny heading for the lobby. He caught my eye and waved.

"Hi kiddo, great show," he quipped. And I also complimented him on his performance. Then he said, "Listen, all the kids from the ice show go to The Purple Cow across the street after their show. Would you like to go?" Well you know the answer.

He continued, "Meet me in the lobby after you change and we'll head over there." I dashed up to my room and took my makeup off and was ready to go. Danny was right; all the skaters were there.

He said, "Follow me." Let me just say, it wasn't hard to follow Danny. As we entered The Purple Cow, he said to the kids sitting in the front booth, "This is Dorothy Dale, the new act in the Patio Room!"

Sonja Henie and Marshall Beard, 1940s

We all said, "Hello." Just as we were about to sit down, another young skater, Marshall Beard, the star of the ice skating revue, sauntered in. And believe me, he knew he was the star! His ego was showing, so I didn't pay much attention to him. But he was good-looking, and I guess that counts for something. I joined in the conversation with Dottie Rodgers and Bob Payne, two of the other skaters, and I liked them right off. We were from two different worlds. The skaters traveled as a group. We (The Variety Acts), on the other hand, traveled on our own to our next engagement and were always meeting new people. I had the feeling Marshall thought we were interlopers.

I thought to myself, "This will be a short-lived friendship!" Little did I know, to my surprise, as we were leaving, Marshall said "Can I walk you back to the hotel?"

I said, "I don't think so, I came with Danny."

But he came right back with, "How about lunch tomorrow? I'll meet you in the lobby at noon?" Noon it was, and as it turned out, he was a very nice, considerate person at 21. And the ego slowly faded away. At one time, he was Sonja Henie's partner, the ice skating star of the 1940s. Sonja was a three-time Olympic winner in 1928, 1932 and 1936. She became a movie star in the 1940s. One of her big movies was *Sun Valley Serenade* in 1942, and

Ken, Dorothy, Marshall, Margaret, 2000

she was responsible for being the first skating star in a touring ice show in the USA. She passed away in 1969 at 57. One of the Henie books was *Queen of the Ice, Queen of Shadows*, in which Marshall is quoted on several pages in relation to the years he worked with Sonja.

After the get-acquainted luncheon, it was love at second sight. So we became inseparable at breakfast, lunch and dinner. He did his show and I did mine. My favorite skaters were Bob and Dorothy. We went everywhere together. I was learning to skate, but my tap shoes still had first priority. It was loads of fun. They never wanted to learn tap. Oh well, too bad. I don't know if my skates are still sharp, but my tap shoes are still clicking. When my contract was up, I knew that it was all coming to an end. I had to move on to my next engagement.

We pledged true love and "all that jazz!" Marshall said he would talk to the agent who booked the Netherland Plaza and asked her to book me back as soon as possible. Off I went, and letters from both of us were in the daily mail. After I closed the show in West Virginia, I headed back to Chicago to a return engagement at the Blackhawk (The Chicago night club "hot spot"). This time it was with the Chico Marx band, which I'm sure you remember as one of the Marx Brothers in the movies. He was the one who played the piano. Guess who the singer was with the band? Mel Tormé. He was just a kid at the time, still in high school. Who would know Mel would become such a sensation in the next few years. We were not that far apart in age. He was around 17, and a little cocky, and I was 19, but I don't believe in cocky.

The dressing rooms were upstairs on the second floor. I heard Chico yell out one night, "Mel, come in here! We need to talk!" I listened. I wondered what it was all about, and then all hell broke out.

Chico continued, "Who do you think you are young man? But whoever you think you are, it is not working for me. You better get rid of that ego, and just perform. I'm going to give you time to work it out. You're suspended for two weeks. And when you come back, I would like to see a different attitude."

One evening, Marshall called to say he had a few days off, and would come to see me. I was thrilled, because Mom could meet him. Just to interject, he was not in the service. Marshall was rejected due to a heart murmur. Remember, it was World War II, so every able-bodied man participated unless a medical issue was present. Marshall arrived, and my Mom loved him, as he did her. It was a mutual admiration society, and I was so pleased. We had a fun time together. He came to see me in the show, and I showed him my favorite places and introduced him to my favorite friends.

Then it was time for him to go back to Cincinnati. Several weeks went by, letters were exchanged and many phone calls transpired. On one call from Marshall, he said the agent had contacted my agent, and they had worked it out that I would return to the Netherland Plaza. So I packed my bag and was very excited that we would be together. It was such fun. With Bob and Dotty, we had something going all the time. They would see my show, and I would see their show, and then over to the Purple Cow or wherever the spirit moved us. Marshall gave me a few pointers on ice-skating, but I needed a lot more. I could never compete with the kids in the show; they were all pros, and I was not about to become one. I was a dancer through and through. After the midnight ice show, when the show room was closed, we would go in and skate. But there were no spins or slides for me. I fell many times. Marshall always picked me up, and we laughed a lot.

On Sundays we would get together with some of the kids from the show, go horseback riding, and have brunch. One time, we went to the burlesque show in town, with the "candy butchers" running up and down the aisle. That is a term from a "bygone era," those were the guys that would "hawk" candy and souvenirs in the aisles of the theatres. It was a new experience for me and I loved it. Many of the future TV comedians came from Burlesque, so you can understand why I was anxious to catch the train back to Cincinnati and "let the good times roll."

When I arrived in Cincinnati, I was back in the Patio Room, but this time it was like old times knowing everyone. The first thing on the agenda was to meet with L.B. Wilson, the owner of the radio station. I had been introduced to him when I worked the Patio Room before, and he was a charming man. So when Marshall told me he would like to meet with me, I wondered why? That's when I made the biggest mistake of my life. We met L.B. in his office. He was as cordial as ever, and went right into why I was there. "So Dorothy, how would you like to be Miss America?" he said before I knew what hit me.

Well that gave me a start, but as I recovered, my response was, "Isn't that a beauty contest? I don't live in Cincinnati. I would have to live here?"

His reply: "No problem! The plan is to rent an apartment for you, and be here for six months. You would have residence here. And then you would participate in the Miss Cincinnati contest, win, and go to Atlantic City for the finals," he finished assuredly.

My next question was, "How do you know I will win?" I was puzzled. Having apparently planned for it, he replied, "Oh, you're a shoo-in. Don't worry about that, we'll take care of everything. You can work here until the time for the contest. Once you win here, you're on your way to Atlantic City and the title."

Unfortunately, in the 1940s, Miss America was not seen by millions of people on TV and advertised all over the world. It just didn't seem that important to me. All you got was the title. There were no scholarships or all the great prizes the young women receive today. You just wore a bathing suit and looked pretty.

So you guessed it, I declined! I told L.B. that I had contract commitments and I had an obligation to fulfill them. Of course, in hindsight and years later, whenever I watch the Miss America contest on TV, I think to myself, "What a dumb move." When TV came in and it was televised all over the world with Bert Parks as the M.C., I would have had the honor of being Miss America, or so said L.B. Wilson, and he was a man of his word. It was nice to know that someone thought I could have been Miss America, but it's like being a little pregnant. You either are or not, and that's the name of that game!

Marshall was talking marriage, which was wonderful and romantic as long as we talked about it. But I was thinking of a long engagement so we could really get to know each other, and could test our feelings. But then you know, when you're young and full of dreams, you go overboard with the love thing. And believe me, it was love on both sides. I just couldn't get my head together with the skating thing. If he had been a dancer, juggler, or comedian, I guess we could have made it. But he would always be in "Buffalo" while I would be in "Boise" with that comedian, dancer or juggler. I didn't need ice to perform. But he did, and so our dream came to an end.

When I finally arrived back in Chicago, Marshall came to visit so we could talk. I tried to explain, but he would have none of it, we took a cab to the airport. He was on his way to New York to join an ice show. We continued to talk until he got out of the cab and said, "Well I guess it's over!"

I don't know how different my life would have been with him, but for a short time, we had magic. I thought maybe along the way, we might get back together, but then I heard he got married to a skater and the magic faded. A couple years later I got a call from him. He was in Chicago changing planes for Hawaii, and asked if on his way back we could get together. Unfortunately, my Catholic school upbringing zeroed in, and I mentioned a little thing like his marriage. He said it was over, but for me it was too late.

Just to add a note, years later I was working in "The Follies." After each performance, the cast would meet and greet in the lobby of the theatre. After one performance, a group of ladies came up to me and said how much they enjoyed my dancing. They told me they had been in several ice shows like the Ice Capades. I asked them if they knew Marshall. They were shocked that I knew him.

The one gal said, "I partnered him." I told them we had worked together in Cincinnati. The one gal informed me that she was friends with his wife Margaret, emphasis on wife! Honestly! They told me that in September there was a reunion of the Ice Capades in Lake Arrowhead and, "Why don't you come? I'm sure Marshall will be there!" I told them I would be on a cruise to Alaska, doing a show, but to say hello to Marshall.

Much to my surprise a month later, I received a call, and the voice on the other end said, "Are you sitting down?"

I said, "No, but I know who this is!" It was wonderful to hear from someone you haven't seen or heard from in sixty years. We had a nice chat, and later on in the year my friend Ken and I had lunch with Marshall and Margaret in Lake Arrowhead where they live. They did come to see the "Follies." They have had a lovely life together and I'm so happy we were able to connect again.

Chapter 15: Vaudeville Died in the 1940s

In 1945, the war ended and show business was not far behind. The war veterans were returning, and if they couldn't take up their old life, they had to look for a new one, which was not easy. It was really amazing how when they were going to save the world and make us free again, the American Flag was flying high; but when they returned, they found there was no place for them after the war.

Show business was also beginning to slow down. One by one, the nightclubs began to disappear. The movie theatres continued to show movies, but Betty Gable, Lana Turner, Eleanor Powell and all of my favorite stars were just a memory. I don't mean to suggest that they were gone, but some went on to Broadway and Las Vegas with big shows. TV had taken over slowly, and the show business as we knew it was on its way out.

The agents were busy trying to find out if this new medium, television, was the way to go. I was still working club dates, and my agents were very loyal to me and kept me working as much as they could. But the interest in TV had definitely taken over. My first television opportunity came with a phone call from a great act I had worked with several times, "Stan Kramer and Company." We were like family. They sort of adopted me. They had worked every big club and theatre in the country. They called and told me, "This new media is for you, and we have recommended you for a shot on WBKB (the first big TV station in Chicago). The station was in the State and Lake Building, across from the Chicago Theatre, on State Street. This was the beginning of TV.

There was a small studio with one camera, and every act in show business trying for a spot before they retired to "the home." When I got the call, I was not ready for the home yet, so I thought I'd give it a shot. The director called and I accepted his offer. Not much money, but a new experience, so "what the heck." I arrived at the studio with costume in bag. They gave me a dressing room and I changed into my short adorable costume ready to set them on fire. I walked on the set. It was a living room, and several people sitting around like they were having a séance. I didn't want to contact the dead. I was only interested in making contact with the living. I looked around and the director said, "Dorothy, are you ready?"

I said, "I'm dancing in a living room? Isn't that a little odd? I've played many strange night clubs in my life, but I've never played a living room."

He thought it was funny, but that was it. "Let's make this your living room debut," he quipped.

I said, "I don't get the point!"

He came back with, "Honey you don't have to, just do it. You're going to be the star of this living room." The people sitting around applauded, so I guess I was a hit. "Thank you very much Dorothy, you will be hearing from us!" Well, I've heard that song before, but low and behold I did hear from them, and did several more spots. TV was in its infancy, and it was great to be part of it at the beginning.

TV programming was not listed in the newspaper on a regular daily basis. The station would send out the listings on a fold-up postcard

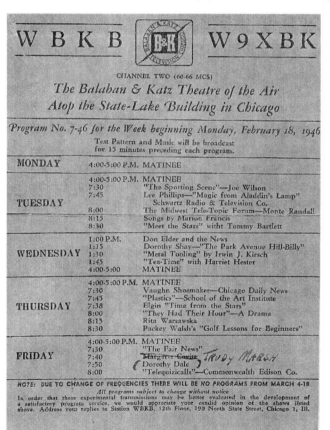

The Beginning of Television, 1946

telling you what time certain programs would be aired. Not everyone owned a TV at this time. It's fun to look back and know that I was the first tap dancer on WBKB, and now at 89, I am the "Oldest Living, Working Showgirl in the World," or so says *The Guinness Book of World Records*, 2009.

A wonderful gentleman named Sabie was married to a gal columnist, and he had a big modeling school in Chicago. He was also a wonderful ballroom dancer. We started giving ballroom exhibitions on TV. We taught all the dances; samba, rumba, fox trot, etc. Unfortunately, I was not earning a lot of money, so I decided to move in another direction.

I continued working a few dates in and out of town, and then embarked on a great opportunity that came my way. I met Elena Moneak, one of the most inspiring ladies I have ever known. She had a fabulous studio called the "Elena Moneak Finishing School, Your Passport to Happiness and Charm." I knew right away I would like to take this trip.

The studio was at 675 N. Michigan Avenue on the "Magnificent Mile" as it was known. The salon was off a beautiful courtyard, with flowers and plants. As you entered the salon, you knew this would be a wonderful experience. Elena never referred to her studio as a beauty salon. It was always a "Beauty Studio."

Elena asked me to come and meet with her; she would like to discuss something with me. So I called her the next day and made an appointment. I arrived at the studio and was greeted by a lovely lady who said "Oh, Ms. Moneak is waiting for you; I'll take you to her office." Elena was a small, elegant woman with a graceful appearance. When she stood up from behind her desk, she extended her hand to me and said, "Dorothy, thank-you for coming. Please sit down and tell me about yourself."

We fell into comfortable conversation. Then out of the blue, she asked me if I would like to work for her. "As you look around, I'm sure you have observed we are a personal beauty studio for women who want to be admired for their figure, skin, and hair, and for her vibrant vital self. We provide all the services to make it happen. I said to her, "I would like that for myself."

Then she replied, "No, No, my dear. I want you to teach it for me. You have most of what I'm looking for, and I will teach you the rest." I told her I was still performing, and doing some TV. "No problem my dear," she continued. "You can work out your own schedule, and have an assistant." So I accepted.

I conducted exercise, ballet, and body coordination for grace and posture, and many other classes were added as I got the hang of it. One day, Elena asked me once more to come to her office. She had someone she wanted me to meet. It was my pleasure. A tall handsome man said, "Hi! I'm Gary!" He worked for one of the Chicago newspapers as a freelance reporter, and was going to join us as a coordinator. Elena said she wanted us to work together, bring new ideas to the business.

Gary and I worked well together. We decided we should promote fashion shows, since I had started teaching modeling classes. I had been teaching part time for Patricia Stevens Modeling School, one of the biggest schools in the Loop, before I started at Moneak's. So I knew what I was doing.

Elena loved the idea, and gave us an expense account to pursue the venues that would be interested in our presentation. It would also give the girls in our classes that had the ability and talent the opportunity to be in the fashion shows. We were not selling our modeling classes to our students with the idea of a fashion career, but the shows would help to give them confidence.

Gary and I set our course with our expense account, and hit all the hotels like the Congress and Stevens. We were able to do luncheon shows on Wednesday and Thursday. We had a success on our hands, and so were our classes.

Elena once again called me into her office. She was very serious, and she jumped right into what was on her mind. "You know Dorothy," she explained. "You have done an excellent job for me, and I will be moving the studio in the next couple months. It will be bigger and better, across the street from the Water Tower (a landmark in Chicago). It's a great location. I just leased one of the brown stone buildings with three floors, so we can expand. You will have the top floor as your studio, and set it up however you would like. It's going to be wonderful."

So, we opened with a bang, and things did go well for quite some time. I was happy with my studio and doing the fashion shows. We would have our Sunday afternoon tea parties and the classes grew. We had built a runway for the in-house fashion shows, and set up movies of each class to show the students their progress. We also had makeup classes for street wear and stage. While we were serving tea, Elena would play the Theremin, a unique musical instrument played without physical contact to the instrument.

All was going well, and then I had the famous call to Elena's office once more. Elena started out with a nice compliment like she always did to set the mood for what she had to say. "Our clients love you, so I have a proposition to offer you. I am getting older, and I need more time for me. So I need someone I can trust to help me run the whole operation. Would you be interested?"

I, on the other hand, had just had a talk with myself about how much time I was spending at the studio. And I didn't want any more responsibility, so this was a shock. I was so appreciative, but I said, "No, I cannot take on any more. But you know I love you, and wish I could, but I can't!"

The biggest mistake of her life was the next one. Elena was very tired, and so she was trying to find her way without giving up everything. She decided to talk to the hair stylist in her salon. He had a good following, but most of the costumers had been with Elena before he arrived. Unfortunately, he was already making his plan to take her clients, and move to another location on Michigan Avenue, along with several of the other hair stylists and the receptionist whom he was dating. It was all very hush, hush, except that he was handing out his cards to his new salon. He didn't inform Elena until he was ready to leave, and this did not give her much time to regroup. This, of course, added to her stress, and she just didn't have the fight in her any more to bring it back. She went into bankruptcy. It was so sad she lost everything. One saving grace: she had a gentleman friend for many years that came to the auction and purchased a few of the things dear to her heart. For one, her mink coat, and the electrical instrument the Theremin she so loved to play.

Elena taught me the touch of beauty is from within. I hope that I have passed on the knowledge I received from that dear woman. My next move: taking over the north shore of Chicago.

I received a call from Dorothy de Houghton, who had a well-known dance school on the north shore of Chicago. The main school was in Evanston, where she had two studios going nearly every hour. She was looking for a teacher to take over some of her classes in Wilmette, Winnetka, Deerfield and Highland Park, not to mention Saturday classes in Maywood, an hour away from Evanston. Carol Lawrence, who I'm sure you are familiar with from "West Side Story" on Broadway, studied with Dorothy for many years, growing up in the Maywood and the Melrose Park area as a child and teen. Dorothy asked me if I would be interested in teaching for her, and after I talked to she and her mother, I decided that I would very much like to be part of her studio along with another teacher, Barbara.

During my years with Dorothy, we must have taught every four and five-year old on the North Shore. Every recital time in June, we had the babies in every color of the rainbow in their tutus on stage. And every Mom, Dad, Grandma and Grandpa came to see their darling perform and say their little pieces. "Mommy went to dancing school. Grandma went there too. Now I go to dancing school, just watch and see what I can do," they would chime. I know it's corny, but the kids loved it, and believe me, it paid for a great house, car, travel and money in the bank for Dorothy and her mom. They were great to work for and always paid me well. We did work our butts off though. I was teaching ballet, point, tap and tumbling classes, plus the babies. They treated Barbara and me like family, so it wasn't a stress. I always loved teaching and watching the students progress through the years.

Dorothy and her mom decided they had enough, and when the school closed for the summer, they took off for Mexico. They instantly fell in love with the casual, laid-back life that they had not enjoyed for fifteen years in Evanston. When they returned for the September sign-up of the season, they told me they would be taking it easy and asked me to take over more classes, which was okay with me. Then they told me that they would finish out the season and would then be moving to Mexico. Dorothy said, "We've bought a lovely house, and I will be teaching, but I won't have to work so hard. When we leave, we will be closing the Evanston Studio, and since the other classes are in rented spaces, the leases will be up in June, so we will just let them go. But we would like to give you Glenview. Everyone really liked you, and would be disappointed if you didn't come back."

So I took over the Glenview classes as my own and it was great. I taught two days a week, regular classes during the day and ballroom to the 7th and 8th graders from the local school in the evening. And now the plot thickens.

I was going along nicely, and then I got a call from Dorothy saying they had come back to Evanston. They found that Mexico didn't work out for them financially. They were working twice as hard to make the same money, so they decided to give it all up and return to Evanston. The hitch, of course, was they asked me to give Glenview back, so I did with no regrets. Dorothy would take over all the teaching to recoup the money they had lost. I decided to open a dancing school in Chicago on Clark Street, in Rogers Park. I leased a store with a bad floor, bad walls and not in a great location, but the rent was what I could afford. The owner was a nice German man and I told him the floor would not work for me, so he said he would put a new one in. But the rest was up to me.

I had a great friend, Betty Hughes. She came to my rescue, and the two of us set out to pull the place together. We decided to paint the walls first. I borrowed a ladder from my brother John, and the two of us got started. It was no small job with the high ceiling. Betty started on one side, I on the other, and we played the radio and listened to music while we worked. Halfway through, John came in and took the brushes away from us, and said, "Do something else!" He finished the walls in record time.

When the walls were done, the floor people arrived and laid the floor. Now we were in business. Before they laid the floor, they removed the toilet and sink and put them in the front window. Talk about a friend. I looked around, and Betty was sitting in the window, cleaning the toilet. Then she sat on the toilet to clean the sink. What a picture to behold. I'm sure that the pedestrians and motorist passing by wondered what was going on, as Betty was waving to them. I said, "Betty get out of the window. You'll get arrested for indecent exposure!" But she just laughed, and continued cleaning.

We were close to the finish when Vincent came by and put up my dance barre and the dressing room partition. John walked in a few minutes later and said, "Surprise!" He had found some old mirrors at a warehouse, and the man gave them to him. So once they were up, we were in business. I placed an ad in the neighborhood paper; registration was in September. Mom was in the front office with a small desk, pencil and paper and signed up the students. It all worked out fine, and then I met Chris.

I usually went to twelve o'clock mass on Sunday. After mass, everyone would congregate on the church steps. Monsignor Campbell, who was still at Our Lady of Lourdes from my grammar school days, remained steadfast, and he always had something to say! "Well, Dorothy, I see you've traveled the world," he commented as he passed me, and then promptly moved on. This particular Sunday, a few of the girls I had graduated with were standing on the steps and came over to say "hello." They suggested we go across the street for coffee. Just as we were about to leave, Mary Rowland said, "Are you free this afternoon? We're going to a cocktail party and open house at Loyola University, across from the Water Tower. It's in the same building as the seminary, where the Jesuits are trained."

I said, "Are they trying to find them wives or take one last fling??"

"No," she said with a smile, "They are having a mixer to raise money for some project."

I said, "Well, thank goodness, 'cause there would be no future in that." So I said okay.

Dorothy Felmen said, "Meet me at the bus stop on Ashland and Wilson, at two, and we can go together."

We walked in, and gave the man at the desk a small fee and he gave each of us two drink tickets. We went right to the bar and ordered a drink. Suddenly, several young men appeared. I remember one in particular, John Kind. Now keep that last name in mind. He was full of conversation and asked me to dance. By the time the dance was over, I was thirsty.

John and I danced another set and another, and back to the bar. But this time, I was out of tickets. This is when I found out that John was not so kind or generous. He asked me if I would like another drink and he would be happy to get it for me.

"Do you have a ticket?" he said in a very matter-of-fact manner. He was the last of the big spenders. I said, "NO thank you. I can get it myself." I took my friend Dorothy by the arm, and said, "Let's get a table and talk!" Little did I know, I was on my way to meet my future husband.

We found a table and sat down. After the last experience, I was perfectly happy just to talk when a gentleman came up and asked me to dance. His name was Chris Kloss. I said, "No thank you, we just want to visit."

"Oh come on and dance with me," he coaxed. "My friend Barney goes to your church and told me he sees you there all the time."

I said, "So you have a recommendation. Would you ask me if I didn't go to church?" It wasn't nice, but I was so aggravated with Mr. Kind. I didn't want to dance again. After awhile, he returned again and said, "Are you talked out yet? Give me a chance. And if you won't dance with me, can my friend and I buy you a drink?" That was the magic word.

"Please sit down," I acquiesced. I found he was very nice, and then he asked if he and Barney might drive us home. I was not keen on that, but Dorothy and Mary thought it was fine, so I went along. The next thing I remember, I had a beautiful ring. We bought a house in Skokie, Illinois, a suburb of Chicago. And were married on June 13, 1953. Then January 19th, 1955, our wonderful baby boy Craig Steven Kloss came along.

Before I got married, I still had the dancing school on Clark Street, but Chris thought I should give it up for the domestic life, and I was happy to do so. I had my last recital in May, and the wedding was in June.

I was a happy housewife. I wanted to be the gardener of the year, but unfortunately, I didn't have a green thumb. The first few years of marriage and many plants later, I got lost in the weeds, and I bought more plants, but no luck. Then I decided to go for something bigger, and my luck would change.

Skokie was virgin territory. It hadn't been too long ago that the Indians had inhabited the area, and ever so often you would find an Indian arrow in the ground. Remember this was 1953, eight years after the war, and the beginning of the big building boom. Skokie was the first suburb outside of Chicago with good public transportation, and that is why we choose the area.

Chris was a doctor, and his schedule was unpredictable, so it was the perfect area for us. There were many vacant lots still available, and one at the corner of our house was filled with small trees, just waiting for me to transplant one of them. So one afternoon, I said to my mother, "Let's go down and dig up one of those little trees!" We got the shovel and headed for the lot. The little tree I wanted was way down in the ground, and it took some elbow grease to bring it up. But I put it in a newspaper and carried it home. I dashed into the back yard and dug a hole. I put a penny in the hole 'cause someone told me it would help the tree to grow.

It was like the tree that grew in Brooklyn. It grew and grew and grew, and I loved watching it grow, until one day the end was in sight. Chris came into the kitchen and told me that the tree had to go. He was exasperated. "I guess you didn't dig the hole deep enough, and I can't cut the grass because the roots have surfaced to the top. The roots are like a snake running though the whole yard. We have to dig up the whole yard." We didn't dwell on the subject, but his last word was, "Please, if you want to plant something, would you consult me before you dig up any other part of the yard?"

I said "Yes, but you know it's a challenge. We can start all over." And then quickly I said, "You know, I think it's four o'clock. Why don't we have a cocktail?"

I did become a fairly good gardener the second time around. I loved it. Unfortunately, life was not a bed of roses as time went by. I decided to say goodbye to Chris; he was a doctor and I was a dancer. It was not a good match. It was the canasta group, and then the mixed bowling group. Not to say I didn't enjoy these activities, but something was missing in my life.

Craig was my love, and he did fill the void. But mostly it was the "Kloss family" I found hard to deal with. They were very controlling and that was hard. I didn't marry until I was twenty-nine and Chris was forty-two. We both were independent, but Chris's father controlled the whole family. He expected me to fall in line. That was something I could not do, and there is the problem, "Dr. Watson."

Anything we bought or talked about was discussed with his father, and he gave his "yay" or "nay." Amazing how things work out for you, or as I always say, "Life is what happens while you're making other plans." Love that saying.

My sister-in-law, Viola, said to me, "I don't understand you Dorothy. You have a nice home, a car, and mostly everything you need. Why don't you settle for what you have and make it work?"

"Viola," I retorted, "It's not about making it work just to have security. I'm getting out of the garden and the kitchen, and making a better life for Craig and me. One that makes us happy."

My brother's daughter, Brandy, was a student at "The Academy of the Sacred Heart" in Chicago, on Sheridan Road. "Hardey Preparatory School for Boys." was also part of the Sacred Heart campus. It was a great school with small classes. I talked to Chris about enrolling Craig before we split. He thought it would be fine, until the Kloss family heard about it, and created a big "who ha" between Chris and me. Their kids all went to public school and once again, they were making decisions for me. "Craig should be going to the public school like our children," they would say. I didn't care where they were sending their children. I, of course, was the bad guy. When I told them to mind their own business, life was never the same.

After many discussions, we decided to separate and give ourselves a breather to see if we could make it work. But in the end, we decided Craig was our one great accomplishment, and to go our own way. So I was back where I began, only now I had this wonderful little person to raise, and every day was an adventure.

I did register Craig at Hardey Prep. and it was the best move I ever made for him, and for me. My niece, Brandy, was a student there since first grade, so I was familiar with the school. I loved all their wonderful traditions. The students learned respect.

I made an appointment with Mother Murphy to discuss the possibility of Craig enrolling at Hardey. We arrived at the school and walked up the front stairs and through the very impressive front door. As we entered, one of the boys from Hardey, in his gray trousers and navy blue blazer with the Sacred Heart emblem on the upper pocket, greeted us. And I could just see Craig in that uniform. The young man ushered us into the parlor and Mother Murphy, with her delightful Irish humor, invited us to sit down. She asked Craig a few questions, like, "Do you like sports?" And of course, she hit on the right question. He answered her right off. A big "YES!" I could see she liked that, but then came the downside.

Mother Murphy looked at me and said, "Mrs. Kloss, you know my dear, at present, we don't have a place for Craig. But I will take all the information today, and if something

Craig in his "Hardey" jacket, 1963

opens up, I will call you." I guess she wanted to soften the blow and put a little humor into the finale. "You know, Craig Steven Kloss," she went on, "That sounds like a movie star." I told her that I wanted him to have the same initials as his father, C.S.K. She stood up and said, "So nice to meet you both!" Out the impressive door we went with little hope.

My brother Vincent, his wife Viola, and their daughter lived across the street from the school in a high rise overlooking Lake Michigan. Craig and I headed over to their place for dinner. Viola had picked up Mom. They were waiting for the news. I told them there was a slight chance, but don't hold your breath. Just when I thought all was lost, a few days before school started, the magic phone call came. Mother Murphy said, "Hello Mrs. Kloss, this is Mother Murphy, and we have an opening for Craig. Can you get him here tomorrow for registration? Order his uniform, and bring your check book." Believe me, it was my checkbook. That last sentence was a little scary, but we entered that same front door. I clicked my heels once again and another door opened.

Craig was going along, and really enjoying Hardey. I answered the phone one afternoon, and the voice said, "Mrs. Kloss, this is Mother Sullivan."

I was a little nervous, and asked, "Is everything alright?"

"Oh yes," came the response. "This has nothing to do with Craig. He is just fine. I just wanted to talk to you. I understand you were in show business, and danced for Merriel Abbott in the Empire Room of the Palmer House. You may not know this, but her adopted son, Frank Lewin, was a student here. He was a little Catholic boy, and as you know, Mrs. Abbott is Jewish. We really loved her for what she was doing for Frankie, raising him in his religion. Every Sunday she would send us lox and bagels with a note: "ENJOY!" Do you think she was trying to convert us?

I wondered where she was going with this, and then as quick as a jackrabbit, she asked if I would like to choreograph a ballet for the students. "We had *Sleeping Beauty* in mind," she quickly added, "and when can you start? We would like to present it as our spring show." How could I refuse an offer like that? So I got my ballet slippers out, limbered up, and the next week I was ready for the auditions. It would be for the lower school. I had no idea how this would change my life.

We started auditions, and Mother Sullivan and Mother Ruggeri were to assist me. It's hard to believe that these two nuns would be doing "point, point, *pas de bourree*." They were young, in their glory, and so full of enthusiasm for this new project. "They were in show business" and while they had the chance, they were going to make the most of it.

The whole school got behind the project, even though it was only open to the lower school. The high school students loved watching the lower school, go through their dance steps. We found the perfect Sleeping Beauty, a girl named Linda, and the young Prince was Sandy. Remember, this is a girl's school. Lucky for me, they both had some training in ballet.

Kathy (Sullivan) and Marianne (Ruggeri) were right on top of things, and after the auditions, it was costume time. The two of them had every book on ballet they could find. It would help them decide on the costumes. They recruited every available mother in the school, plus the nuns that could sew. They had put on many shows at the school, but this was going to be THE production. It was not *Hansel and Gretel*, or *Madame Butterfly*. It wasn't even *H.M.S. Pinafore*, the operetta that Craig was in at Hardey Prep. He was one of the three maidens. I'm glad he didn't become too attached to that part, although he was a darling girl with his Japanese wig. They did a great job, but *Sleeping Beauty* was something new for them. No singing or speaking; just dance and movement. It was fun watching Kathy and Marianne trying to get the steps so they could rehearse the students. It did become a problem that had to be dealt with though, due to Kathy's newfound "career" in dance. Her whole life had taken on new meaning.

As time went by, Kathy would decide to change the choreography. I would come into a rehearsal and notice several changes. When I asked why the change, the dancers told me, "Mother said she liked what SHE gave us." I would slowly burn. I was working so hard to give the children steps that they could do, and make them look like they could dance. Most of them had never studied dance.

I told them, "You will not change anything I give you!"

"Oh, but Ms. Kloss," they implored, "We can't tell Mother that."

I said, "You won't have to. I will!" I could hear the snickering in the background, and I knew they couldn't wait to hear what I was going to say to Kathy. I really wanted her to be part of it and have fun, but she just couldn't stay out of it. She would interrupt me with some little critique. I knew I had to stop her quickly, before she became the "choreographer," and Marianne and I would be sewing costumes. I waited for her to arrive. She came in with a big smile on her face, and said, "How are we doing today?" My reply was, "Mother, WE are not doing well. I understand YOU have become a choreographer. That is a very ambitious undertaking. I'm sure you have some great ideas, and I'm very happy to listen. But you're just confusing the children. I cannot spend my time redoing everything when I should be moving forward. School will be closing for the summer, and we'll never get the show on. So please try to understand my commitment to make this a wonderful production. Otherwise, I can't continue." She was VERY apologetic, and all was well.

The school had a small theatre, but not adequate for this production. So it was decided to give the show in the tennis courts. It was the perfect place, and the weather would be wonderful in June. The school was buzzing with activity, and the students were excited, telling their parents about their special part in the show.

The day of dress rehearsal, everyone was buzzing around, getting the sets in place, and trying on costumes. I saw Kathy and Marianne standing on the side. They seemed to be arguing about something. I sauntered over to see what was the problem. They had a photo from one of their ballet books. The page was turned to a picture of Sleeping Beauty. Marianne was trying to convince Kathy that Sleeping Beauty should wear her hair in the period of the ballet. Kathy was saying, "No, I don't think so. I think she should let her hair fall naturally."

As I arrived on the scene, Marianne said, "Why don't we ask Dorothy what she thinks?" Marianne was right, and the decision was made. I don't think I gained any points that day.

Thanks to the parents' participation, and great applause for the show, they sealed my livelihood for the next ten years. As they left the theater, better known as the tennis courts, they filled a lovely glass bowl at the exit with money for future productions.

I was hired to teach dance two days a week. After my first year of teaching, I was asked to teach at their school in Lake Forest, Woodlands Academy of the Sacred Heart. They had decided I would be a great addition to Woodlands, since it was a day school and boarding school. I became part of the faculty, part of the physical education department. I had all the benefits, plus dancing and choreographing shows. It was a nine-to-four job.

Woodlands Academy of the Sacred Heart, Lake Forrest, Illinois, Dance Class, 1966

"Gypsy," Sandy McDonald as Baby June, Drake Theatre, Woodlands Academy, 1970.

The students were from first grade through high school. Barat College, a Sacred Heart School, was on the same campus. The Drake Theatre was on the college campus, and we had the good fortune to present our productions at the Drake. We had everything we needed to do a show. It wasn't like the tennis courts, but I will always love that first show and the tennis courts will always be dear to my heart. It gave me a future I never dreamed of at the time, and one I needed at the time.

We did all the great book shows like "Carousel" and "Gypsy." Then came the most exciting adventure for the middle school. Father Banahan, moderator of the television program, *The Catholic Hour*, came to Woodlands to see one of the dress rehearsals for the Christmas show. And he was so impressed with the talent and the way it was conducted that he decided to incorporate the second act into his hour-long TV show on WBKB, Channel 7. With it being the Christmas season, you guessed it: the show was *The Nutcracker Suite*.

The children taking part in the performance arrived at the studio, in Chicago, on December 14th and taped the show. One outstanding little girl was Kathy Grant, who was a boarder at the school, and had dance training. She was my ballerina on point for Sugarplum Fairy. She was a real pro at twelve. I've often wondered if Kathy continued to pursue dance. I hope so, 'cause she was a natural.

During this time, Craig graduated from Hardey, and enrolled at Loyola Academy. Every year, Loyola had a talent show. It was the big event of the year. The students at other Catholic schools would participate. Most of the time, the glee club from Woodlands would be the talent. This year,

Sacred Heart in Chicago decided they'd like to have an entry, but it was a little late to do a group number. So I suggested my niece Brandy do a number from *The Sound of Music*. It was the movie of the year, and the song was perfect. "I am Sixteen Going on Seventeen." It didn't win, but she was thrilled to be in the show. She really did a great job. Some of the nuns were a little concerned about how short her skirt was, but I assured them it was perfectly fine. It was a pleated skirt just above her knees. They would really be in shock at today's costumes.

Rose Wolden was the head of the physical education department. She and I were great friends. She came in the faculty room and told me that she was getting married. It didn't mean much to me, except that I would be going to a wedding and I was happy for her. She didn't mention that she would not be back the next year. She and Harry wanted some time off.

Mother Dennehy called me into her office; she told me about Rose leaving and it sent me into shock. She said, "Next year, we would like you to take over the gym classes."

I said, "Really? I'm not a gym teacher, basketball coach, softball coach, or have any experience in any of those sports. What about my dance classes?"

"Gypsy," Mary McCoy with the "Newsboys," 1970.

"You will continue with your classes" she continued, "And we will work out a schedule for the gym classes."

"What about all those rules?" I asked.

"Don't worry about it," she said confidently, "You've been going to games with Craig for years. You must know some of them, and the students will help you through the year. Anytime you need help, just give the whistle to one of them." She handed me all the rule-books to study during the summer. My decision: you have to do what you have to do.

I did enjoy coaching the teams, but we had a losing year, unlike when Rose was coaching. The girls took it all with good humor. At the end of the year, we had the banquet, and one of the girls gave a little talk about

MRS. DOROTHY KLOSS

Yearbook, Woodlands Academy, 1970

the year. She said, "You know, we may not have had a winning year with Ms. Kloss, but when we went for a jump shot, we pointed our toes." They presented me with a lovely emerald pin. Rose returned the following year.

One of the last shows I did at Woodlands, before moving on after approximately ten years, was "Carousel." Craig got several of his buddies from Loyola to be in the show, which was a plus. When you're doing a show at a girl's school, you need some guys to fill out the cast. Craig never had a calling for show business, but that was okay with me. He did hang in for eight years of piano lessons, so I figured he paid his dues. Basketball was his forte, and he did excel in most of the sports he went out for.

The end was in sight at Woodlands. The school brought in consultants to decide what they could do to bring in more money, and cut back on things they thought unnecessary. I was one of the unnecessary ones, so I got my pink slip. The school started getting grants, but the ironic part is that they paid a fortune to the consultants. I had a good run, and it was time for me to move on. Craig was graduating from Loyola, and so I picked myself up, brushed myself off, and clicked my heels one more time.

I decided to rent space and teach. So I contacted the Winnetka Community House, in Winnetka, Illinois. I rented the space, put an ad in the community paper, and waited for the phone to ring. At first, I was a little disappointed. I asked the newspaper to do a story on me and they said "No problem." After the story came out, the phone did start to ring, and I was in business. Back to my first love, DANCING! But a big change was in the wind. A warm breeze was blowing me southward.

Life with Vincent was always catching a plane, train or bus. He would have a new restaurant or a show that I had to see, but whatever it was, it was a Vincent experience and I loved every minute of it. He would call me and say, "Can you be in LA tomorrow, or New York or Milwaukee... I have a surprise for you." His surprises made my heart pump a little faster. His surprises were always big and had an element of adventure.

I remember being on the road, I had Mom with me. After four weeks, we got a call from him with one of his surprises. He said, "When are you two coming home?" I told him that it would be about two weeks. "Gosh, can't you guys hurry up? I have a great surprise for you."

I thought, "Here we go again." I said, "The surprise will have to wait, I have a contract." Two weeks later, Mom and I arrived home, and two boxes where waiting for us. I opened my box and there was this beautiful silver fox jacket. Mom's box had a lovely silver fox stole. We put them on and headed for one of his favorite restaurants.

During dinner I mentioned how much Mom and I loved our jacket and stole. Then I had to go and ask him where he purchased them. "Well you know Dart, I have some good friends in the business and they called me to say they were over stocked and could give me a deal that would be hard to turn down." Conversation closed. I didn't ask any more questions and Mom and I enjoyed those furs for many years.

Unfortunately, Vincent was in the gambling business, he had good days and bad days. I had always thought if he had a chance to go to college, he would have been a brilliant lawyer. He was so quick and bright with a memory that never stopped. I'm still counting on my fingers and he's already added up a column in a flash. But remember, he was figuring those numbers and odds. I was just figuring the 10% to my agent.

I'm sure most people reading this book have seen "Guys and Dolls." There you have Vincent, and I mean this as a compliment to him. For people unfamiliar with a bookie's life, let me explain. First of all, it's illegal to bet on a horse race with a bookie, but not at the racetrack. If you're at the racetrack it's okay because the government can keep track of you and like everything else in life, if you win a lot of money, they have a document waiting for you to sign so they get their share. The bookie lets you have it all. You have to remember that the bookie has a lot of expenses. His business is constantly on the move from one apartment or store to the next, and their customers find them wherever they go. You see, bookies don't have business cards.

The government is always trying to find them and sometimes they do. It's a no-win situation. The government's case is that bookies don't pay taxes. But if they did, they would know where they are, arrest them and close their business. So the bookie has to keep moving, and they have to be quick!

Vincent was a big mover in Chicago and one day they caught up with him. He canceled his lease. They confiscated his books. Now they had him. He went to court and they indicted him for bookmaking. He was out on bail until the court date. He and his wife Viola decided to move to Las Vegas after this was all settled. He was offered a job at the Riviera Hotel. Viola packed and moved their belongings into my basement until they got settled in Vegas. In the mean time Vincent could not leave Chicago, due to the indictment.

Our Uncle Phil came to Chicago from St. Louis, where he lived with my Aunt Mae to help drive Viola to Vegas. At this point, Vincent and his daughter moved in with Craig and me. My Mom had passed away in 1966. Brandy had just graduated from high school and would be going off to college in the fall. Once again, the plot thickens.

I was home alone one day when I heard the front door bell. Two young men in dark suits where standing there, with the storm door between us. At first I thought they were Mormons, but quickly I reassessed my thinking when the one said, "Dorothy, how's everything going?" They flashed FBI badges. "Is Vincent home?"

Then the one jumped in quickly and said, "Don't get nervous, we just want to ask you a few questions."

I told them, "I'm not nervous. What do you want to know."

"May we step in for a moment?" they inquired.

I told them NO, I can answer any questions right through the door. "When will Vincent be back?" they asked.

"I really don't know, I'm his sister not his wife or mother, I don't keep track of his every move," I responded.

The next one: "Is Brandy around?"

I said, "You know very well she's not, and no doubt you've been tracking her. You know where she works, and if you don't then you're not doing a very good job for the FBI. I really don't appreciate you coming to my door unannounced, thank you very much."

When they left, I hopped in my car and went to the store, where I called my brother John and told him to pick up Brandy at work and bring her home. I found out later the dark-suit guys had gone to my neighbors, asking questions.

Vincent arrived for his court date, paid a fine and left for Las Vegas and his new job, legal gambling. Ain't that a kick! Years later, Viola told the story how two FBI agents would stop by to check on Vincent. Why, all they had to do was go to the casino. He would be there in his silk suit and his lucky diamond ring. After a few years of these visits, Viola was losing patience. The one would always ask her if he could have a glass of her good water. Finally, one day she had enough and told him "No, I'm sick of you coming to my house and making small talk, so make your case and get out." They never came back.

Chapter 16: The Big Move

Jack and Bob arrived from New York and moved me out of my house in Skokie, Illinois. I had lived there for 20 years. I did everything that most people do when they sell their home of many years. First, you're excited about the move, and then that sentimental moment hits and you wonder if you did the right thing. It all happened, and it was the beginning of a new adventure in my life. But I digress...

I had known Jack for a long time. He was from Chicago, but was moving to New York. He was offered a very lucrative job. I would see him at family events and parties, and I knew his mother and father. This was a goodbye party for him. He was very handsome, and had a great sense of humor, which I enjoyed immensely. I never paid much attention to him, but he did seem to gravitate in my direction and he used his wit and charm to engage in conversation. We all said goodbye, and he was off to "the big apple" with our good wishes.

Several weeks later, Jack called me one morning and said, "I thought I'd say hello, and see how you're doing." Yakety-yak, Yakety-yak.

The next morning, he was on the phone again, and I said, "Are you calling from work?"

He said, "It's no problem, I have a WATS line. I can call anytime, it goes with the job." So I didn't think any more about it. He kept calling, and I kept wondering why. Then one morning, he called again, he said, "I'll be in Chicago next week, and I'd like to stop by, okay?"

What could I say? So I said, "Yes, stop by." And guess what? He did! Full of wit and charm, I found myself really enjoying his company. More to come!

The calls continued, and then one morning he called to ask if the mail had arrived. I said, "No, why?"

He said, "I'll call you later." When the mail arrived, it was an invitation to the world's most prestigious sailing competition, the America's Cup, in Newport, Rhode Island. I was overwhelmed. He called back a couple hours later, and said he had invited six other friends. And my ticket to New York would be arriving shortly. We would fly to Rhode Island from New York in a private plane, and all stay together in a coach house. It all happened just the way he said, and even more so. The second day after we arrived, he whisked us away to Nantucket in the same private plane. We stayed at this lovely old Victorian hotel, from the whaling days. The island was so quaint, and we spent two days eating, drinking and being merry. Then back to Rhode Island, and the big dinner at the tennis club, for the American and Australian crews that would be competing in the race. Every night was a party, or a disco, and I came home feeling like Cinderella, except my shoes were black to match my grown. Jack kept involving himself more and more in my life. And I was beginning to look forward to his visits, and all the wonderful events in which I was included. One such event was flying to New York to see *No, No, Nanette*, and then off to Puerto Rico, for "rum and coca cola!"

The most amazing thing happened. The musical, *No, No, Nanette* was on Broadway. Jack knew I loved Ruby Keeler, the star of the show. Ruby was in the original *42nd Street* movie, and was married to Al Jolson, who made the first talking picture, *The Jazz Singer*. She was older, but still had that sweet face, and could still tap her heart out. When I arrived in New York, Jack said, "I have a surprise for you. I have tickets for *No, No Nanette* tonight." It was a wonderful show, with Bobby Van doing the old soft shoe. I liked his style. In the front row of the ensemble was this young dancer, dancing like Gene Kelly. I didn't know it at the time, but thirty years later he would be my roommate in California.

My son was at Loyola Academy in Wilmette, a suburb of Chicago. He was busy playing basketball, tennis and having a good time in his last year of high school, and looking forward to college.

Jack called to say he was coming in for Thanksgiving, and asked if Craig and I would have dinner with him. Since I'm not big on cooking, I thought it was a grand idea. I had a sign in my kitchen, "This kitchen is closed due to illness, I'm sick of cooking." So I said, "Yes."

Jack arrived, and made reservations at a new restaurant on Rush Street, a trendy street in Chicago. We were shown to our table, and settled in for a new dining experience. Little did we know what a new experience it would be, within the next few minutes; we ordered a drink and started a lively conversation. An older, rather plump gentleman was escorted to the table next to us. He looked so lonely. Gosh, here it is Thanksgiving. "No one should be alone on a holiday," I thought. "Aren't we lucky to have each other!"

Well by the time we had another drink, we had decided to invite the gentleman (the poor soul) to join us. We elected Craig to invite him. So Craig made his way to his table, and we were straining our ears to hear. We thought he would thank Craig and decline, but before we knew what happened, he was at our table with his plate and saying, "Thank you for inviting me. I'm Ralph." We introduced ourselves, and had a lovely dinner. After dinner, Craig was going to meet some of his buddies from school, so he excused himself and left.

Ralph was very chatty, and good company, so when we finished our coffee, we decided to go to the Prudential building, on the top floor, to have an after dinner drink. Ralph invited himself along, and it was fine with us. We parked the car in one of the upper parking areas, which had several floors, and took the elevator to the top floor where, there was a lovely view of Chicago.

When it was time to leave, Ralph told us where he lived, and we said we would be happy to drive him home. We took the elevator to the parking area, but could not remember which floor we were on. Ralph and I sat on a concrete slab, and waited for Jack to find the car. Once he did, we hopped in and headed for Lincoln Park West to find Ralph's house. It was a large brownstone. He invited us in. At first we declined, but he insisted, and so we helped him up the stairs and entered the front foyer, which was out of Dickens, but beautiful. We said our adieus. As we were leaving, he said, "I want to thank you for a most enjoyable Thanksgiving."

We said, "Our pleasure." Then he said, "I heard you talking, Dorothy, about joining Jack in New York for Christmas, and wondered if I could tag along?"

We were quite surprised, but we thought, "He's such a nice old man, why not?" So we gave him our phone number, and said okay, but to think it over. He called the next day and asked if we really meant it. We said yes, and he told us that he would be in touch.

A week passed, and Jack had gone back to New York. Ralph called, to ask for a resume. I said, "What are you talking about?"

He said, "Well, you see, I have a lawyer and trustees that take care of me. And I told them that I wanted to go to New York with you for Christmas. They said they would have to investigate you and Jack before I could make a commitment."

I said, "No Ralph, that doesn't work for me! We just wanted to do a kind thing on Thanksgiving. If you recall, we didn't ask you for a resume. So I'm truly sorry." I guess there is a price to pay when you have a trust fund. Of course, I will never know. But I'm glad we made one old man happy for a day.

Before Jack left for New York, we were sitting in the kitchen having coffee when the doorbell rang. I went to the door, and saw a gentleman I didn't know. It was the day after Thanksgiving. "Who is this person?" I thought. He was looking at me through the storm door.

He introduced himself as being with a local real estate company. He said he would very much like to sell my house. This came out of the blue, but then I guess life has many surprises. He said he could get a good price for my house, so I said, "Step right in and lets discuss the possibilities." I don't know what possessed me, but I was ready to talk turkey. Before he left, I had signed a 90-day contract. I was on a roll, and never stopped.

I guess I figured Craig would be going to college, and I could use the money. I needed a change, but never thought it would be such a big one. I would put the money in the bank, get a nice little apartment, and continue teaching. Not to be! What a challenge! I knew I was up to it. I was only 52.

Jack went back to New York, and a few days later he called, and said, "How do you feel about moving to Florida? I'm really fed up with New York, and if the pace keeps up, I'll have an ulcer. I'll resign my job. Bob would like to join us." Bob was a friend from New York. I had known Bob, and liked him. I told Jack, we need a plan. Bob was a landscape architect. He had serviced many buildings in New York. He had just finished designing a new restaurant in Chicago, so he would be a great addition to our little twosome.

After thinking it over, I said, "Jack, we need to focus on how, where, and when. And I would want to know the plan." Jack had a personality that made everything bigger than life, and everything he pursued was something exciting with great expectations. I was not hard to convince. I was so ready for a change. I was teaching at the Winnetka Community House, and had many classes. But my thinking at the time was, "Is this all there is? A change would be good no matter what." So after much discussion, we decided to take a chance.

Florida seemed the perfect place, especially after living in below-zero weather in Chicago most of my life. I didn't have a lot of options. I never had a straight job. I only knew the old soft shoe. I would think to myself, "Well, maybe I can get a job at Marshall Fields. I'll get my little black dress and pearls, and hope they find a place for me in cosmetics." After all, my mother was a hairdresser, and I knew makeup from show business. My first concern was Craig, and how he would feel about leaving Chicago and selling the house. I wondered if he would be okay with moving across the country. Craig grew up in this house, and all his roots were here. I asked him how he felt about it, and I will never forget his answer. "Mom, I think it's your turn," he replied. "Don't worry about me. I'm going off to college and would come home one weekend a month. Now, I can look forward to sunny Florida at Thanksgiving and Christmas, so let's get packing."

For our next holiday, I drove to Dayton, Ohio to pick up Craig. He was enrolled at the University of Dayton. We were on our way to New York, and after the five hour trip from Chicago to Dayton, I was glad to hand over the driving to Craig. We arrived in New York and as usual, Jack's first words were "Let the fun begin." He had a wonderful apartment on the top floor of his building with a view of Manhattan that was spectacular. His apartment had a wrap-around terrace; it was lit up with Christmas lights like a premier of *It's a Wonderful Life*. He had many invitations to Christmas parties, and I met several of his friends and colleagues from work. It was a magical Christmas for both Craig and me. Christmas Eve morning, we went out for a walk, had breakfast, and waited for the shops to open. It was like *My Fair Lady*. We picked up flowers, wine, and all good things for Christmas Eve dinner. Back to the apartment and Jack started cooking. We did have a space problem, so decided to put one table on the terrace until the dinner hour. We set the table and thought, "Aren't we smart?" The other table was in the small dining area, and we would bring the big table in for dinner. The guests arrived, and all was well. The oven was on, we served the wine, and we all gave a Christmas toast.

It was time to bring in the table; dinner was ready to be served. Suddenly, the lights went out. We thought it was just our apartment, but it was the whole building. We knew, because Jack went to his neighbors, and they were sitting in the dark. Jack invited them to join us. He said, "Why sit alone in the dark, when you can be in the dark with all of us merry makers?" The big problem was the table we had set on the terrace. When they picked it up, all the dishes and glassware started to slip off, and several dishes broke. No one seemed to care if they had a dish or not. It was such fun. We found candles, and we sang all the Christmas songs and told stories. It was a most enchanting evening!

Christmas Day we spent with Bob's parents, they lived in Montclair, New Jersey. They were delightful people. It was a lovely day except for one thing! I had this silk print dress on that I thought was smashing, perfect for Christmas. Unfortunately, it had static cling. It clung to me all day. As hard as I pulled, it would not let go. Of course, they thought it was very funny! I was the comic relief. Finally, I just let it stick. The clinging dress did not stay in my closet very long. The last few days of our New York visit was coming to an end, and we had that long drive back to Chicago. We would leave New Years day.

I got a call the day after Christmas. It was the real estate office. The agent had a thing about the day after holidays. He said, "Your house is sold!" I was in shock. I thought it would be longer. "As soon as you get back," he went on to say, "we can sign the papers, and you need to be out by June!"

"This is a wow!" I said. "Okay, see you in Chicago."

Craig and I drove back in record time, and arrived safe and sound. Luck was on our side. When we drove into the driveway, the car began to smoke, but we made it home. Craig went back to school.

I told my brother John about my plan. He thought it was terrific. But my other brother, Vincent, didn't think it was a good idea. He said, "Do you know what you're doing?" I said, "Yes I do, and why not? There's nothing here for me!"

This move would be my Oz. When Jack and Bob arrived, they packed the U-haul, the door closed, and it was party time. All my old and dear friends came to say adieu! We all sat on the kitchen floor, laughing and remembering, all the fun times we had together. They all said that I would be back. Guess not!

June 1975! Early the next morning, after our party, I said goodbye to my house on Keystone Avenue, and I never looked back.

We hit the freeway; Jack was driving the truck, car number one, was driven by Bob. Car number two by Craig. I was the 2nd driver of my car. Louie, the dog, was very happy in the back seat. We arrived in Miami, pulled into a motel, and it was a new beginning.

We called a rental agent the next morning. He gave us the address of a house that was available on Palm Island. We liked the sound of that, so off we went. The house was waiting for us. It was, five bedrooms, three baths, and a lovely fireplace. It was off the McArthur Causeway. The view from the upstairs was glorious. You could see the cruise ships leave port. One bedroom had an outside door that had a small bridge leading to a small apartment, once the servant's quarters, if you had servants. Now the catch! The owner had an elderly father who loved to fish. She lived in New York, but she bought the house so her father could come from New York for three months during the season to fish and have someplace to stay. It had a separate entrance. If we agreed to let him stay in the apartment, we could have the house for $500.00 a month. We drew a deep breath, and said, "Yes, we would be happy to have him." We signed the lease, and moved in the next day.

Our plan was to get a job and pursue our dream. We did wake up sooner than we thought, but no matter. While the dream was still a dream, life was good. We all had a special talent that would blend together, and make our dream come true. We looked for locations every weekend to find the right spot to open a small restaurant and gift gallery. Jack had the marketing skills, Bob the design, and I had dabbled in art, and had talent and style. Before we left Chicago, my brother John, who was the artist, had taught me to silk screen and gave me all the necessary materials and tools I would need to design scarves and whatever else I came up with. This would be a partnership.

Decorating the Palm Island house was a real challenge, but we had a ball doing it. Saturdays and Sundays we would go "junking" as we called it, and find all these "treasures" that would not go in any other house. The reception area, was bigger than a breadbox, believe me. It was a small ballroom, with a beautiful staircase to the second floor. We decided that the stairs needed a new runner. Jack would install it, which was great. We pulled up the old carpet, and found the runner we liked. And he started

to lay it, when I heard this loud scream. He had stepped on an old nail. It went into the bottom of his foot. Panic set in, and we rushed him to the hospital. They removed the nail, and gave him a shot. I don't know what was in that shot, but he was back to the carpet job the next day.

The following Sunday, we happened to pass by a gallery, and saw this very large painting in the window of a gypsy woman. She was quite wonderful. We had to

Craig with our Gypsy Lady. The Palm Island House in Miami, Florida, 1976.

have her for the foyer, if the price was right. Well, it was, and we put her in the convertible and rushed her home to hang in a place of honor. We didn't know who she was, but she must have been someone important, and full of life. We wanted her to be part of our family. She became a con-

157

versation piece. When we had a party, we would give everyone a notepad and ask them to name our lady and write a story about her. It was amazing how everyone saw her in a different way. She now lives in San Diego with a friend who took her off my hands. My wall space grew smaller after I left Florida.

We had decided that once we were settled, we would look for a job, and work on our dream project on the weekends. This was a real challenge for me, since I had never had a straight job before. I was in show business, and then a housewife and mother. So what to do? Well, get the want ads and pursue. One ad caught my eye. Under sales, "Fountainbleau Hotel!" Right off, I liked the sound of that. So I put on my best sales outfit and drove to the hotel. I asked for directions to the Alicia Ruth shop, and went downstairs. It was a lovely shop, and several women were waiting, I assumed, for the job I wanted. "They have a nerve," I thought. But I went right up to the counter and introduced myself to the lady behind the counter, Barbara.

"I'm Dorothy Kloss and I'm here about the job." She stopped me cold when she said, "Did you make an appointment?" I told her that I didn't know that was required. It didn't say anything about it in the ad. Just then, a gentleman came from the back to summon one of the other ladies. He looked over at Barbara, and she said, "Will it be okay if I put this lady on the list? She didn't have an appointment, "Yes, have her wait." It was the beginning of my nine-to-five life.

Chapter 17: The New Job

I waited, and talked to Barbara, I thanked her for placing my name on the list. She told me that he usually never adds a name without an appointment. "I think he likes you," I said, "We'll see..."

He came out of his office, and introduced himself as Mr. Sassoon (Ralph). "Please follow me," he motioned. He was quite charming, and I knew I wanted to work for him. "Please sit down, Dorothy," he indicated. "Tell me about yourself."

I said, "Well, right off I should tell you, this is the first time I have ever applied for a job. I was in show business until I got married, and then I taught dancing for years. So I hope I qualify."

Next, he wanted to know what made me think I would qualify for a sales job.

So I thought a moment and then said, "Well being in show business most of my life, I had to sell myself. So I'm sure I can sell your linens and lingerie."

He followed with, "You know my sister was in show business. And my first wife and I lived in Jane Froman's house." Jane Froman was a very famous singer in the 1940s. He continued, "So I guess that would qualify you for this job. We walked to the front and he told Barbara to start training me on Monday.

I said, "Oh, is it okay if I start on Tuesday? I have an appointment on Monday."

He looked at me with surprise, and said, "That will be fine, 10 a.m."

I went home, clicking my heels, and thanking "the man upstairs" for this real job. When I told Jack and Bob, they were a little surprised, but said, "We need to celebrate."

We did, most of the evening. Bob was a hoot. I had great fun with him. He owned an antique shop on the Cape. His girlfriend managed it for him. Sometimes Jack got a little annoyed with us. I didn't realize Jack could be a little depressed at times. I never noticed it before, and this did start to bother me. He was also very fastidious. If you smoked and put the butt in the ashtray, he removed it immediately. Give me a break!

I thought, "He's just nervous." But I think there was more to it. I just let it ride, like on the night we all went to the marina for dinner. Afterwards, we decided to continue on to disco, but he said, "No, let's go home." So Bob was driving and we let Jack out, and went on to the disco. I'm sure he was angry, but we didn't care. Our attitude was, "Come to the cabaret!"

I reported to work on Tuesday, and Barbara was great to work with. She started to train me. All went well, except for the cash register. It was the old kind, so you had to count out the change to the customer. I thought, "I hope I don't make any mistakes." They left me on my own, and I was having a great time chatting with the costumers and learning the merchandise. It was a new thing for me. The other ladies that worked there had different hours, but I did get to know them, and they were very nice and helpful. So I was happy as a lark.

Mr. Sassoon was a born salesman, a very classy gentleman. After I got to know him, he decided I was doing a good job, so he told me a very funny story. "When you told me you were in show business, I knew you were the right person for this job," he confessed. "I have always loved show people. They have such zest for living. I could see that in you right off. You are a people person. That is what makes you a great sales person. Even though your first week, you cost me $50.00 due to cash register mistakes, I knew you would not steal from the register, but you were so busy talking and making friends with the customers, that you didn't watch what you were doing. I knew you were nervous, so I just marked it up to experience. Once you got it, you got it, and that is what I like."

He had four beautiful daughters by his first wife, and I did meet two of them. They were as nice as their father. His second wife was Miss Memphis. I understand she was beautiful. Barbara filled me in on everything. He had met her in New York, when she was a hatcheck girl at one of the famous restaurants. Mr. Sassoon told me she was true blue. I guess, at one time in his life, after being a millionaire, he went broke. They had been together for several years, and he had given her the world. If that meant jewelry, furs or whatever made her happy. So when he could no longer afford all the finer things in life, he became very depressed. She came to him, and said, "I have always been a shrewd person with money. Before I met you, I saved my money and invested. I'm giving it to you, to get started again because you were so good to me." Now that's some gal.

They married and moved to Miami, and through his connections, were able to open "The Alicia/Ruth Stores" in three hotels. They had a lovely home in Bal Harbour. They had a great life until her death, a year before I came to work for him.

One of the most amusing things I remember was the table linen story. Mr. Sassoon would never let the sales ladies sell the table linen. That was like opening night for him. I wondered why. They were exquisite cut out embroidery and appliqué tablecloths. They were also very expensive. I guess he thought we would blow the sale, but I was determined that one day I would get a chance to make a sale. We had a very wealthy Latin clientele. Ralph, would sit down with them, display the table linens on the counter, and go into this wonderful "spiel" about how they were designed and handmade by the little nuns in the basement of their convent in Spain. He told them that he would make a trip to Spain every year to select each table linen for his collection.

I have to tell you, they came by UPS. I could hardly keep a straight face, but I controlled myself, and listened to everything he said. I thought, "This is a learning experience." He knew I was watching. I could see a little grin on his face, and a twinkle in his eye.

One afternoon, a customer came in and inquired about the table linens. Mr. Sassoon, or Ralph, as I called him now, was not in at the time. They said they could not wait, and asked if I could show them. I said, "Well — yes!" After all, I had taught dance at a Catholic school for ten years, and knew many nuns. Except my nuns were not in a basement appliquéing table linens. So I asked them to have a seat. Barbara was looking at me like, "Is she crazy?" But I just continued, and told them all about the nuns, and I made the sale. When Ralph came back, I told him what had happened and I thought he would be angry, but instead he said, "I knew sooner or later you would beat me at my own game."

I said, "Well, I knew some of those little nuns!"

He laughed and said, "Come on, have dinner with me!" That started a very close relationship. He taught me many things about selling and management that were very beneficial to me in the coming years.

Ralph decided I could be on my own in the store, so he asked me to work three nights a week. And it was fine with me, because things were not going well back on the island with Jack. Mr. Clean was getting on my nerves.

161

All the retail shops were on the lower level of the hotel, and all the sales people were great fun. We all knew each other. Unfortunately, we didn't do much business after 7 p.m. Most people were in the showroom or at the Poodle lounge. So we would stand in our doorway, and talk across the lobby area. When it was quiet, we would do crazy things like play window mannequins. The dress shop always changed windows once a week, and placed the mannequins in these abstract positions. So we would come out of our doorway, and strike a pose to match the mannequin. Everyone would laugh. I was back in show business, only I didn't have taps on my shoes.

Things were not going well at "the palace" (the ole homestead). We came to realize that we had to wake up from our dream of a business in Florida. Nothing was happening there in 1975. The Cubans were coming in, and had their own area in Miami. Outside of the few tourists, nothing was happening.

The "want ads" all said bi-lingual, very depressing. This was not working for Jack, or Bob, who had big-money jobs in New York. But I loved Miami, and I had made friends. I even found the Avery Dancing School, which hired me on my day off to teach. So after several discussions, we decided to "hang it up!" I decided to stay until the end of the lease on the house.

The only sad thing that happened was Louie, my dog. The living room had a beautiful fireplace and we never used it. Florida had lovely weather most of the time, so we just admired it. Then one evening, the weather changed and it turned very cold. We decided to light the fireplace. Big mistake! It must have opened the flue, 'cause the next morning, Louie was barking like crazy. We ran downstairs to see what was happening. He was barking at the fireplace. A pigeon was sitting in front of it. In our excitement, Jack said, "I'll open the front door, and the pigeon will fly out." Wrong!! Louie headed for the door, and was gone in a second. We ran out after him, but he had vanished. I was so upset. We tried everything. We went to the waste department, to the pound, and asked everyone on the island. We even advertised in the newspaper, but nothing; my Louie was gone. And I was sad for a long time. But then, as they say, when one door closes, another opens. That is what happened. Goodbye Jack and Bob!! Thank you for giving me a new adventure.

The house was a little big for me alone, even though, the father of the owner was still upstairs. I continued my job, and teaching dance, then one day the phone rang. The lady introduced herself. "I'm the head-mistress, Ms. Handley at the private school here. Your neighbor suggested I call you. She is our French teacher." I could not imagine why.

162

Then she explained. "I have a young man who will be graduating in June. He is from Iran, and his parents are looking for a private residence for him to rent a room. His sister, and her family live in the area, but he doesn't want to live with them. Nicole (my neighbor) thought you might be interested. He was a senior in high school. The parents are here, but will be going back to Iran in a few weeks, and would be happy to meet with you."

So, I met with them, and they were charming, as was the young man. They were willing to pay $500 a month. I clicked my heels, and said, "Okay." Hussein moved in a couple days later, in one of the upstairs bedrooms. He was no problem. One day a week, I would take clean towels to his room. He had photos of the Shah, and Farah Diba of Iran, in these beautiful jeweled frames on his dresser. I wondered, but I didn't think any more about it until Easter.

My son called, and said that he would like to bring three of his friends from school for the Easter spring break. They arrived, and Hussein thought this was great. He got friendly right away, and they liked him!

They took him with them if they were going out, and he was always ready to go. He had a great car and one night, said, "Let me drive tonight!"

So they said "Okay."

At the end of the night, Craig recounted, "Wow, he was going 90 miles an hour, and he was stopped by the police. They took him in, and he had diplomatic immunity."

His parents called me from Iran and apologized and said, "He will not be driving again."

The next week, Craig's girlfriend Joni, was arriving. I was going to paint the bedroom she would be staying in. I got my bucket of paint, and started to paint. Hussein came into the room, and said, "Why are you painting, Dorothy?" I told him about Joni. He said, "Oh, let me do that for you!" I said, "Okay!"

Spring Break with Jim Horvath's friends from college, and me. Hussein on right, 1976.

Well, he tried. He had a problem with straight lines, and where the ceiling and wall come together, forget it. The ceiling had more paint on it than the house, but it was nice of him to offer. I don't think he ever painted a room in the palace. His sister and family came over about a week after that, and asked me about the paint job. "Hussein tells us he painted a room for you," they boasted. "We are so proud of him, and that he had a chance to do something like that." I didn't tell them he would never make it as a painter.

After Joni and Craig went back to school, I got another call from Jim Horvath. He wanted to know if he could visit and bring three other kids from college with him. He thought maybe we could work on some tap. What to say — well of course "Yes!"

He came with three non-tappers. We danced in my living room and the kids had a great time in Miami since it was also their spring break. To backup, his Grandma Jean was the one who helped my mother through beauty school. When I was still in Chicago, teaching at the Winnetka Community House, Jim would come to class every week at the center and to my house during the week, to work on his tap. This kid meant business. Great enthusiasm. As I

Jim Horvath with friends at Palm Island House, 1976.

mentioned earlier, he later danced himself into Bob Fosse's *Dancin'* and several Broadway shows. When I go to New York, even now at 88, Jim is always there to take me to dinner.

Chapter 18:
Go West, Young Gal, Go West

My time in Florida was coming to an end, only I didn't know it. After Jack and I decided it was over, I continued living in "the palace," on Palm Island, and having a great time with Ralph. He took me everywhere; dinner, the dog races, the country club, and last but not least, he asked me to marry him. I was only fifty-two at the time, and he was in his seventies, a very young seventy, I must say. He was full of life, very good-looking, generous, and a very classy man with great charm, but not for me. Now that I think about it, was that a dumb move? I was betwixt and between, due to the lease on the house that would be up in June. As Jackie Mason would say, "I looked at the house. The house looked at me. Should I go? Should I stay?" What a dilemma, but not for long.

Alicia Ruth sold wonderful lingerie, and this lovely young gal, who was a buyer, would stop by to see if we needed to place an order. Her name was Jane, and we became friends. On one of her visits to the shop, she invited me to dinner. She and her husband were having a dinner party with friends, and unfortunately the wife of one of the gentlemen couldn't make it. And she thought it might be nice if I took her place. That way, her seating arrangement would stay the same. So, kidding, I said, "So Jane, I'm a fill in?"

She hastily replied, "Oh, no Dorothy, I didn't mean it that way!"

"I know," I said, and then I told her, "I would be delighted." The evening arrived, and I drove to their beautiful house. The age of this delightful group, about twenty-seven. We had drinks, and then took our places at the table. Jane was serving Greek. Everything was perfect.

The house had a cathedral ceiling, with a wraparound balcony completely covering the living and dining room. There was a beautiful staircase leading up to the balcony. After dinner, they decided to have coffee in the upstairs library. I followed the group, and found myself in this exquisite room. Everyone found a comfortable chair, and "let the conversation begin." The next thing I noticed, everyone seemed to be smoking. I figured they were young. I had stopped smoking in 1966. They asked me if I would like a cigarette. I said, "No, thank you. I don't smoke." Jane served a very strong coffee, I thought was espresso. It was then I began to feel a little strange, so I excused myself and went to the bathroom hoping I could lose the feeling. But it persisted, and when I returned to the den of iniquity, full of smoke, I decided it was time for me to leave. I told Jane that I had to open the store in the morning, and I thought I should go.

I had saved the day for Jane, and then went on my way. I know you're wondering what this had to do with my decision to leave Florida. I arrived home and hit the couch. I was so ill, I had to up-chuck and I thought it was the Greek food Jane had served, although it seemed everyone else was fine. I finally fell asleep, and the next morning I was still ill, but I got myself dressed and got to the store. After awhile, Barbara came in and said, "You look like death warmed over!" I told her about the Greek food. She told me to go home.

I was lying on the bed thinking, "How I would like a cup of coffee," but I didn't have the strength to make it. I was alone, and feeling sorry for myself, but the feeling continued. I said to myself, "Get over it, Dorothy!"

I thought, "It's time for a new adventure. What am I doing here, anyhow?" Like a flash, I thought, "Why don't I move to Vegas? Vincent and Viola live there, and I would have family." So I picked up the phone, after I had coffee, and called Vincent. I told him I would be moving there in June. He said, "Great, I'll find you an apartment." I guess "the Greek food" played a big part in my Vegas move. It was worth getting sick to move me along.

To put an end to the dinner party mystery, Barbara talked to Jane the next day and asked her if any of her other guests had gotten sick. "Barbara, she said, it wasn't the Greek food that made Dorothy ill. It was the marijuana she inhaled." A great song in the 1940s was "Smoke Gets in Your Eyes." It went something like this. "They asked me how I knew, my true love was true. I of course replied, something here inside, cannot be denied…Smoke gets in your eyes." It did get in my eyes, but also in my lungs. Jane came in a couple days later to apologize. She said, "I thought you knew — I'm so sorry." All was forgiven, and I made the decision I needed to make. But didn't know it at the time.

I did like Jane. She was young, and on top of all the new fashions, and makeup, she was a real, *Women's Wear Daily* gal. One day, she said to me, "How do you like my eye lashes? Aren't they wonderful?"

I asked her what was different and she just looked at me. "I just had false lashes put on," she said triumphantly. "What do you mean"? I questioned. "They stay on about a month. It's like getting a hair cut every month," she boasted. "You don't have to wear mascara — look how long and full they are." I gave her another look. I did think they were quite nice. So before I could say "No," she was on the phone making an appointment for me.

I kept the appointment. The eye expert had me lie back in the chair; she then placed a linen towel on my chest and placed the separate eyelashes on the towel. She picked up each lash with the tweezers, and placed each one slightly above my eyelash. When she finished, I thought, "They are quite lovely." I left the salon, got in my car and at the next stop sign I stopped. I was so busy looking in the mirror at my new eyelashes. I hit the car in front of me. The man got out, and came back to me.

"Lady, what are you doing?" he said as he angrily approached.

I said, "I'm so sorry. I was admiring my new eyelashes."

What a dumb thing to say, but he took a deep breath, and said, "No damage, but forget the eyelashes." My friend Jane, again! If I had stayed in Florida much longer, with Jane's influence, I wonder what would have happened.

Craig would be leaving Dayton and arriving in Florida in a few weeks. When I called him, I said, "We have a change of plans. We're moving to Vegas!" It was no problem for him; he loved Vegas. "So come as soon as you can. I'll get the moving van and start to pack."

I went to work, and told Ralph and Barbara! Ralph said, "I know you have family there, but I could be family!"

My thought was, "But I wonder, for how long?"

Barbara said to me, "You know, you're crazy. All this could be yours. He's crazy about you, and would give you anything you want." I said, "Barbara, I know, but what I want is not here." Ralph gave me a lovely going away party. Craig arrived, and we hit the road. A year later, Ralph died. It could have all been mine. The choices we make! If I had married Ralph and stayed, Barbara would have said I killed him.

We decided to stop at Disney World in Orlando on our way to Vegas. It had just opened. The landscaping was not even completed, but we spent the day, and then onward to Vegas.

When we went through Boulder Dam, we knew we were in Las Vegas and almost out of gas. There was no air conditioning in the car. We had purchased ice sacks for the front of the car, to keep the engine from overheating. The heat had started as soon as we hit the desert. Boy, it was hot!! But we knew we were almost at our destination. Vincent and Viola, lived at the Las Vegas Country Club Estates, on the golf course. But they had decided to move out further in the desert, a new area, where they were building new homes. They sold their place and moved in the new house by the time we arrived. Craig and I would be staying with them until our moving van arrived. One of the reasons for their move to the new house; they had their own swimming pool. Vincent was sensitive about swimming with other people since he lost his leg.

We settled in with Viola and Vincent and then Vi told me we were having a family reunion, and a house warming. My brother John, his family, and several friends from Chicago would be arriving. It would be a "hot time in the old town tonight." It was a fun time, and I would get to see John and his grandkids. John had two sons, John and Vincent.

Lorraine was a friend of Viola's from Chicago. I had known her slightly from Sacred Heart Academy. Her daughter was in my dance class. Lorraine had written to Vi and said she would be on her way to Los Angeles, and would like to stop in Vegas to visit. So there she was, with a suitcase full of vitamin pills that she immediately placed on Viola's kitchen sink. Not a good move on Lorraine's part. Every time I went into the kitchen, Vi would look at me with an evil eye, and I would say, "Don't look at me, she's your friend!" Vi loved to give parties, and have people stay with her. But three days was her limit. And Lorraine's three days were up, this was an over stay. During her three days, we became friends.

To reiterate, after Craig and I arrived in Vegas, Vincent said to me, "You know, Dorothy, I don't know if you're going to like Vegas. It's a small town, and you're a big city girl. Put your furniture in storage, and go to Los Angeles, stay in my apartment in Beverly Hills. Check out L.A. before you make a decision."

Lorraine and I were talking over coffee, and she told me she would be driving to L.A. the next day. She had a niece there, who worked at the studios. She was getting a divorce after many years of marriage. She had two sons and Mary, her daughter, a beautiful home in the suburbs, and her husband had a big power job, but the marriage was over. She had to get away and think about her new life.

"When you come to L.A., Dorothy, call me," she said. "We can do lunch!" Craig had gone back to school. A few days later, I drove to L.A. and got settled in Vincent's apartment. I loved it there, and called Lorraine who was happy to hear from me. I had a beautiful blue convertible, which was perfect for Beverly Hills. I thought I was a movie star. Lorraine and I had the best time. We were on vacation, going and coming every day without a care.

One day, she said to me, "You know, my niece knows this great psychic, and we should go!" I was not thrilled with the idea, but she convinced me that it would be fun. So she made an appointment. The psychic would meet us at a restaurant in Beverly Hills. I was waiting for this woman to come in, with a turban on her head, carrying a crystal ball. But instead, this beautiful blonde came over to our table, and introduced herself as Tamara. She sat down, and we talked for a few minutes. Then she said, "Dorothy, why don't I read for you first?" She laid out the tarot cards. The first thing she said: "Why are you leaving L.A.? This is where it's at for you."

I said, "Well, I made the decision to go back to Vegas, and I'm packed."

Then she went on, "You will be back!" She told me, many positive things, but it was all too positive. You know, kind of like the old joke, "you're going on a long trip." Then she shuffled the cards, and started to read for Lorraine. Wow! Right off, her first prediction was negative, and I was in shock. She told her things were not going the way she had planned. It was going to be a long road, and financially disappointing. At this point, I was beginning to feel really good about my reading. At the end of Lorraine's reading, she asked me if there was anything I would like to ask her.

I said, "Yes, it's about my dog, Louie." She said, "Say no more. Louie did not get killed! He is perfectly fine with a nice family, but he does miss you." I thought that was nice of her to say.

Lorraine went back to Chicago and we did keep in touch. What Tamara told her came to pass. When she got back to Chicago, she wrote to tell me that her husband was under investigation for fraud within his company. They had to sell the house. They went back together, for financial reasons, and eventually moved out of Chicago. I never heard the conclusion of the story.

Before my reading with Tamara, I knew Lorraine was leaving, and my only other friend was the nice little Japanese lady that managed the building that Vincent was renting. Vincent was losing patience with me. I guess he thought I was having too good a time in Beverly Hills, and not making up my mind what I wanted to do. He came up for the weekend, and said, "So Dorothy, what are you going to do?"

I said, "I'll have to give it some thought."

And I did. I thought about what Tamara had said and decided to give L.A. another try. I decided to look for a job. I bought the newspaper, and went immediately to the classifieds, employment opportunities! And I thought, "I'll find something in no time." I looked down the list to see what would appeal to me. One opportunity hit me right off: "Well-groomed lady to work at exclusive Beverly Hills store, Geary's." I called for an appointment. I had been in Geary's several times. It was a fabulous store, where many of the movie stars bought their china and silver. The ad said, "well-groomed," so I put on my Sunday best, and off I went. The gentleman that interviewed me said, "You're just what we're looking for!" Well, I was very pleased with myself. He had me fill out the work papers and told me to report the next day. My first day was uneventful.

One of the other sales ladies filled me in on what was expected of me. If you have never been in Geary's, let me explain. As you come in the front door, and walk straight ahead, you will see two staircases, one on the right, and one on the left, leading to the second floor offices. You can view the whole store from the second floor.

At first, I thought it was the staircase in "Gone with the Wind," and that Scarlett would appear at any moment, with Rhett Butler. But to my surprise, it was not Scarlett that would be climbing those stairs; it would be me. "If you have any kind of problem," I was told, "or need to check something, or somebody, take it upstairs."

Then I said, "Oh, then you have to come down. I guess you don't have an elevator?" There were about twenty stairs.

Then she told me, "We do not sell merchandise off the floor. You take the number off the piece, and go downstairs to the basement to find it."

I thought, "This is a real stair job. I'm so well-groomed, and I'm going to the basement and drag all this merchandise upstairs. Well, let's give it a try." Two days later, I heard raindrops falling on my window. I thought, "Do I really want this job?" And very quickly, I said, "No." I called Geary's, and told the nice man that hired me that I had decided to move on. He said, "But Dorothy, we really do like you. Are you sure? What is the problem?"

"First of all, it's raining, and there are too many stairs," I explained. He laughed, and said, "I know they are a problem." Then he said, "Just come in and I'll give you your check." I got my check for the three days, cashed it, and went shopping.

While I was in Beverly Hills, I took a dance class with Dom Salerno at the Beverly Hills Dance Academy. He was teaching a jazz class. I had very little training in jazz — remember, I came from the tap period — but I really wanted to learn more. I loved his class. Most of the young people in the class were half my age. Dom said to me, "You were in the business. I can tell the way you move." I told him earlier that I had very little jazz. He was so nice, he told me to come to another class to catch up for no charge. I did miss his classes when I went back to Vegas.

I drove back to Vegas. Vincent found an apartment for me in the Las Vegas Country Club Estates, where they lived before moving to the new house. There were lovely homes on the golf course, and the group of apartments I would be living in had been there before the houses, and they remained. It was a lovely apartment overlooking the ninth hole on the second floor.

I moved my furniture in, and I was ready for Vegas. In the meantime, Viola was living in her new house without a care in the world, until one day she heard a loud scream, and went flying out the patio door. Her neighbor was yelling across the wall, "Call animal control, there is a big snake in my pool." Viola looked over the wall, and almost went into shock. But she got on the phone. The next conversation with Vi was all about the snake, and how she couldn't live here any longer. "We have to sell," she insisted. And they did, quickly, and found a house in their old area, Las Vegas Country Club. I was now in walking distance to their place. Viola loved to cook. So once they got settled, she would invite me to dinner. At that time, Vincent was working at the Stardust Hotel.

Vi knew exactly the time Vincent would be home, and she was ready for him with the feast of the evening. She would set up a little snack before dinner, which would be enough for my dinner; several kinds of cheese, crackers, fruit, and whatever else she could find. Both she and Vincent were putting on weight. I guess they didn't notice but I did. Vincent was straining to walk on his prostheses, and he was on his feet all day at the casino. Vi would say to me, "You eat like a bird!"

I would say, "That's okay, I'm happy."

We would sit at the dining room table and look out on the golf course and the street. I would laugh at the two of them. They would look out the window and see the residents jogging. Their favorite statement, "Will you look at those darn fools out there jogging?!" As they put another burger on the fire, and another pound on "coming up the rear!"

I thought it would be a good idea for Viola to get a bike. I already had a bike, and since she was not a physical person, this would be a good idea to get her going and lose some weight. I called her, after she got her bike, and said, "Let's go riding, I'll be right over." We jumped on our bikes and started to circle the complex. Vi was gung ho the first few minutes, then I could see her slowly fading, and suddenly she took the lead. I thought we were at Santa Anita racetrack. She was heading toward the back gate as fast as her legs would go. I followed along and wondered where she was going. Well, not surprisingly, she flew out the gate and pulled up in front of Swensen's Ice Cream Parlor and said, "Let's get an egg salad sandwich."

I said to myself, "I guess this isn't working. I'll have to take another approach."

My next approach was golf. I said, "You know, Vi, I think golf is your game. Let's go to the stop and sock and hit a couple practice balls. If you like it, you can take a few lessons. It would be such fun to play with you on the golf course."

My Sister-in-Law Viola, and Vincent Hunn, with Dorothy and Ken

"Okay, here we go again," she said, "but I'm not making any promises."

After a few days of hitting the ball, she did decide to take lessons, and I thought, "You got her now."

She bought the golf shoes and a great outfit and a new set of clubs. Craig had just arrived home from school, and we were going to play nine holes, I thought this would be a good time to take Vi out to play on the course. Craig called her and said, "Aunt Vi, mom and I are going to play nine holes today. Come along!"

We picked her up in her new outfit (may I say at this point, I was in tennis shoes), and off we went. We played the first hole and she did have a good arm, so I thought we were in for a good game. At the start of the second hole she began to fade, turned around and yelled, "I'll see you back at the clubhouse." When we arrived at the clubhouse after our game, she was enjoying a nice big sandwich. I just couldn't find an exercise that she would enjoy, so I gave up.

One day I was walking around Las

My niece Brandy, with husband Richard Knowles, and my brother Vincent

172

Vegas village, and I saw a sign, "Beauty School." I thought about my mother at that moment, and thought, "Maybe I'll go in and sign up," so I did. I decided to take the three-month manicuring course. This would be fun, since I could do a manicure when I was nine years old. The course was $300. I signed the contract and I was off to another adventure.

I made a lot of new friends. The cosmetologists always wanted to cut and shape my hair, and I had a lot of it. But there was more to the course than just cutting hair, I had to study so I could pass the state board exam.

When it came time to take the test, I arrived at the school, and was given a manicuring kit, and assigned to a desk, which is a lot different than a manicuring table. It was a chair with writing space on the side. We were told to bring someone with us to demonstrate our skill giving a manicure. Well, I took "the biker" and "golfer" with me, my sister-in-law Viola, which was the first mistake. I sat down in the chair, and set up my utensils. Viola sat across from me, and immediately started telling me not to be nervous. "Don't be nervous, she cautioned.

I said, "Viola, be quiet. I'm not nervous."

The cosmetologists were being tested at the same time as the manicurists, except their timing was different from ours. The clock was set, and we started. I was going along just fine. I was about to start the polish, and they announced that we had ten minutes to finish. But it was for the cosmetologists not the manicurist. Whereupon, Viola yells out, "Oh my god, don't get nervous, Dorothy!" The aftershock of her yelling threw me, and I knocked over my set up, water, and the polish hit the floor. There was no saving it, and as we both took to the floor trying to pick it up, Vi smudged her nails. They called time, and I was done for. It was a comedy of errors.

I did pass the written test with flying colors: 90 on the written test, and 79 on the skill test. I was unable to finish the manicure, so that brought my score down. But it didn't stop me from getting a job. Now I had my license, and I hit the "Employment Opportunities" section of the newspaper, once again! There was an opening at the Riviera Hotel beauty salon, "Annie of Paris." That sounded like my cup of tea. "Maybe I'll learn to speak French," I thought. It was located on the top floor of the hotel. I took myself up there, and asked for Annie. The girl at the desk motioned for me to take a seat; she would see if she was available.

Well, she was available. "Can I help you?" Annie asked.

"Well I don't know, but I'm here about the manicurist job," I replied. Annie was a tall blond, with a French accent and a French attitude. It was amazing how my attitude suddenly changed. "Come over to the table and sit down," she said. "File one nail, push back the cuticle on another nail, do a nail wrap, and polish one nail with a dark polish."

As soon as I started, her haughty attitude was getting to me. When she critiqued one little thing, I decided this was not the job for me. I stood up and said, "I don't want to work for you!" and walked out.

She had my employment record, with my phone number. She called the next day and said, "This is Annie. Now don't hang up. I'm sorry we got off on the wrong foot. Please come back — I'd like to offer you the job." I did go back, and I was with Annie for several months.

One of the gals did great porcelain nails, which were new on the market. You didn't need a license at that time, and Annie asked her to teach me. There was big money in porcelain nails. All the showgirls wanted them, and not everyone could do a professional job. At that time, it took about an hour and a half for a set of nails, but the money was terrific.

One day, Annie called me at home. She asked if I'd do her a favor. "Raquel Welch is at the MGM Grand Hotel, and needs a pedicure. I know it's your day off, but I really would appreciate you doing this for me. Unfortunately she can't get anyone in town to do it, due to her bad behavior."

I said, "Okay." I arrived with my clippers and nail file. Her assistant met me at the elevator and ushered me into her room. Raquel walked into the room in a stunning sunshine yellow terrycloth robe. I said, "Hello," and she looked past me like I wasn't there and sat down. "Be sure you don't cut too short!" she warned. And I looked at her, and thought to myself, "B - - ch, you better be nice, 'cause the clippers could slip...I didn't mean that."

She picked up her book and began to read. When I finished, I gave her the bill. She paid me the exact amount, and no tip. Her assistant walked me to the elevator, and said, "Don't let her get to you. She is very difficult. I will never work for her again." She was a temp...

Connie Stevens, on the other hand, was adorable. She needed a couple of nails fixed, and was really under pressure, since she was opening a new show that night. When I entered her hotel room filled with people and her two little girls, who were just as adorable as their mother, she was very gracious. "I'll try to be with you in a moment," she apologized. Everybody was friendly and nice, and actually, they were rehearsing. She would sit down, and then up again. I tried to get one nail fixed, and she was up, and the kids were jumping around. She still remained nice, and apologizing every time she had to leave me. When I finished, she thanked me, paid the bill and gave me a big tip. One classy lady!!

Tony Orlando's wife came in for a repair on her porcelain nails. She said, "Look at these nails, they're unnatural looking. Can you do something with them?" I said, "I'll try. I'll sand them down." When I finished, she was pleased, since she was going to a party that evening. During our conversation, she told me she was there with President Ford and Mrs. Ford. I jumped right on that one. "Do you think Mrs. Ford would like a manicure?" I hastened. I thought to myself, "Gosh, to do the First Lady's nails! Would that be something!"

Mrs. Orlando said, "I'll ask her, Dorothy." And she did, but due to the security, she was unable to come to the salon. After she left, she called the salon to tell me how sorry she was. How nice.

The other joy of working at the salon was meeting and getting to know this beautiful, talented woman, Pia Zadora. She was married to the owner of the Riviera Hotel at the time, Riklis Meshulam.

Pia, one afternoon, made an appointment for a manicure. She sat down at my table and we talked right through to the end of the polish. She told me about her career and being a child star on Broadway, and now here she was a young married woman at twenty-three. A couple days later she was back again, and again, and again. I really looked forward to her coming in and we exchanged many conversations. She even talked her husband into coming for a manicure. He was a charmer and I could see why, Pia married him even with a thirty-year age difference.

Moving along to 2012, Pia was opening at The McCallum Theatre in Palm Springs. Ken and I decided to attend. As the saying goes, "She knocked them dead." She received a standing ovation. After the show we went back stage and after twenty-five years, she was still that adorable woman who greeted everyone with such love, including me!

My friend Dorothy from Chicago had moved to San Diego. She called me about coming there for Easter. I had not seen Dorothy for a long time, and I thought it was a great idea. I went to Annie and told her I needed the Saturday, before Easter off. She told me that would be impossible because the salon would be too busy. I said, "You have plenty of coverage," but she would not listen. So I said, "Okay, find another girl." And Craig and I went to San Diego.

When we got back, I found another salon that hired me. And on my third day of work, I got a phone call that threw me into panic. My sister-in-law, Eleanor, called to tell me my brother John had passed away. I was devastated. Vincent and Vi picked me up, and we left for Chicago immediately. Craig came in from school, and the family was together for a sad reunion. John's wife, Eleanor, and his sons John and Vincent, and their children, were all there to bury John next to my mother. Eleanor followed a few years later.

A young man came to me at the cemetery, introduced himself, and said, "You're John's sister Dorothy, right? He talked about you all the time." John worked for the art department for the city of Chicago. The young man told me he loved John. He said that he was like Peter Pan, always flying high and making everyone feel good. "He helped me so much and gave me encouragement. I will surely miss him," he said. Me too!

After we returned to Vegas, I decided manicuring was not for me. Just the smell of the stuff we worked with would kill you. I said to Viola, "I think I will look for something else. Maybe at one of the hotels."

She had a skeptical look on her face. "What can you do?" she said in an imperious tone. "You're fifty years old, with very little experience. They want young, good-looking girls with great legs!"

"I'll show you legs!!" I thought. I could not believe what she was saying to me. She, who was sitting in her lovely home without a worry in the world. But those words gave me a challenge. I said, "Thanks for the encouragement," and left.

I went right out, and bought the newspaper and found, what else, "Job Opportunities." And there was one with my name on it, at the MGM Grand Hotel. I called the number, and a nice gal said, "If you can come right now, we can talk. Today is the last day to interview." I changed clothes, and within a half hour I was in the office.

This nice gal said, "I see you were in show business," after reading my resume. "The position's at the MGM Hotel in the Serendipity, on the lower level of the hotel. It's collectibles and artwork." She asked me to fill out the paperwork, and I put down Vi and Vincent's phone number, in case I wasn't home. She gave me a smile and said, "We'll be in touch."

I left the office, and went shopping to keep my mind active. After about an hour, I was at home and Viola called. "Where have you been? I've been trying to reach you, and so is Mr. Smith, about a job. He lives here on the golf course, right across from our place. He would like you to call him."

Gosh, what a change in attitude. I said, "Okay," and took the number. George Smith was the owner of the Serendipity, and the clock shop at the MGM Grand Hotel. He asked if I could come over to his house, just a short distance from me. I said yes. When I arrived, he and his wife met me at the door. His wife, Francine, was very attractive. She had long black hair, and always wore mostly white. She had been a June Taylor dancer and, of course, we immediately hit it off when I told her I knew June and Marilyn Taylor (June's sister) from the Abbott years. George Smith was a nice man to work for, and so was Francine. I loved working with all the art, and unusual collectibles, it was a very busy store.

It was the first time I learned about "ups" (like, your turn). You would wait your turn to wait on a customer. When a customer would enter the door, all the sales girls were like eagles. They would quickly check to see who was "up," or in other words, who should get the customer. They would say, "it's my up." It was like life and death to them, but I did finally get the hang of it, and knew I had better be on my toes or I would be left behind. You had a base salary, and then after a certain amount of sales, you got a commission. That was what they were after, that commission.

I did have fun working there. I used to visit the MGM lion on my lunch hour every afternoon. He was just down from the store, with his trainer to control him. He was a big attraction; everyone would have photos taken with him. Once in a while, they would ask me to go down to the clock shop and fill in for Dennis, who was George's son. If he had something to do, I would watch the shop. I loved looking at all the clocks. If there were no customers, I would watch the lion from the store door. We never became friends, but I knew he was there. And he knew I was there!

One day, Francine came in and said, "June Taylor is in town with Jackie Gleason. They are taping a TV show from here." She asked me to fill in while she did the show.

I said, "How great!"

Francine added, "I told her you were working for me." The next day, June called and came over to the store. We had coffee, and talked about the good old days with Abbott. Then we went back to the present, she was on TV, I was waiting for "ups" to pay the rent. But everything changes, doesn't it?

Francine was fun, and she wanted to know if I was dating anyone. I said, "No, not at this time, why?"

"Well," she confided, "a friend of mine would like to date you. He came by the store to check you out, and he liked what he saw, and asked me how he should go about asking you out."

I said, "So now I'm a check out?"

"Can I give him your number?" She plowed on!

I told her yes, and the call came that evening. He asked if 7:00 o'clock was okay, and I told him that was fine. "You have to go through the gate. I'm just a short distance from there." I instructed. He arrived the next night, but was late. He called, and I walked outside my door and waved to him. At least, I assumed this was my date. And it was a good guess on my part.

I got in the car, and he immediately started "yapping" at me like I had known him for years. Right off, I knew this was not for me. We went to a steakhouse where all the locals use to go. He sat there for an hour, telling me about himself. It was like having dinner with a dummy. All I did was nod.

As we left the restaurant, he asked me if I would like to see his collection of slot machines. I thought that was a new approach, but I said, "Okay," and off we went to his house in a lovely area. As we walked in, I saw a pool table in the living room, and I wondered who decorated this house. He took me down a long hall to the slot machine room, and on the way I noticed that hanging on both sides of the hall wall were photos of him, every few feet. I said, "You told me you had a grown son. Is there a picture of him?"

"Oh, yes, here is one," he pointed out. I don't know how he found a space for it.

We sat down in the living room and I was very uncomfortable. He started telling me about his TV antenna. He turned on the TV and asked me if I thought the sound was good. "It sounds okay to me," I said.

"You know," he said, "I had the TV man out this morning. And he had to climb up in the area above the ceiling to check it out. He nearly gave me a heart attack; he fell out and landed on his back. I was so upset with him falling that I got him out of here as fast as I could. You know, they can sue you for anything today."

I asked him, "Did you even ask the man if he was hurt?"

"No, I just wanted him out," he said without hesitation. "And that is why I'm still not sure about the sound on the TV." I stood up and said to him, "I would appreciate you taking me home, I can see you're all heart."

When I told Francine the next day, she roared with laughter, and I did too. She told me that he was very affluent. He owned most of the slot machines in Vegas. I hope he was happy with the slots, 'cause I would not want him.

I started to teach dance classes part time at a new studio associated with a new venue, "Meadows Playhouse." It was off the strip, theater in the round. It was backed by, Peter Lind Hayes, and his wife Mary Healy. They were both in show business, and had big careers in movies, theater, and TV, and lived in Vegas. I taught on my days off, and I loved doing what I love to do. I also was the choreographer for some of the shows that had a dance sequence, but it was short-lived. The theatre just couldn't make it, and closed after a couple seasons.

My best friend in Chicago was Dorothy Contursi. Dorothy's husband, Joe, was a great trumpet man, who played with *Theatre of the Air* on WGN radio. When I was teaching modeling in Chicago, Dorothy was one of my students. And when she heard I was in show business, she asked me to one of her ongoing parties. Every musician in the big bands would stop by. Jump ahead to the eighties, Dorothy decided to visit me in Vegas, and I was really looking forward to her visit. But I had no idea she had gained so much weight. When I picked her up at the airport, I was shocked. She must have been over two hundred pounds. The first night, I took her to the strip. I parked the car, and when we tried to cross the street, she stopped traffic. Horns were blowing, people were leaning out of their car windows shouting "Hey lady, get out of the street," along with several other superlatives. I didn't want to hurry her, I was afraid she might fall. We finally made it across. Then she had to sit down. Where? I kept thinking, "How am I going to get her back across the street, to get the car?" Guess what? I got a cab to drive us to the car. What are friends for?

That night, we got back to the apartment and thank goodness Craig was there. I gave her my queen-size bed. I slept on the couch. We all got into bed, and then we heard a loud crash. Craig and I jumped out of bed, and ran to the bedroom. Dorothy was sitting on the floor, in the middle of the bed. She had broken the slats; the mattress went down to the floor. She was laughing uncontrollably. Craig and I were trying to get her up, but every time we tried to pull her up, she would start to laugh again, and fall back down. We finally had to roll her on her side, off of the mattress, so we could get her up. Then Craig pulled the mattress off of the slats. We were afraid one of them might stab her in the back, and we would be brought up on murder charges. She had to sleep on the mattress on the floor.

It was not a great visit, even though I tried to show her a good time. Every time Dorothy sat on one of my chairs, I was afraid she would break it. We had a good time, but I was glad when I took her to the airport for her return flight. It was kind of like the three bears; "Who's been sitting in my chair?" Dorothy was my matron of honor when I got married. We were friends for fifty years.

Chapter 19: California, Here I Come!

As Al Jolson sang in the thirties, "California, here I come, right back where I started from!" Well, I didn't start in California, but I certainly made my mark there. Just like the psychic said, remember?? After three years in Las Vegas, I knew I had to move on; there was no question. Craig was graduating from college, I went back to Chicago for a few days, and then off to Dayton for the big event. When I arrived, I did meet his father, and it was nice he could be there. Craig took us around the campus, and his fraternity house was the surprise of the day. As we walked in, I thought I recognized a piece of furniture that looked familiar to me. Not only was it familiar, it was part of his beautiful bedroom set at home. Now, a dog was sitting on top of the nightstand, "I thought you wanted that for your room?" I asked him.

Craig explained, "Mom we didn't have enough room for it! It was my contribution to the fraternity house." It was hard to believe my little league player was a man, soon to be out there in "the big league" starting a new life. The graduation dinner was wonderful, and I was really surprised when he and some of his buddies got up, and sang, "I did it my way!" My thought was, "I hope you can always do it your way." After he graduated, he arrived in Vegas. It was so good to have him home. I could see him every day.

After a few weeks, I walked into the living room one day and he was sitting at the coffee table with a deck of cards in his hands. This made my heart skip a beat. He was dealing and shuffling, I started wondering what he had in mind. He said, "Mom. I have an idea I would like to run by you.

I was thinking, Uncle Vinnie has connections, and maybe he could get me a job at one of the downtown casinos. I could work as a dealer for a year or so, save my money, then I could open a bar."

I looked at him, like the witch in *The Wizard of Oz*, and said, "Are you nuts? It doesn't work like that, Craig. First of all, you wouldn't save your money. You would probably go to another casino, and lose it." I thought, "I have to get him out of this town." How? Well, all good things happen to those of us who believe. He went out to UNLV (University of Las Vegas) and checked on the interviews for new grads. He saw one for Campbell Soup, as a rep. He made an appointment.

I said, "You know, you need to get out of those jeans and get a nice suit." So we went shopping. The day of the interview he got all dressed up with a white shirt, tie and his new suit. He looked perfect, or so his mother thought. He came back from the interview and said, "I think they liked me, mom. And guess what? The job in Las Vegas has been filled, but they asked me if I would like to go to California." My prayers were answered. The next week we drove to L.A. and he went to the Campbell Soup office, and then we found him a motel until he could get settled. I stayed for a few days, then drove back to Vegas, and went back to work.

After a couple of months, Craig called one evening and said, "Mom, why don't you move here? You can get a job."

I said, "Are you sure?"

"Yes," he said emphatically. "We can get a nice apartment."

So I drove up and we found an apartment in Covina. He would be working out of the Covina area. Then I got the newspaper and found my favorite section, "Job Opportunities!" I saw an ad for "Rossmeyer Gallery" in Glendora, which was just a short distance from Covina. I sent them a resume, and they called me for an interview. I got the job, but I was still in Vegas, 'cause I couldn't get in my apartment until the first of the month. I had to go back for my furniture. They said, "Why don't you move early? We will store your furniture until you get in the apartment." So back I went to Vegas, one more time. What a move!! I was on the second floor, not with a dog or cat, but a piano and a glass top table.

When I arrived in Vegas, the movers took it upstairs, but now Craig and some of his buddies were going to help me move to California. Craig went out to UNLV and found a sumo wrestler, about 300 lbs. or more, willing to move the piano and glass top table. They got both down with no trouble at all and it saved Craig and his friends' backs. When we arrived in California, we drove to Glendora. My new boss, Jerry Ross, and some of his crew, helped us move the contents of the truck into their warehouse. When it was time to move into the apartment, we got it back on the truck. On the first, we moved to the new apartment. The next day, Craig and I both went to work.

I reported to the gallery and loved my new job. Behind the gallery was the porcelain and bronze factory. We produced collectible plates. They were the big rage in the eighties (the 1980s). It seemed everyone had a passion for collectibles. Hummel's were a big sell, and since one of the owners happened to work for Hummel, we got all the most desirable ones. The artwork was mostly Western. Richard Myers, one of the owners, did wonderful western bronzes, and was a well known sculptor. His work was in many prominent homes and businesses.

The gallery was in a small mini-mall, with a restaurant, travel agency, and a few other stores. The gallery was doing quite well, but the rest of the stores where having problems. The complex hired a public relations man named Bob Floury. We were asked to meet at the restaurant to discuss the possibilities of bringing in more business to the complex. Bob was sitting at the bar listening to the discussion. He didn't seem to have any input, and I wondered what he was doing there, maybe just someone having a drink.

After the meeting he came over to me and said, "How about a drink? You have a lot to say."

Bob Floury, are we having a fun time? You Bet!
1980

"Yes, I do," I said with a snappy reply, "and may I ask, who you are?"

He introduced himself, "I'm the public relations man for the restaurant and the complex."

I came back with, "Our business is doing fine! Do you think maybe it's because I have a lot to say?"

"I'd like to hear more of your ideas," he said with interest. After the drink, he said, "How about dinner tomorrow night?"

And I said, "Okay." It was the beginning of a five-year relationship. Bob had the greatest sense of humor I've ever known, and I guess I was attracted to him because of that. He kept me laughing all the time, plus he looked like Benny Hill. He eventually was hired as the Director of Advertising and Public Relations at the Marina City Club, in Marina Del Rey.

I learned a lot from Bob. He had this wonderful way of presenting himself. Every project he worked on, he made exciting. He also was a restaurant critic for *The Star News* in Pasadena, and several other papers. That, of course, took us to all the good restaurants in town. I'm getting ahead of myself, but would like to give you an example of Bob and his wit. After I left the gallery I went to work at the Los Angeles Chamber of Commerce.

I was working for the women's council at the Chamber, I asked Bob to help me get some PR for the women's council. It was the opening of the new season for the Pasadena symphony orchestra. He said he would be happy to call them. He made an appointment with the manager of the civic auditorium.

Ruby Murillo, my boss, along with Bob and I, arrived and toured the theatre. I took notes for the press release. Afterwards Doris, the manager, invited us to lunch at the Hilton. Ruby had to leave, but Bob and I accepted. We never turn down lunch. The three of us sat in the booth and started talking. I got on a "roll," telling some story. Doris was sitting across from Bob and I. There was an empty seat next to her. As I told the story, Doris really got involved in it. I would look over at the empty space, and I would say something to Doris and then as I was making hand gestures I would kind of include the invisible person sitting next to her. I did have a habit of talking with my hands. I would say something, look at her, and point to the empty chair to make my point. Every time I did this, Doris would also look at the empty space, like someone was there.

When we finished lunch, we said goodbye to Doris, and thanked her for lunch. When we got in the car, Bob said to me, "That was quite a story you told at lunch."

"Oh, did you like it?" I asked. "It was amazing to watch Doris," Bob said. "She was so fascinated with the invisible person in the empty seat that you kept referring to. You would look at the empty seat, and Doris would immediately look at the empty seat, and shake her head like someone was there. I just hope Doris didn't pay for the invisible person's lunch."

I said, "At least I didn't have someone interrupting me, like you!" But I had to laugh. I had no idea I was acting this out.

Bob saw the humor in everything, and life was not dull with him. Sunday would come along, and he didn't have to work, so I would say, "Why don't we drive to the beach, have lunch this afternoon?" He would be on the couch watching a game, and just look at me. Looking briefly away from the game he would reply, "No, why don't you go shopping, we'll go to dinner tonight?" What could I do, after he handed me fifty or hundred dollars, and say, "Go buy yourself something."

Bob did have some issues that I had not recognized in the beginning. He had highs and lows, and towards the end of our relationship, he was mostly on a lows. Due to his temper, which I had never really seen, he lost his job at the club. That brought on the depression. What I didn't know was that he had been seeing a psychiatrist. He was so over-medicated that he lost all sense of living. When I found out, I told him to get rid of the medication. But he just couldn't do it, even though I told him that if he didn't, it would be over for us. He lost all his sense of worth.

Lisa, my friend from Vegas, was coming to L.A. I told her that I would meet her at the Huntington library in Pasadena for tea. After some conversation, she said, "Is something wrong with you and Bob? You're not yourself!" I told her the problem.

She said, "You have to stop this right now. He is bringing you down with him." She did us both a great favor. I went home and told Bob that he needed more help than I could give him, and it was over. He checked into the Veterans Hospital in Westwood, and after nine months he came out with a new outlook on life.

He did try to come back in my life. He rented an apartment down the block from me. One Sunday morning, he knocked on my door with coffee and donuts. He thought that would get me. We did remain friends, but I had gone on to other things.

Bob was at the beginning of my adventure with Rossmeyer Gallery, and when I left for another job, we were still together.

The owners of the gallery were great people. Richard had a lovely wife, Maureen, and I liked her a lot. She would come into the gallery and we would talk about the collectibles. She would help me unpack new merchandise, and I would place them on the glass shelves, or in the glass cases. The Hummels, Lladro, Swarovski, Snowbabies, Rockwell figurines, and all the collectibles were displayed, each in its own display case. We never mixed merchandise. For instance, Lladro was displayed in one case, Swarovski in another case; each collectible always had its own area and special spotlight.

Maureen came in one afternoon, and as we were talking, I mentioned that a friend from Vegas was going to stop by the next day for a visit. She said, "Why don't you go to lunch? I can watch the gallery."

"Oh, Maureen that would be nice," I replied. "But what if someone comes in? You need to know how to do a credit card, and answer questions!"

185

"Just show me," she eagerly said, "If I have a problem, you're just across the street. I'll call the restaurant."

Reluctantly, I said, "okay!" After all, she and Richard were the owners. The next day, Lisa arrived, and we took off for lunch. I didn't hear from Maureen, so I figured everything was fine. When I got back, Maureen said, "You're going to kill me!"

"Why would I want to do that?" I thought. She walked over to a glass case. I followed, as she opened the door, there was this beautiful sculpture, the bust of an Indian maiden. She had a feather on the top of her head pointing straight up. As Maureen picked her up to move her, the feather hit the top of the shelf and broke it off. I'm sure she was in panic.

She moved the merchandise around to other areas. She thought it looked better; she was "playing house." I tried to tell her, "You keep each collectible in its, own area. We're not playing house, Maureen. This is a business. You have to abide by the rules. Jerry and Richard will really be angry with me for leaving you alone.

"I'm so sorry, Dorothy," she said apologetically, "I was trying to keep busy, and do a little dusting!" The sculpture was priced at fifteen hundred dollars. The subject was never brought up, and I guess all was forgiven. As you can tell, my life has not been all about tap dancing.

Another time, Maureen called and said, "Dorothy, a truck will be arriving, delivering some groceries in boxes. Just put them in a corner; some of my friends will be picking them up within the next week. It will be good for business. They will look around and maybe make a purchase when they pick up their box."

Maureen and Richard were Mormons. They were restocking their shelter (a practice of stocking food by the Mormon religion) for the coming year, but what did I know? I figured a small truck would pull up to the gallery, and drop off a few boxes. After all, this is a gallery, not to be confused with a gift shop.

Saturday arrived, one of our busiest days of the week, and this humongous truck arrived in the parking lot. The driver came in and said, "I have a delivery. Where should I put the boxes?"

I casually said, "Oh, just over by the side of the wall." I stood there in amazement, as he started bringing in the boxes. There must have been a hundred. The other owner came in and I could tell it was over for Maureen. He was furious!

He said, "Dorothy, do not let this happen again. Whenever Maureen wants something, you tell her to call me!" It was hard to say no to her because she was so lovable. The following week, all of her hundred friends came into the gallery to pick up their boxes. Not one of them made a purchase, but one did ask me if I had a stamp.

I was at the gallery for three years. Craig was still with Campbell Soup. His boss, the young man that had hired him, came over to our apartment to pick up Craig one day. He told me about Craig's interview for the job in Las Vegas. He amusingly began, "Craig came in, all full of enthusiasm, looking very dapper in his suit. And we knew we liked him right off. He was very well groomed, but we did laugh after he left. He had shaving cream behind his one ear." We all laughed, but at least they knew he was a clean young man.

Steve and Maureen Tobia graduated from Dayton with Craig. After they got married, they moved to California from New York. They were living in north Hollywood in a small apartment. Maureen was working for a large company, and Steve was getting his masters degree. They didn't have much money at the time, and they would come out to our apartment every Sunday for dinner. I really loved those kids. Now Craig announced he is getting married to Joni Champa, who he met in college. Joni was from St. Louis, but when she was in high school, her father was transferred to Cleveland. The wedding was planned for September in St. Louis. Craig said, "You know mom, you've been talking about moving closer to L.A. Now would be the time, before I get married."

So, I found a lovely townhouse in Arcadia. The shopping mall and Santa Anita Race Track were in walking distance, if you needed to walk. I was only fifteen minutes from Pasadena and about forty minutes from Beverly Hills, where I had a good friend who introduced me to all the good restaurants in the area. Ruthie Podnos was her name. All the above people changed my life. You will see how.

I was still at Rossmeyer gallery, but I was itching to move on. Steve Tobia had gotten his master's, and was working at the Los Angeles Chamber of Commerce on Third Street in downtown L.A. He was in government, and doing well. On one of Steve and Maureen's Sunday evening dinners at our apartment, I happened to mention that I was going to look for another job. I needed to make more money. Steve was listening.

I had met a fun gal, Dot Swanson who owned the travel agency, down from the gallery. She and I would go to dinner, the movies, and play golf together. Dot had a colorful life. She belonged to the Burch Society, volunteered at the Pasadena Playhouse, and had a psychic. Here I go again with "the psychic!" There was a bookstore in Glendora. On certain nights, they would have group readings. Off I went with her one evening to hear my future. The psychic asked for several people to give her a personal object. Dot said, "Give her your ring." I was not thrilled about it, but Dot was very forceful. The psychic right off said, "You will be changing jobs in the next couple of weeks, and in the coming years you will be on top of a pyramid, reaching the highest heights."

I thought, "I'm going to Egypt!!"

A week later, I was sitting in the gallery and the phone rang. The lady on the line said, "Dorothy Kloss, please. I'm calling about a job opening. Steve Tobia has given you a wonderful recommendation. We are looking for someone to fill the position of, administrative assistant of the Women's Council at the Los Angeles Chamber of Commerce."

"My, this sounds very important," I thought to myself. The lady continued, "Would you be interested in applying? If so, I would like to set up an appointment. We've heard wonderful things about you from Steve."

I thought, "What could he have told her? I make a great dinner on Sunday, and I'm a great tap dancer?" But her next statement did not thrill me. "How about Monday at one for an interview, with Ruby Murillo, the president of the council? Then we can do the typing test."

"Well gee," I interjected, "My typing skills are a little rusty."

She said, "Don't worry about it, please come in."

My next thought was, "Should I call the psychic? She sure hit this one on the head."

Monday arrived, and I headed for the chamber without a clue what I was doing on the Pasadena freeway. I found the chamber on Third Street and clicked my heels. When I entered, I asked for the personnel department, and asked for Marit. She said, "I'm so happy to meet you, Dorothy." She explained briefly, about the Women's Council and then we moved on to meet Ruby Marillo. I liked her right off.

Ruby Murillo was the President of the Women's Council. She was also the representative for General Telephone Company. There were 300 members in the council. It began when wives of the chamber's Executive Board decided to form a group to hold service teas. It had grown, through the years, as more women found their way in the executive world. The teas were replaced with executive women who were CEO's, and in management.

We provided information on women's clubs, organizations, seminars and special events sponsored by the women's council. We sponsored "The Man of the Year" awards. I would arrange, a three-day trip to Sacramento, make appointments with the legislators, where the group would discuss their issues. It was great fun for me. Once a month we had the Executive Board meetings. Most of the time, the meeting was at one of the great restaurants, like Jimmy's in Beverly Hills. I made all the reservations, took the minutes of the meetings, took photos for the newsletter, and wrote the press releases.

Ruby and I became friends. She would call and say, "Dorothy, how about lunch?"

Since she was my boss, I would say, "What time?"

"Ten minutes?" she would say, "Meet me in front." My neighbors in their little cubicles would see me freshening up my makeup, and my phone would start to ring.

Dorothy Kloss, administrative assistant to the Los Angeles Women's Council, and Ruby Murillo, President of the Women's Council, joined by Congressman John Roussellout, (R-26), David Deacon Jones, NFL Football Hall of Famer, and Ben Davidson, formerly of the Oakland Raiders with William Howell, President of Miller Brewing Company.

"Going somewhere? Out to lunch again? Boy, have you got the job!" And then they would all wave to me, on my way out to one of my favorite restaurants, "The Dining Car."

My two best friends at the chamber were Jean Converse and Marie Steinbough. When, I didn't have lunch with Ruby they where the chosen ones. I loved both of those gals. We may stay in for lunch, and if so, we would get a group together downstairs. I taught a tap class in the basement. One 4th of July, we even put on a show; it was a great hit. We also did a Christmas show. We were very busy having a good time.

Jean was married to Bill Converse, who was the comptroller for the L.A. Athletic Club in downtown Los Angeles. Jean, Marie, and I, would dash over to the club for lunch. Jean would say, "Let's stick the old boy for lunch." She had a great sense of humor, and we laughed a lot!

Marie had been married for twenty-five years. Then her husband left her for a gal they use to double date with. Just don't trust the girl next store. Marie had never gone anywhere during her marriage. She raised five kids, and told us he took her to McDonalds for their anniversary. What a love match! And may I say, she was a beauty. Jean and I decided to take her in hand and show her the world. I had just made reservations to go to Europe. I said to her, "Why don't you go with me? Do something for you! See how happy I am? I'm always doing something for me!" So my friend Dot, with the psychic, booked our "get away trip" to London and France. It was the best thing that ever happened to her. Both she and Jean are gone now, and I truly miss them.

After 50 years, the Women's Council had their final luncheon. I could see job opportunities just around the corner. It was a wonderful Christmas luncheon, at the Beverly Wilshire hotel, celebrating fifty years of the Women's Council. Disneyland provided some of the entertainment, and I was responsible for the 1800 to 1980 fashion show. Some of the ladies modeled, and it was a great success, though a sad one for many. The council had become an independent moneymaker in 1977. The chamber didn't think they could make it on their own, but the council proved them wrong. The chamber didn't want to integrate them into the chamber, but rather eliminate the council. The women's council flourished, and the chamber discovered that they were in competition for the money from companies. When the council planned a spring production, "Salute to California's Elected and Appointed Women Officials," it was over, and the ladies became members of the chamber.

The Christmas luncheon was the last hurrah, my last hurrah. When I received my last paycheck, we all went to Lawry's for Mexican food and several margaritas, and I said goodbye. Time to click those heels again, and tap dance "as fast as I can!"

Chapter 20: So Where Do I Go From Here?

After the Chamber of Commerce, what else was out there for me? I discovered many things were available, if you just put your mind to it. And that's exactly what I did. I pulled out those "Employment Opportunities" in the newspaper and saw a job opportunity in Pasadena. I called the number and asked the gal that answered about the position that was being offered. She said, "Can you come in this afternoon?"

And with a quick "Yes," I had an appointment. It was really weird. I looked at the address to be sure I was in the right place. The small sign on the front read, "Las Encinas Hospital." I drove through the open gate, and all these lovely little cottages were set apart from each other, with large oak trees shading them. I thought I was in a forest, and some wonderful creature from *Grimm's Fairy Tales* would appear. I was reluctant to continue. Just then, I saw a person who seemed to know where he was going, and I flagged him down. I told him I had an appointment, and he said, "Don't let the grounds throw you! Go straight ahead to personnel."

I walked in, and a really nice gal took my name. I sat down. Within a few minutes, another lady came out of the closed door of the office that said "Director of Personnel." She filled me in on the job. "First of all," she informed me, "Las Encinas Hospital has been here since 1904. It was referred to back then as a sanitarium for nervous diseases." Their approach to treating mental illness was "not just to live but to enjoy living." It was a revolutionary idea in those days. Years later, it focused on psychiatric and substance abuse. They had horses and donkeys on the grounds, and grew their own vegetables. But in 1950, the department of health realized that the hospital was running a small farm, and informed them they had to make a change. So they donated the animals to a new theme park, called Disneyland. They had 27 acres, and the original shingled bungalows were for the staff.

In 1981, one piece of land at the corner of Del Mar Boulevard was vacant. Bob Tonry was the administrator of the hospital, and he suggested to Dr. Stephen Smith, the medical director, and his wife, Dr. Terry Smith, that they should build a very exclusive apartment complex on the land. Many Pasadena residents were selling their large homes; this would be ideal for them. The project was finished with a swimming pool and tennis courts, offering luxury in every way. They were looking for a manager to run the complex, and make the people happy. I always want to make people happy, so I thought, "I would like this job." But they had interviewed many people, I would have to wait and see.

The next morning, I got a call to come in and meet with Dr. Terry; she was just the best. She talked to me very casually, about what I had done and then she thanked me for coming in, and I left. I didn't hear from them for a couple days, and then received another call to come in. I was on my way. "Mr. Tonry would like to meet with you," the voice said. What a charmer. He was tall, very good looking, and made you think all was right with the world. He had been the administrator of the motion picture home, so he knew his way around. We had a fun interview. He asked me a lot of questions about my career in show business. Now to explain, the Oaks was next to Las Encinas Hospital, but the only connection the Oaks had to the hospital was the emergency call system. The patients were not allowed at the Oaks, but sometimes they would wander over and find themselves in the Oaks area. They had very good security, so it was not a problem. The last question Bob asked me, "So tell me Dorothy, how would you handle a lecherous old man?"

After a slight pause, I said, "Very carefully." He laughed, "Good answer. I think you have the job." The next day I received a call, congratulating me on being selected for the position of Manager of the Oaks of Pasadena.

I loved working at the Oaks. The staff, from housekeeping to the kitchen help, was terrific, which made my job easy. We hired a French chef. The dining room was exquisite. I eventually talked to Bob about having our own credit cards, and inviting the business people from Pasadena to enjoy our sumptuous business luncheons or dinner. We purchased two limousines that would be available to the business community; they would not have to look for parking. We would pick them up with a reservation. It took off like a house of fire. The residents loved having outside people come for lunch or dinner. It made them feel like they were not dining in the same place for every meal. Even though these were rental apartments, going for $2500 per month (quite a hefty sum then) in the 1980s, we wanted our residents to have the elegance of fine living. They were allowed to bring in their own decorator, with my okay, on what they wanted to change. I usually let them have their way, and had fun helping a few of the residents choose their fabric. They could not tear down a wall, but the drapes, their color choice, or whatever made them happy, we would accommodate. There were 300 apartments, and you could take a long lease. We were pretty full. It was no problem to entertain the residents. They were up for anything I wanted to do. I had a "happy hour" every evening from four to five. It was short. I didn't want them staggering into the dinner room, and dropping a few hors d'oeuvres on the way. They loved it, and got to know each other. I brought in enter-

tainment on certain days, like St. Patrick's Day, or the holiday of the month. I entertained, and had sing-a-longs. It was my kind of thing.

One afternoon a gentleman came to the desk and asked Betty, my secretary, if I was available. He gave her his card. It read, "Great moments in the theatre," Allan Gruener. Well, that got my attention, I said to

Allan Gruener and you-know-who!

Betty, show him right in. A tall, distinguished looking man with the charm of "prince charming."

"Thank you so much for seeing me," he said. "I want to introduce you to my program." He handed it to me, and proceeded to tell me about his one-man show. He would select a Broadway show, and he played all the parts. Great idea if it works. Believe me, it did for him. He was a wonderful actor. I looked over the program; it was filled with ads of restaurants and businesses from all over California. He played every woman's club in California. Each year, he would do a new show, and he was booked solid. He asked me if I would be interested in taking out an ad. I told him that I would have to think about it. Then he asked if I would give him a tour of the Oaks. Before the tour was over, he had an ad, and an invitation to lunch in our dining room the next day.

Allan was always on the go, and before I knew what happened, I was on the go with him. Every day I had off, he had it planned. Most of the time it was going to the racetrack and dinner. It was fine with me, 'cause I loved the track. I only bet $2.00. Allan, on the other hand, bet big, and often. He had won the "pick-six" once and never got over it. He kept thinking it would happen again.

There was a great show in L.A., *Torch Song Trilogy*, a very funny take off on a gay guy, with an over-protective mother, who would like him to

Estelle Getty (The Golden Girls), Ruth Podnoes, and Dorothy, 1992

find a nice girl, get married, and give her grandchildren. The actress that played the mother was Estelle Getty; she later became Dorothy's (Bea Arthur's) mother on *The Golden Girls*. She was hilarious. We went to see the show, and afterwards met with Estelle. Allan and I took her to lunch several times. She was such a nice woman. She didn't belong to SAG (Screen Actors Guild), so Allan sponsored her. She was from New York, had done a lot of Jewish theatre before arriving in California for *Torch Song*.

I had the chance to watch Allan perform his one-man show; he was brilliant. He asked me to go with him to one of his performances, at the Ojai Valley Inn in Ojai, California. Unfortunately, he had chosen a rather "downer" show for this performance, but the audience thought he was great. The presentation was *'night, Mother*, a very serious piece. But the comments were "A superb reader of dramatic literature." At the end of the play, the daughter commits suicide.

Now this is the kick. He asked me to shoot the gun backstage when it was time for her to go. I must tell you, I was brilliant. It's not easy to shoot a gun on cue.

Allan was fun if you had a sense of humor. One day we were on our way to Hollywood Park, for the one o'clock race. He said, "I want to stop off at the cemetery for a moment."

I inquired, "Is something special going on at the cemetery today?"

"Yes," Allan said, "I would like to introduce you to my mother."

I said, "Does she have a condo there? Allan, your mother is dead."

"Yes, I know," he said with ease and charm, "but she will know you are here with me."

I thought, "Whatever floats your boat, Allan." It's the actor thing. So we arrived at the cemetery and found the Jewish section.

We stood in front of her grave, and he said, "Mother, this is Dorothy." I said, "Hello," just to please him, and off we went to the track.

We went to a preview of *Yentl*, with Barbra Streisand. Phil Silvers, the comedian, was sitting in front of us. He and Allan exchanged words before the movie began, and then it was lights out. At the end of the movie, whatever possessed Allan, he jumped up, and started applauding like it was a live show and yelling, "Brilliant, bravo!" Phil turned around and said, "For gosh sakes Allan, sit down, it's a movie!" But he went on and on. We left the theatre, and walked to the car. We no sooner got into the car, he turned to me, and very nervously said, "You know, I'm Jewish!" I just looked at him, and said in a Jewish accent, "So, vats the big deal?"

The Oaks was a great job, and I have many fond memories. The movie star Robert Young, and his wife, had an apartment at the Oaks. They had leased it for five years. Mrs. Hoover, of the famous vacuum cleaning family, also lived at the Oaks. She was a beauty even at her age, around eighty.

Many of the residents would stop by my office, stick their head in the door and say, "Dorothy, are you busy?"

I would say, "No," and in they would come for a little chat. They would tell me about their children, husbands, and their travels. One lady, in particular, came in and asked me if I liked to travel. She then went on to tell me about her last cruise. "You know, Dorothy, my first husband was a brute. He never had a kind word for anyone, and my life was hell with him. After he passed away, I never thought I would marry again, but I met Charlie, and he was a prince. Both of us were in our golden years, so we decided we would see the world together. We booked this wonderful cruise going to Greece. I had never been there, but Charlie had. I was so looking forward to seeing it. We were having a lovely time on the ship, having dinner, dancing, and meeting interesting people. Out of the blue, Charlie had a heart attack, and died. I, of course, was devastated! What to do? After talking to the captain, it was decided at the next stop to ship

Charlie back to the USA. I just didn't know what to do. Should I go back with him? Or go on and see the beauty of Greece that he had told me about. I thought to myself, "I may never get another chance. So, I sent Charlie on his way, I got back on the ship, and enjoyed Greece. Do you think I did the right thing?"

I said, "You know, I'm not here to judge." I think she wanted me to justify her actions. My reaction: live and let live. I guess you might say I was a psychiatrist without a license.

Search continues for 'Rosebuds' dancers

The Army has found about 14 young girls for its "Rosebuds" dance troupe, slated to perform during the Army-Navy extravaganza this November. But about 10 more are needed to make an even two dozen, and local girls are encouraged to audition tonight.

"The Navy's taking care of their own party out at LAX (Los Angeles International Airport)," explained spokeswoman Dorothy Kloss. But the Army, which will host its post-game party at the Convention Center in Pasadena, wants two dozen girls to do "a dance number at the hop," ride in the pre-game parade and perform other entertainment during the festivities, Kloss said.

"It's a cute gimmick for the cadets," she added.

Dancers between the ages of 18 and 25 are invited to try out between 6 p.m. and 8 p.m. today at Bushnell, 2828 E. Foothill Blvd. in Pasadena.

Search continues for "Rosebud Dancers."

I did get involved in many community events. The Army/Navy festivities for the football game on November 25, 1983 would take place at the Rose Bowl in Pasadena. The sponsor was Bushnell. The gal from human resources at Bushnell was my contact. Together, we planned the event. Our priority was the Army cadets from West Point. The midshipmen from Annapolis were sponsored by, another company.

Edna Krueger and I had a grand time working on the project. I thought it would be a great idea to audition the young girls from the area, and create a number to honor West Point. We held auditions, and twenty-four girls became the "Pasadena Rosebuds." We then

The Pasadena "Rosebuds." Army/Navy Games, choreographed by Dorothy Kloss, November 1983, Pasadena, California.

invited 24 cadets to accompany them on stage, as they danced, and sang to them. Each girl wore a West Point hat. They sang, "Hello West Point, well hello West Point, it's really great to have you here." They sang it to, what else, but "Hello Dolly." The event was held at the Civic Center in Pasadena.

I was at the Oaks for three years. We heard a rumor that the hospital, and the Oaks, would be sold. My heart skipped a beat; it was true. Hospital Corporation of America and Beverly Enterprises, in a joint venture, would purchase the property. It didn't take them long to take over, like any company that buys a new property. They started to restructure. That's a scary word. What it really means is, many people would be let go. Mr. Tonry was the first. They kept me on for another eight months. I did not have a geriatrics background, I just knew a lot of old people, and a lot about old people. They told me that wouldn't work. My thought was, "You're going to make these people old. I was keeping them young." The whole concept of the Oaks would change. The head honchos did give me a letter of recommendation, and that goes a long way when you're looking for a new job. I could do a whole book with my letters of recommendation.

The Los Angeles Times "Employment Section" was my saving grace once again. The *Queen Mary* (the famous ocean liner docked in Long Beach) was looking for a guest services manager. I sent them my revised resume. I had many jobs to add. I got the call, and headed for the *Queen Mary* hotel. The hotel manager was Jack Applequest. Jack was a man with a jolly personality. I liked him immediately. He clued in on my show business career right away. He had worked at Caesar's Palace for several years, so you might say he knew show business. Jack explained that this would be a new department, and I would be responsible in many areas. The job description: responsible for hotel guest complaints, the concierge, arrange the tour of the ship for the guests, and sign-ups for bus tours. I also was responsible for restaurant recommendations, and recommendations for attractions throughout California, including TV shows, VIP requests, gift certificates, maps and directions; just whatever made the hotel guests happy. I just knew this was my job. I left his office with great expectations, and my dream came true. I started working the next week. My biggest problem was living in Arcadia. It was a forty-minute trip to the *Queen*. I had to be there at 8 a.m., First we had to start hiring concierges to get going, and then it would all come together, I told myself. We were set up in the old purser's office, from days gone by, at the front of the hotel. In the beginning, it was Hertz Rent-a-Car, a desk and me. Personnel started interviewing for the concierge position, and they would send the people to me for my approval.

The *Queen Mary* was managed by Wrather Port Properties. Jack Wrather was an oilman from Texas. He was married to Bonita Granville; she stared in many movies as a child, and adult. Joseph F. Prevratil, was President of the Queen. My five years working for him were outstanding. The *Queen* and Spruce Goose (the attraction built by Howard Hughes) were at their best during his tenure. It was an honor to work for him.

Cynthia Silk, Captain Gregory and Dorothy Kloss, the Queen Mary, Long Beach, California, 1988.

There were some interesting happenings on board! Besides the mystery of the ghosts on board ship, there were rumors of "strange happenings!" I heard many stories; some I believed some…

The Queen had a schoolroom. The teacher was Ann Agular. It was a work placement course in hotel management. Her job was to place the student in one of the departments on the ship: reservations, front desk, sales, and my department, if they qualified. Ann asked me if she could send over a student to see me. "I really need to place her," she confessed, "and you would be doing me a big favor."

I said, " I'll be happy too, if she is presentable with a nice personality. You know, Ann, she has to be a people person."

"Oh yes, I think you will like her," she assured me.

In walked the girl and she said, "Ms. Agular sent me," and then she smiled. She was missing three front teeth. When I asked her what happened to her teeth, and would she be getting them replaced, she said, "No, not at present. I have no money."

Captain Gregory, on his ship, The Queen Mary, 1988.

I did feel badly for her, but I told her that another department would be better suited for her. When I saw Ann, I said, "Are you crazy, sending me that girl without teeth?"

She shrugged her shoulders and said, "I didn't think you would notice."

Jack was great to work with. He never interfered, or called you down on anything. Working on the *Queen* was like going on a cruise every day. I finally got the department together, hired the concierges, and we were in business.

Reunion on The Queen Mary with "my crew," Maria, David, Dot, Jan, Cynthia and Mark, 2004.

Joining the *Queen Mary* was this incredible aeronautical wonder, Howard Hughes's "flying boat," The Spruce Goose! It was the largest plane ever built. Its location was on the other side of London town, a shopping section, with its restaurants, shops and nightlife. During my years at the *Queen*, business was booming.

The Queen's Salon had a gourmet Sunday brunch. There was also the Sir Winston Churchill restaurant, and the wedding chapel, where Captain Gregory officiated at the weddings. The captain was a darling man. He would call me to make a reservation, for his dear friend June Lockhart, who would be coming for the weekend. Then he would say, "Let's have lunch!" We would go off the property to one of his favorite restaurants for lunch. Zsa Zsa Gabor's last marriage to the count was officiated by Captain Gregory.

I finally got my act together and I found an apartment in Long Beach, two blocks from the ocean. It was great. I could walk to Belmont shores, with all the shops, and bike down Ocean Boulevard along the beach. But best of all, I was ten minutes from work.

After six years at the *Queen Mary* I resigned. Craig and his wife Joni asked me over one evening for dinner. They jumped right into the reason for the dinner. They had decided to go in business with their friends Dennis and Liz. "We would like you to come and work for us." I was a little hesitant. I had a job I loved. They continued, "Mom, you would be your own boss; it would really help us out, since we want to continue in our present jobs. This is an investment for us."

Was this an investment for me? I was changing jobs and moving. I never gave it a thought. I guess my karma kicked in, and I said, "Yes."

Leaving the *Queen* was with a heavy heart. They gave me an outstanding going away party, and I moved back to Arcadia. We heard a rumor that Disney was taking over the Queen Mary. Jack Wrather had passed away, and his wife didn't want to continue with the operation. I guess I made the right decision to move on. Mr. Wrather built the Disneyland hotel at the time Disneyland was getting started. Walt Disney and Jack Wrather were friends. Walt suggested Jack build a hotel, "I'll give you the name: Disneyland Hotel," said Walt. Jack took him up on it. Disneyland Corporation did not own the hotel. When Mrs. Wrather decided to get out, she offered Disney the Queen Mary Hotel, Spruce Goose, all the *Lassie* TV shows that she owned, and the Disneyland Hotel. It was a done deal. I had already left before Disney came in.

"Special Handling," Craig and Joni's new business, opened in a shopping mall in Arcadia with Vons, and several other businesses. We did FedEx, UPS and just what the name implies: gift wrapping, engraving, and faxing. It was one of the first mail stores in California. I did have help. It was okay, but it was not the Queen. We had the grand opening with a bang. It was a hit. A couple weeks after the opening, I came down with what we thought was the flu, or a virus. One Sunday morning, I could not get out of bed. I called my son, Craig, and he called the ambulance. I arrived at Methodist Hospital emergency room. Dr. Delavoy, after some discussion with my son, came in and told me there was a blockage in my intestines, and that it could be colon cancer. They needed to do surgery.

I said, "Okay, how about now?" And that's how it happened. Everyone has their own way of dealing with things. St. Theresa, has always been my saving grace, along with St. Jude and St. Anthony. Have I got it covered? Cynthia Silk was one of my concierges at the Queen Mary. I loved Cynthia, and she was pretty and bright. After surgery, the doctor came in and started to tell me my chances for the years ahead. I stopped him cold. I told him that I didn't want to hear his diagnosis of my future. "Life is a mystery, and I'd like to keep it that way," I said emphatically. After he left, I received a beautiful basket of flowers from Cynthia. Right in the middle of the bouquet was one red rose. I knew I would be okay. I never had a doubt, and here I am almost 25 years later. Thanks to St. Theresa…did I mention, she is the Saint of Roses.

The plan was to have six weeks of chemotherapy, but I did so well, I was finished in four weeks. I didn't lose my hair, just my eyebrows and eye lashes. I went back to work at "Special Handling" until they decided to close the business. It was a lot of work, and not that much profit. What to do? Buy a newspaper.

I was reading the *Pasadena Star News* when I came across an article about the Pasadena Senior Center. Betty Kay, formerly from Skokie, Illinois, and now a resident of California, was the guest speaker at the Pasadena Senior Center. Could this be a coincidence??

Betty Kay started a dancing school in Skokie, a few blocks from where I lived when I was married. I knew about the school, but had no interest. I had been taking jazz classes in Evanston at Gus Giordano's studio. Gus was one of the first jazz teachers in the Chicago area. This was in the 1950s, and jazz was a new form of dance. Betty Kay had called Gus to see if he could recommend a teacher/choreographer for her studio.

She needed someone to set the June recital numbers. Gus recommended me. I started working with Betty after observing her classes. After a few weeks, she asked me to take over some of the classes. I really didn't want to get too involved, since my son was small, and needed my attention. But my mom was taking care of him, and I could use the money. I started teaching on a full time basis.

Betty had a partner, Alice, who took care of the business side of the studio. Alice came to me, and told me that Betty was moving to California. She asked if I would continue teaching for her, since she was taking over the studio. I agreed.

Fast forward to 1989-90. I took myself down to the Pasadena Senior Center with the article in hand. I asked to see the Activity Director. I introduced myself, and told her I had read about the guest speaker, Betty

Kay. I would like to get in touch with her, since I had taught dance for her back in Chicago. Would she give me her phone number? Yes, of course, but "dance" was the magic word. The next question came very quickly. "Would you be interested in teaching here at the

The Pasadena Tappers, "Tops in Taps," 1994.

center?" The activity director asked. "We're looking for a teacher. Danna Lou, the tap teacher, is pregnant, and would like to leave as soon as possible."

I told her, "Yes, I would like to give it a try." I met with Donna Lou the next week. She was a pleasant young woman, not quite ready for delivery, but it was time for her to go. Since I would be taking over her class, I asked

My Senior Center Tap Group, Mary Cantrell, Esther Brassinton,
Mary Lou Hensley, Clair Dreen, Lillian Hill, Dee Mead, Gwen DeYoung, Francis?,
Dorothy Kloss, Helen Gamet, Pat Yankowsky, Clara Gomez, Barbara Pankey,
Pasadena California, 1995.

her what she was teaching the class. She told me she was teaching "Tappersize" by Ken Prescott. Ken had made a great tap tape, but I was not about to teach from his tape. I had my own method of teaching. Little did I know, he and I would be living together in a few years from then.

I started with about ten people in her class, and as time went on, I had several classes a week, with different levels for each class. Mary Cantrell, one of the ladies, was very pretty, and a good tapper, but Mary was also a perfectionist. Mary was in the back row one day, and annoyed that she could not get the step. She said, "Dorothy, I'm not getting this step!" I told her to come up front; I would show her.

She was beside herself, and finally I said, "Mary, settle down, don't have a heart attack over a tap step. Just let it go, you're not going to Broadway! So do what you can do, have a good time. Anyhow, it's almost coffee time." I don't know if the ladies came for tap or for coffee. Before class they would say to me, "Are we going for coffee?"

I got together the best dancers, and choreographed several routines for them. They decided they wanted to perform. I called the group "Tops in Taps" from my old days, and let me say, they were good. Gwynn DeYoung was the promoter of the group and booked them into every rest home, school and library in town. Tap dancing filled their life and gave them a feeling of accomplishment. Lillian Hill had tapped her whole life and had taken from every tap teacher in California. But when you would talk about doing a show, Lill, would say, "Oh, I can't do that," but she never missed a show.

Pat Yankosky and Thelma Rotonde were the youngest in the group. Dede was from Holland, I called her my front row girl 'cause I could never get her out of the front row. She would not move to the second line. I would call out rotate so everyone would have a chance at the front line, but Dede was glued to the floor and stood her ground. Claire Drean was so easy to work with, as were Jane Evan, Mary Lou Hensley and Darlene Henderson. There were others, but through the years we lost them. They were all great gals.

Gwynn's son had a wonderful place in Carlsbad. Every year, he would give up his paradise on the water to the "tops in tap" girls. We would go to the races at Del Mar, Shop and, of course, lunch. Let me explain, our sweet Mary had lost her husband and not long afterward had a breakdown. It was an awful time for her, but all of us watched out for her. She was on the way back and we were so pleased she would be with us again. In the meantime, Dede had moved to Las Vegas and was probably annoying some tap teacher there. We were outside at a big round table having lunch and discussing Mary and Dede. A man came by and sat at the next table from us. We didn't even know he was there. When he got up to leave, he stopped by our table and with a smile on his face he said, "I heard your problem with Mary and Dede, and I have the solution. You can work with Mary, but get rid of Dede," and he walked away. We roared with laughter.

Craig and Joni were married ten years when the word came that I would be a grandma in February. Miss Jamie Kloss was born on St. Valentine's Day. My world was complete but, not completely, because another bundle of joy arrived seven years later, Miss Megan Kloss, who is a Scorpio, just like her Grandma Dorothy.

Joni had a job she loved and made fabulous money. Craig had changed jobs several years before, working for Corning Inc. The two of them had it made until Miss Jamie came along. What to do? I asked Joni how she was going to handle both the baby and the job, and she said, "Well, Dorothy, we're going to hire a nanny."

My Son Craig and his wife, Joni,
Pasadena, California, the 1980s

I thought, "Good luck," but, then I raised my kid. I did say to her, "If you have a problem, I would be happy to help you out," and then I quickly withdrew from the drawing room.

She started interviewing nannies, and it was a "revolting situation." First, the money was out of their league, even though they both made above average salaries. The nannies started at $100 a day. The last nanny that arrived for an interview was in a tight leopard skin jacket, and pants with matching purse. That was scary enough — can you imagine the poor baby looking at all those spots? It would be okay for a night at "Jungle Jim's," but not a night with Jamie. Then the call came from Joni.

"Did you mean it when you said you would help out with Jamie?" she asked.

I said, "Yes!" So we set a schedule, and it worked for both of us. I had Jamie for five years, and what a joy. She was a very sweet child. I went from singing "Hello Dolly" to lullabies. My only regret is that I never had the same time with Megan, to instill all of grandma's idiosyncrasies. You know, don't take a baby for a walk with a top hat and cane. Only kidding, I guess!!

Chapter 21: Life Happens When You're Making Other Plans – And What A Folly – "The Follies!"

CAST of CHARACTERS, HEREAFTER REFERRED TO AS:

The Producer – Mr. P

The Choreographer – Mr. C

The wife and then the ex – Ex

The girlfriend – Lala

Public Relations – PR

People in the cast – cast members

The Location – the town or desert, where the sun shines every day

The following is MY RECOLLECTION (After all I am 89!)

Teaching at the Pasadena Senior Center was great fun. The ladies, and some gentlemen, in their fifties and sixties, still had the joy of living. Tap dancing gave them the exercise and enthusiasm of a younger person. Since I was in the same age range, I understood there need to put a little fun in their life. My fun came from watching them laugh and smile with me, and enjoy every class. Of course, the best was coffee afterwards so we could hang out. As I said before, I don't know if they came for the tap class or for the coffee. Most of them became my best friends, and still are to this day, even though our birthdays seem to come faster. It was six years I cherish. Most of them have continued to tap dance and stay alive. I used to tell them, "It keeps your heart pumping, don't you know," an old Irish expression.

In 1994, Craig called me one evening and asked if I would be home. There was something he wanted to discuss with me, I said, "Come on over."

Then he said, "I'll jog over!" That's when I knew it was serious. Craig never jogged anywhere if he could drive. A few minutes later, he was at the door, and he certainly wasn't out of breath. He jumped right into the serious business at hand, and covered the future events to take place. "Mom, I've been transferred and we're moving to Philadelphia. I have three months to sell the house, pack up, and move. We will be out of here by January 2nd. Joni and I have to go to Philadelphia and find a house, we'll be gone for a week, and I hope you can take care of Jamie." Jamie had just hit five years old. "We figure, we'll get settled, and then by next year, you can move back east, and we'll find you a nice apartment." It was a nice offer, but I decided to leave it open. I had, something else in mind, it wasn't in Philadelphia.

One of the senior dancers had been to a show in the desert, she had seen The Follies, featuring performers fifty-five and over. All had been professionals in show business, performing on Broadway, theatres and nightclubs in their younger years. This sounded very appealing. She mentioned that I should be in the show. At that moment, something snapped in my brain. I filed it away just in case. But it was not until my visit from Craig that I opened the file. After Craig, Joni and Jamie left on January 2, 1995, I decided to give it a try. I sent a tape and resume to The Follies. I received a call a short time later asking me to audition.

I received the audition date and place, the Marilyn Clark Studio in Burbank, I packed my tap shoes. The studio was filled with dancers, both men and women, but mostly women hoping for a spot in the show. Everyone handed in their photos and resume and entered the studio. Then the juggling for a front spot began. I didn't feel like a fight, so I just moved to a back spot, and waited for them all to settle. I remember years ago, being at Rickett's Restaurant in Chicago, after the last show. Bert Lahr was there with his wife, and we were invited to join them. He told us how he met his wife. He recalled, "She was in the back line of the chorus. You know how she got moved to the front line? She met me." He of course was the STAR of the show. You see being in the back line is not so bad. If you give them what they want, they will find you.

The choreographer was up front talking to his assistant, she had been the lead dancer in *Jubilee* in Las Vegas, and sitting at a table was the producer. We started with a jazz combination with the assistant. Next, it was a tap combination, which Mr., C gave from his chair due to a bad foot. After a few minutes, he pointed to me in the back row, and said, "Please, come forward. I have a bad foot, and you seem to know what you're doing. Could you help me out?" The assistant didn't tap. Mr., C said, "Just stand in front and I'll give you the combinations."

After we finished with the tap, he came over and asked me, "Do you sing?"

I said, "Yes. I'm not Judy Garland, but yes…but I didn't bring music."

He laughed, and said, "Just sing 'Happy Birthday.'" Then he said, "I really want you in the show. Don't move." He went over to Mr. P., and when he came back, he said, "Mr. P. would like to speak to you."

So I walked over to him, he asked me a few questions. "Are you really 71?" he inquired.

I said, of course, "Yes!"

"Are you married?" he asked.

I said, "No."

He came back with, "Would you like to be?"

I came back with, "We'll talk."

He laughed, and I started to pack up my belongings to leave when Mr. C yelled after me. "Dorothy, do not go anywhere over the weekend. We'll need to get in touch with you." The call came the next day; I was in the Follies. The apartment in Philadelphia was not in my future.

Craig arrived back from Philadelphia to move me from Arcadia to the desert. I spent the summer packing, and now we were on our way. We arrived in the desert, and what a great beginning. We pulled into the motel, and immediately took half of the overhang with us; it was lower than Craig anticipated. It came tumbling down. The man at the desk said not to worry — it happens all the time.

I said, "Why don't you fix it?"

He said, "I really enjoy watching the people look and go, 'Oh my gosh, what did I do'?"

I said, "That's really sadistic." But he just laughed, and gave us our key.

The next morning, we went to the Follies, got the key to the Villa, and moved into a very nice furnished apartment. I had a truck full of furniture, so we had called ahead and rented a storage space. That was our next stop. I settled in, Craig left for Philadelphia, and I waited for the next word from the Follies, it came the next day. The assistant called me to say that Mr. C had asked her to get in touch with me, in regard to a week of tap dancing for the cast, a "warm up" before we started rehearsal. "Will you teach the class?" she asked.

I was flattered, and told her that I'd be delighted, but that was short-lived. Someone at the Follies rescinded Mr. C's request. I knew at this

Larry Kern, holding up in the forest, 1997

point that I was going to have to hold my own. But then remember the old saying, "The first day in show business is the first day of rejection." Someone's nose was out of joint. I love the old story about Bill and Jim.

Bill said to Jim, "I guess I'm just a "has been."

Jim said, "Were you ever anybody?"

Bill said, "No,"

Jim said, "Then how can you be a "has been?"

A couple of days later, we were sent to a local dance school to limber up and get our feet going. There were three new people in the show and yours truly. The cast from the year before, who had been invited back sat in a row waiting for the class to start. When we walked in, they looked at us like we were from Mars. Not one person said "Hello," They just sized us up. Not a welcome in sight. We hit the floor for five days. At the end of that time, we had learned names and were civil to each other. But that's about it.

Mr. C was a taskmaster who was full of energy, which I loved about him, he gave me more energy. We started working on the show. They had teamed one of the cast members and myself together in a tap number, "Begin the Beguine." He had worked in the movies for many years, and was a very handsome man, but very competitive. During the first three days of rehearsal, he didn't speak

Jerry Antes and Me, my first FOLLIES show, 1995-96

to me. It was all about him. He seemed to resent me. I guess he was irritated when he heard a good tap dancer was coming into the show. Don't quite understand this thinking. I mean why would they hire a bad tap dancer? I really did try to communicate with him, but it was not to be. Then on the fourth day, I decided to try another tactic, because I couldn't live with this kind of situation.

I said, "You know, that last step, I'm not sure of it, could you show it to me again?"

I guess his male ego was satisfied. He still would try to critique me, right up until the last day of the show. One of my favorite sayings that I live by, and became one of my trademarks, is "Just let it go."

Coming into the Follies at 71 years young, I never thought there would be any kind of competition. When you're young, you're out there working for that prominent spot, but not at age 71. Wrong. It never changes, no matter what age. It's still there pushing you into being competitive. When I had my own act, I didn't experience jealousy. In the 1940s, working in nightclubs and theaters, you only stayed in one place for a limited time: two, six, eight or ten weeks. The lineup of the show would be a tap dancer, dance team or a novelty act, a comedienne and a star. When you're in a show like the Follies, the cast is jockeying for a solo spot, and the best way to get one is to suck up to the choreographer, I guess. I hate that word, but in this case, it is the only one that truly fits.

Today is not a dress rehearsal, 2009

In my second year, I had a wide awaking. We were given our scripts. Each routine and vocal has your initial next to it. Lala, (Mr. P's girlfriend and fellow cast member) came over to me before rehearsal started. She said, "Did you see your steps in the corner?"

I said, "Oh, wow."

211

She continued, "Those are for you and your partner for the stair number, "Shuffle Off to Buffalo." Mr. C will start the number after lunch."

I had worked on steps, and was really excited about the number. I was standing next to one of the lady cast members, I told her about the number. We were friends, and together since we came into the show. Several times, she had mentioned to me that she never gets a chance to do a solo.

I asked her if she had ever been a soloist, she said no! I didn't think any more about it, but I did think she was getting a late start for a solo. I guess it's never too late. It would be like me wanting to be a brain surgeon at seventy-one. After lunch, she came up to me and said, "I just wanted to tell you, I'm doing the step number." I was in shock. Lala saw her talking to me, and called me over to the side. She told me how sorry she was, but the choreographer who the lady had gotten very friendly with, had gone to Mr. P. and told him he wanted to give her a chance at the solo part. Since he was the choreographer, Mr. P had to acquiesce to his wish.

I didn't know that Mr. C and she were so chummy. She was baking him cookies, and met his parents, all the while I was looking at TV. Mr. C was a nice man, and a good choreographer. I didn't ask for anything special. I just took what he gave me. Mr. P. looked over at me when he came into the room and said, "Dorothy, you don't bake cookies."

I said, "I don't intend to either. If I can't get it on my talent, I don't want it." I was annoyed, and it really did piss me off! I hate that word, but sometimes it makes you feel better. I liked this lady, and we remained friends, but from then on I knew I had to be alert.

A former cast member came into the Follies as an understudy, not part of the regular cast. She was expected to learn everyone's routine, so she could jump in at any time in anyone's place. Now think about it. There are 16 people doing approximately five to six routines a show. She was expected to jump in a new spot every day. It was mind-boggling. She had been a Rockette for 27 years, a good dancer with a fast mind. I thought she was doing a great job, but I guess the man at the top was not happy. At Christmas, she was going back to New York for our ten days hiatus. Before she left, she was handed a letter telling her when she returned, she had to know every routine, or she would be let go. What a Christmas gift. Incidentally, she was Mrs. Claus at FAO Schwartz, the famous toy store in New York City, every Christmas.

The entrepreneur of the Follies will remain nameless or Mr. P.

He started the Follies four years before I arrived. The main street coming into town, was a graveyard. The street had lost its charm; most of the businesses had moved out. The City Council was looking for some way to give it a lift, and so The Follies was born.

The Theatre is in the center of town, and had been empty for several years. It was built in 1936 as a movie theatre. At that time many of the movie stars built homes in the area, and would drive down on weekends and stay at the famous Racquet Club, but that was by gone days.

There was a smaller version of the Follies already established called, *The Golden Girls*! Mr. P knew the man who produced it, and contacted him. At this time, the show was performing in a casino in Atlantic City. The idea of older performers struck a nerve in Mr. P, and it became HIS idea. From what I have heard in talking with some of the gals that worked in the show, Mr. P, and this gentleman were going to be partners and bring the show to the desert. But in the end, it was all about Mr. P, and the other guy was left out.

In the beginning, Mr. P. hired local performers, some with professional experience, and a few with just local experience. Later on he hired a choreographer and got the show going. And although it did not catch on at first to "waiting in line crowds," it was holding its own.

A few of the girls in the chorus line that had experience were generous with their knowledge, and they passed it on to Mr. P. He was a fast learner, and took it all in. I'm sure he read every book on "The Ziegfeld Follies" and "George White Scandals." They produced their "Follies" type shows back in the 1920s and 1930s. "This Follies" is a knock-off of their concept. The only problem: if you read these books from the 1920s, not only has Mr. P, used the "beautiful girl" and "showgirl" idea, he even adopted how they ran their business. They were originals. But I do give him credit for taking an idea and making it HIS idea, and making it work. I've heard people say what a genius he is. Sorry, putting The Follies together is not brain surgery. The difference, these Follies girls are called the lovelies; Ziegfeld's girls were "the long stemmed American beauties." You see, I've read these books too. For a guy who started out as a clown, he's made millions and kept most of it.

Most of the things that occurred were before I arrived on the scene. But when things happen in a group situation, everyone is ready to tell you about it. And as a new kid on the block, I was ready to listen. That was before I decided to write this book. Boy, did I get an earful.

Mr. P was married to a nice gal, for several years. She helped him get things together, when they got the "Okay" to go with the Follies from the City Council. Mr. P hired a choreographer. In the second year, they held auditions again, and two new people were hired: Lala and a gentleman.

Lala had been a Latin Quarter Showgirl in New York. The gentleman and Lala became great friends. She was well endowed, and this became her stairway to a "star." On the other hand, I had to dance my fool head off to finally get a real star, on The Walk of Stars in 2010. Mr. P, and Lala became more than just friends. She herself tells the story of how Mr. P, was looking at her at the audition, and I'm sure she looked back. It was time to decide on the girls for the new show. Mr. P and the choreographer were going over the résumés and checking out girls before making a decision. Mr. C, pulled out Lala's photo and said, "No, I don't think so!"

Mr. P said, "Yes, I think so!" A star was born, at least in the Follies. She was his star. This was the beginning of her new career.

The choreographer and director started out on a positive note. But the relationship slowly went downhill. Mr. C, and Mr. P, had several disagreements, and after the show opened a few months later, Mr. C, pulled several of his people from the cast, and took them to do a show in Branson, Mo. Mr. P, scurried around to find performers to replace the ones that left. One of the girls who auditioned was from the desert area. They called her to come in, and she learned the show quickly, and became part of the show. After the show closed for the season, she auditioned again, but they didn't bring her back. Talk about loyalty.

When Mr. P, and Lala's relationship became the gossip of the Follies, Mr. P's wife's happy life became a nightmare. The cast at the time had known her from the year before. When this liaison between Mr. P, and Lala became public, it could not be ignored. The cast, of course, thought it was outrageous that his wife had to be subjected to this every day when she came to work. Unfortunately for the cast, who had great respect for her, were mostly gone the next year. I don't know exactly when it happened, but a divorce was in progress, and in the end she got part of the Follies. Lala made the statement that all the people who were against her would be gone. "I'll get rid of them! Just you wait, Henry Higgins, just you wait!"

Well they didn't have to wait, she did. Fifteen years later, she is still getting rid of people that don't dance to her beat. First, she was made the dance captain of the cast, which gave her the start she needed to advance to the next step, and I don't mean a tap step. Through the years, I watched how clever and manipulative she was to get her way. She would blatantly say in the dressing room, "I sleep with the boss!" What a claim to fame! But that was the signal that you better beat to my drum. I thought talent was the name of the game, but I guess she had a talent we weren't aware of until it reared its ugly head. Casually she would say to me, "Don't you think 'Jean' is putting on weight?" At first, I didn't catch on.

And being honest I might say, "Well I guess," never thinking that I was helping the process.

Then she would go to Mr. P, and say, "You know, even Dorothy said she's putting on weight." He would start to notice Jean more closely. Truthfully, I think he was still in the bedroom when these statements were made. His imagination got the best of him. He actually did think she was putting on weight. This would continue throughout the years, with just small things, "I don't think she's dancing as well as she did before." So the seed was planted. How can you play with someone's livelihood?

Right after the show closed in May, auditions took place for the next year. This is when the bomb would fall, and it fell on "Jean." I thought she was better than some of the people that joined the cast after the auditions. Jean was a sexy gal, a former stripper. Now come on, the girl knew how to move, and Lala moved her right out. Jean would come on to Mr. P, and believe me he enjoyed every minute. Not a good thing if you want to keep your job. Especially when someone is working against you.

Jean's departure was the beginning of the power climb. Remember the "ten little Indians, and then there were nine?" Lala started picking on Jean before her departure. One instance I remember very clearly. Lala did not deal with things in a diplomatic way. She told her that she was not doing something correctly in a routine, but poor Jean didn't understand what she was saying. So when she started to question her, all HELL broke loose. Lala yelled at her, "Don't question my authority!"

Jean said, "Lala, I'm not!"

Lala pulled her over to the side, and said to her, "Don't you f*** with me, I'll have your job!" Is that harassment? I should think so, but of course, it would not matter. It would be her word against Lala's.

We had several human resource people in and out of the department during the year, and I'm sure they quit or were fired because they were ethical and would not surrender their integrity.

Speaking of human resources, Mr. P, always made a point that one of the crew would escort us to the parking lot, after the evening show. Now I had no problem with this, and it was a safety measure. One year, we had a new HR person, a young woman who had been a parole officer. Now I'm sure she meant well, and as a humanitarian she wanted to help the under-privileged in life, but all convicts are not underprivileged, and they did commit a crime, and that's why they were incarcerated. It was commendable on her part, but give me a break. When they started to hire the crew for the year, we would say "hello and welcome aboard." This year was different. She brought in ex-cons for the crew jobs. I'm not saying

215

every guy that comes out of prison is a bad guy, and should not have a chance, but I found it rather strange that they would be walking us to the parking lot, in the dead of night. You know, one of them could have a "relapse," and since we didn't know what their crime was, this could be a dangerous situation. But then, "*C'est la vie.*" That's the Follies way.

This is not an exposé on Lala; it's just that working with her for 15 years brought a love-hate relationship between us. In the beginning, she was not quite sure of me, and I do believe she liked me. She treated everyone as a threat to her position, and she was holding on for dear life. She didn't think I was a threat because of my age. Her attitude towards the cast, men or women alike was the same, "Don't f*** with me," and of course they didn't. Everyone really wanted the job. Believe me, it wasn't for the money. Dancing and singing had been their life; they wanted to catch that last bit of glory before they said "Adieu!" Mr. P, knew this, and used it to his advantage. He has absolutely no respect for the cast. One incident a few years ago was during rehearsal, working from 10 a.m. to 6 p.m. We were standing on the stage, dead tired, when he entered the theater. "Cast step forward, I have something to say," he said in his usual quasi "Ziegfeld" manner. "After reviewing some of your work, all I can say is — you suck!" Can you believe it? Well, believe it! Now remember, this is a cast comprised of 16 performers, a dog act or ventriloquist, the star of the show, and Mr. P. The cast is the lifeline of the show. Mr. P comes out, tells a few jokes, harasses the Jews, Catholics, the gays, and Mormons, and tells the audience how awful they look, and then he has the audacity to tell the cast they suck. Well Mr. Ziegfeld, or whoever you think you are, No, the cast does not suck. This little group of performers made you several millions of dollars.

We received step out pay for a solo part, or to understudy the other cast members. On payday, we would get our checks, and try to figure out how much we were getting for the step outs, but could never figure it out. Everyone thought we should have a meeting with Mr. P, and question him about it. So I went to Lala, and told her that the cast was not happy, and she said she would take care of it. After lunch, Mr. P appeared in the green room and sat in his favorite chair. Then he started admonishing the cast. He looked at one cast member, and took him apart with his insulting statements. He told us that whatever he decided to pay us was at his discretion; he didn't have to explain himself to us. When did you ever have a job you had to guess at your salary? In other words, he would give us what he thought appropriate. A great singer and beautiful lady in the cast had worked at the studios, and was in several movies, including

Funny Girl and *A Funny Thing Happened on the Way to the Forum*. She was sitting on the other side of the room listening, Lala looked over at her and said, "do you have something to say, you look like you would like to say something"? She responded, "Well yes, when I tried to figure out my paycheck for the step outs, it came to fifty-three cents a show."

Now Mr. P was really in a huff. Sitting on the floor were several cast members. He looked over at each one and with fire in his eyes, said the famous words, "just where would you be if not in this show?" Let me just say, this cast member had been many places, and done many things in the business, but he just shrugged his shoulders and let it go. Then he hit two of the ladies with the same question, they had no answer. Any answer you would give him would bring out his anger, and he would put you down even more. Finally he said to me, "Ms. Kloss" (Oh, I forgot to mention that we were always referred to as "Ms." or "Mr." rather than our first name), "where would you be?"

I came back with, "Probably on Broadway!" That ended the meeting; we never did find out what we were making.

A documentary was made of the Follies in 1996. Six girls were chosen. It was nominated for an Academy Award. We came in second. There was much "to do" about it, and Lala and Mr. P, at this time, had moved in together, living up on a hill. After we were nominated, Lala came in and told us she and Mr. P, would be giving a small get together at the house. We could watch the awards together. A few weeks later, she announced there would be no party. They were attending a party in some hotel in Hollywood after the awards, but they were not going to the actual awards. I was surprised that the six girls involved in making the documentary were not invited. We put a lot of our own personal time in, without pay, to create this documentary. When they showed clips of the documentary at the awards, guess who was the one strutting across the stage? Lala! It was all about her. No one seemed to care, and it didn't make her a movie star, or a star of any kind.

Now that the two of them were going to L.A. they canceled their party at the "house on the hill" the night of the Academy Awards, it left the rest of us on our own. I said to one of the other gals, "Why don't we have our own party with a few people? We can watch it on TV." So we decided that would be our way of celebrating the big event.

One of the gals said, "I'll make a casserole." I said, "Let's not make a big deal out of this. It's going to be wine, cheese and crackers! We will be working all day, and we don't need all that. We don't have the time." Lala heard us talking. When I left the dressing room, she captured this gal, and started to question her.

"Is Dorothy going to invite the whole cast?" she asked.

No she said, "I don't think so. Just a few of the people that participated in the documentary

Lala said to her, "Listen, take the frozen turkey in the freezer upstairs, and cook it for your party!"

The gal said, "I don't think Dorothy wants to go to all that bother!"

Lala came back with, "Take the turkey and cook it." She wanted to get rid of the turkey in the freezer. It had been there for two years.

I came up to the green room where everyone hung out, and they told me what had transpired, I said, "No, no — NO TURKEY! We're just having wine, cheese, and crackers."

With that, Lala was standing there and said to me, "Dorothy take the turkey, and don't f*** with me. Do you hear me? Don't f*** with me." Now first of all, let me explain this was an old, old turkey, almost as old as me. It had been in the freezer forever. Old or young, I was not taking that turkey, or her abusive language. I just looked at her, and walked away. We finished the matinee, I went out to dinner, and when I returned she was waiting for me. I guess she thought about what she had said to me. The cast had heard her, and she decided she had made a big mistake, "You know, we need to talk."

I said, "Yes we do." Then I told her, "Don't ever speak to me like that again. I don't use that language, and I don't appreciate you speaking to me in that tone. It's not acceptable, and our plans for the Academy Award party are none of your business. When we step outside the Follies door, we have no obligation to you, or the turkey, or the Follies."

She came back with how much she loved me and, how I was her favorite. And so we moved on. That was the beginning of the power struggle to get to the top of the mountain. It took her nineteen years to accomplish her goal, and run the show. My way of looking at it, nineteen years of being subservient to someone who only needs you for the moment, but then, different strokes, for different folks.

Each year brought changes and new cast members. A few were really full of themselves, and you wonder what they did in life that made them feel so important. I didn't know this person, but my friend, Ken Prescott, knew her from New York. So when I mentioned the new girl in the cast, he said, "I know her!" At this time, she was living in Kansas City. When I met her the first week of the rehearsal, I mentioned it to her. Ken and I invited her to dinner after rehearsal one evening. She and Ken renewed old times here, there, and everywhere. In the rehearsal script, I noticed she would be my understudy for my tap solo. I mentioned to her, that Ken had choreographed my routine. It would be fun working with her on the number. I just happened to say that Ken and I had worked on it during the summer; the number was set.

The next week, we had a time set aside so I could give her the number. As I started to show her the routine, she had this look on her face like, "There's nothing to it," and then she really pissed me off (again, I hate that word, but it fits).

She looked at me and said, "It took you all summer to learn this?"

I hit back with, "No, we worked on it this summer. It's not how long it takes you to learn it, it's how you do it after you get it! Do you have it?" It really pleased the heck out of me when she had trouble getting some of the steps. As I always say, don't judge if you don't want to be judged.

We had a German gal in the show, she had worked all over Europe, and had worked for our choreographer, in Germany. Every summer, she would go back to Germany for the summer. She had family in Munich.

In May of 2002, we were just finishing the season at the Follies. A very popular magazine in Germany called "Maxi" wanted to do a photo shoot on some of the Follies girls. It was due to this cast member that made the shoot possible. The people from the magazine had seen the show, and they knew the girls they wanted for the shoot. They made their choice. You see this was really this cast members gig. She was a friend of Kathryn Seidel, the production coordinator, and Kai Peters, the photographer. She told me they would like me for the shoot, and I was thrilled. It was a $1,000 a day!! BOY, what a gig. The shoot would be after the "Follies" closed, so we would no longer be under contract, and be free agents. Unfortunately, Lala, got wind of it and immediately went to Mr. P.

Almost immediately, Lala came into the dressing room. She informed us that if we took the gig, we would not be invited back to the Follies the next year. The cast member that had set the shoot up didn't know what to do. Then, she did what Mr. P, wanted her to do. She gave the project to him so he could control it. I'm sure if she had not told us about the money, he would have taken it. I know from whence I speak. I had a similar situation but that comes later so hang in; it's interesting.

We did the shoot, and he sent Lala and the PR guy, to oversee every move that was made. It really annoyed Kathryn and Peter, putting their two cents in every time we moved. We did three days in different homes in the area. One was the old Sinatra house. The clothes featured were small European sizes. None of them fit Lala, and would not fit many of the

Follies girls. That is why they made their selection of a certain few. Mr. P was determined to choose the ones he wanted: When Kathryn objected, due to the size of the girls, it came down to three of us. They used one other girl he forced them to use for one shot in a fur coat, and let her go home, but they had to pay her for the day.

Every time we started to shoot, Lala or the PR guy would say to Peter, "They can only stand so long," or, "They need a break." anything to hold up the shoot. I'm sure Lala was pissed…. because she wasn't in it. What was her problem? Mr. P, had her on all the brochures, and in all the media he could get her in for the Follies. Why not give other people a shot? Not their way. We couldn't all sleep with him, and why would we want to? Just to get your picture on the brochure?

The magazine came out in September, and it was wonderful. I had three full pages in color. It was titled "Oldies but Goldies." Not much was said about it, but it gave the Follies great press.

I'm sure you've heard the term "a coffee table book"

I first met Carol Saline when I was greeting patrons in the lobby of the Follies after the show. Later, I learned that Carol was observing me, and the way I was engaging in conversation with the patrons.

It first began when she contacted Mr. P. She was interested in me being part of her book. She had seen me on numerous interviews. She decided I would be perfect for one of the twelve women featured in her book, each one with a different profession and walk of life. I was thrilled to be chosen and an honor to be in a book written by this well-respected author.

Here was the plan. First Mr. P, informed me about the offer. Then he informed me that Carol would be coming out from Philadelphia to interview me at the theatre, and at my home. Notice, I said informed, need I say more? Everyone was all a twitter and much ado about the upcoming project. The PR man was involved, and he scheduled Carol to come to my home for coffee and croissants, and photograph me in my condo, walk the grounds and on and on…you get the idea. The book went south and Carol went back east. Let me reiterate. Besides flying her own photographer out, Carol was in constant communication with me due to the fact she wanted to get a real sense of who I was. That did not go over well with Mr. P. You see they wanted to tell her who I was.

At the eleventh hour, Mr. P canceled the whole shoot and interview. He gave me some cock and bull story that the contract was suddenly unsatisfactory. What a crock! Not true, Carol was in contact with me and was very apologetic; she told me she tried everything to make it work. This would have been great publicity for the Follies, but there we have that control again. I may have lost the book but I made a great new friend in Carol.

My first brochure cover was in season 2007/8, after I did "The Today Show" in 2005! Remember, I had been in the show twelve years already. And much to their surprise, "The Today Show" was a huge hit, so they decided to give me a shot. Up until then, it was all about Lala,

When I came through the office area, Mr. P said, "Did you see the brochure?" He plucked it from the holder to show me. What struck me and several friends and fans, Lala was still on the front, and I was on the back!! You see he just couldn't give it to me. It wasn't about talent. He was making me second best, even though I had a multitude of loyal fans that came to see me every year, from the beginning. I had danced my heart out, but remember what I said: competition is the name of the game. Age doesn't mean a thing. The following year, they did the same thing with the brochure. Another cast member was on the front, I was on the back. I do believe that started me thinking I should leave the Follies. At the end of the year, the show was closing, and they asked me to stay after the show one evening to get a few shots for following year.

They wanted to do a life-size cutout of me. They would display it at the visitor center, hotels around town and the Follies lobby. I had to stand in a position that would be easy to cutout. Much to my surprise when the new season started, there was a big cutout of another cast member in the lobby! I got trashed. Now what really hurt, they had made several of these cutouts unbeknownst to me, and had them in the greenroom before

taking them to their destination. They took the cutouts of the other cast member and lined them up in a row in the green room. She stood in the center holding one of the brochures showing me on the back. The brochure is nine inches by four. She is sur-rounded by all of her life size images, and holding "little old me" like I

On the UCLA panel on Health and Aging, with Dr. Small, 2008

didn't matter. How unkind! But then, talent is not measured by size.

In May 2007, KCET did a symposium on "Living Better Longer" with Dr. Gary Small from UCLA. The theatre was set up for this special event, and we had a sold out audience. Four of the oldest performers were asked to participate: We were the panel, with Dr. Small. Mr. P was the moderator of the discussion on aging. It was just getting too serious for me, so I did try to lighten it up a bit. Dr. Small said to me, "Dorothy, you are an amazing woman to be so healthy at your age. Performing nine shows a week! And it seems, living life to its fullest." At that time I was eighty-four. He continued, "How do you do it?"

I looked at the Dr., and in a Jewish accent said, "I don't know, you're the Doctor, I'm a dancer, you tell me!" The audience loved it. Since I was on a roll I thought, "Let's keep it up," so I broke into John Travolta's "Stayin' Alive," and then I said, "Don't wallow in your lost youth. Keep moving and most of all, keep laughing, and keep shopping. You can't help getting older but you don't have to be old!"

The Follies decided I could speak, with a sense of humor. They asked me if I would speak at several luncheons in the area to publicize the Follies. "People are interested in your career, and aging," they explained. I told them I would be happy too. My thought was, "I'm always talking anyhow, so let it do some good." One event was at the Eisenhower Hospital. I really had fun with the audience. I talked about how I got started in show business, my life in Chicago, and about the USO tours during World War II. The most amazing thing happened. I finished the lecture, and several people came up to talk to me. I had mentioned that many of the people in the audience where probably my age, WWII people. I told them about Vincent being injured in Metz. One lady and gentleman came up; she had tears in her eyes. She told me her brother was killed in Metz, and she loved hearing me tell the story. Another lady was stationed at Great Lakes, Naval Station. She had been in the service during the war. She loved the Eddy Duchin story about me being the last act to perform with Eddy, the night the band broke up, and Eddy being inducted into the service. The PR guy taped me. He showed it to Mr. P, and that is when he decided I should do several of these lectures, which I did for several months. I even did a few on my day off — remember, these were for gratis, or in other words, "no money." He has it in the contract that anything we do outside the Follies is part of our job, and therefore we cannot be compensated for it. He wants it all.

Example: a wonderful organization, W.O.W., knew me from the Follies. They heard I was doing lectures. The president got in touch with me, and asked if I would do their Christmas Luncheon. The pay would be $3000.00, a tidy little sum for ninety-minutes. Unfortunately, I was under the Follies contract, and there comes the rub. I went to the PR man, I told him about it and what great publicity it would be. They had heard about the other lectures I had given. I also told him about the fee, and said, "We could split it with the Follies." Before the sun set in the west, I was summoned to Mr. P's office. It was going to be another "Ms. Kloss" day. As I walked in, there sat Lala and the line captain on the couch. The inquisition was about to begin. The very idea having them sitting there, judging me! The ex wife who also was there had a right to be there; she's a partner. But these two chorus girls PLEASE! I was infuriated.

He started with the usual, "Ms. Kloss, let me just say this event you would like to speak at, what is it again?"

I told him.

"Well, you can do it if you would like, but you can't have the fee. You see we don't take fees."

I was thinking to myself, "Wanna bet?" but I held my tongue. He kept saying to me, "but if you want to do it, you can!"

I said, "All these ladies in this organization come to the Follies and support it."

"Well," he continued, in his condescending tone, "I think you should do it, since you have made a commitment."

Right then, I knew he wanted me to do it for the Follies, but nothing for me. What really riled me was when he told me to give the fee to my favorite charity. I told him that I was my favorite charity, but it didn't move his hard, hard heart. Right then I decided, "Why should I do this on my day off when they'll get it all?" I told him, "I don't want to do it any longer."

"Are you sure Ms. Kloss?" he asked.

I said, "Yes, it's too stressful." Subject closed.

Some stories have a happy ending, and this is one of them. I called Vickie the President of W.O.W., told her I couldn't do the lecture, but I mentioned that my roommate Ken has a terrific act. Why not book him in my place? She loved the idea. Ken was in Australia at the time so I sent him an email to be sure he was available. He said, yes and it was set. He did the show, got the money, and we lived happily ever after. Or so said, "the spider to the fly" as we flew away with the fee.

My meeting was not over, only I didn't know it. The next subject for discussion was my star on "The Walk of Stars!" Several friends and fans decided I should have a star. Lisette and Boyd Haigler, and Ken Prescott, my roommate, started the whole thing. They put their heads together, and made a plan. Lisette e-mailed Mr. P, about the venture she would be taking on. She thought, "Surely, the Follies would like to be involved." Guess again. He e-mailed her back that they could not participate, since there were other people in the cast that were just as deserving as Dorothy.

She told him, "We're not interested in the other people." Mr. P told Lisette that he didn't want to be involved, but to "keep him informed." Right! Why should he be kept informed, since he didn't want to be involved?

The meeting now turned to the Star. The inquisition continued! "Now, Dorothy, (all of a sudden, I'm Dorothy) why would you want a Star? People walking over it."

Honestly? I looked at him and said, "It's the honor of being selected, and voted on." I was the only *Guinness* person in the cast, and the only one that had their own act when I was in the business, and had many other accolades. Why would he think the rest of the cast, deserved to have a Star. No, one offered them one.

His next remark, "I just want you to understand that the Follies cannot be involved, and you cannot use the Follies name."

I fired right back, and said, "I don't need the Follies name. I had my name in lights sixty years ago!" That ended the meeting. I'm sure he never thought they could raise the ten thousand dollars for the Star. Believe me, I didn't use the Follies name.

Mr. P was not invited to the Star celebration.

It was a wonderful day for me with Ken, my two granddaughters Jamie and Megan, Kaye Ballard, Rita Coolidge and Bill "Bulldog" Feingold, who has a great local radio show. Bob Alexander is the President of "The Walk of Stars," along with Susan Stafford, the first *Wheel of Fortune* girl, and an accomplished lady. After the other speakers, we unveiled the Star.

When Lisette, Boyd, and Ken had the fundraiser, they raised the money in one night. Now, I am forever immortalized in cement in front of the theater, where the Follies perform from October thru May. How fitting, don't you think? Mr. P probably walks over it every day and says to himself, "S.O.B.!"

If you're not familiar with," The Walk of Stars," it started in 1992. It's very much like "The Hollywood Walk of Stars!" Bob Alexander is the president, along with twenty board members, who select and vote on the candidates. The first inductees were Earle Strebe, who ran the Follies Theatre back in 1936, Hollywood actors, William Powell, Ruby Keeler, Charlie Farrell and Ralph Bellamy. Charlie and Ralph owned the famous Racquet Club. What an honor for me to be in the company of these great legends. I have the 330th star that reads, "Dorothy Dale Kloss, Tap Dancer Extraordinaire, *The Guinness Book of Records*, 2009."

Other stars honored through the years: Marilyn Monroe, Rock Hudson, Kaye Ballard, and many more. As the song from "Sweet Charity" goes, "If they could see me now!"

Chapter 22: Flash! Bam! Alakazam!

As the song, "Orange Colored Sky" says:
> *I was walking along, minding my business*
> *When out of an orange colored sky,*
> *Flash! Bam! Alakazam!*
> *Wonderful you walked by.*

That's exactly how it happened.

It was 1999, and the Follies' new show was going into rehearsal. The new people were settling in, getting ready for the first day of orientation, which was the next day. One cast member and her husband had the condo next to me, and next to them was another cast member, who was new this year. It was twilight, and the four of us were standing in front of my condo talking about the upcoming season, getting acquainted.

The Villas, (where the cast was housed) are quite nice. The grounds are lovely, and the whole area is very hilly. I always felt like hitting a high note, like Julie Andrews, "The hills are alive, with the sound of music." But instead, one hill leading down to my condo was alive with a handsome man, coming in our direction. When he reached the bottom of the hill, I thought, "Who is this person?" We didn't have to wait very long to find out.

He extended his hand to the one gal and said, "Well we meet again. Gosh how long has it been?" By this time, we realized he must be the new man in the show. Too good to be true! So we introduced ourselves. He had this wonderful smile, and was full of energy. I invited them in for a glass of wine, and whatever I could find in my refrigerator.

The one gal and Ken Prescott had been in "No, No, Nanette," together on Broadway, in 1970, with Ruby Keeler. We sat around the dining room table and had a great time reminiscing about our careers. I thought to myself, "This is going to be a great year!" Little did I know, just how great, until the show got going — but that comes later.

Ken and Dorothy rehearsing, 1999

Rehearsals started at 10 a.m. sharp. Most of the people arrived a little earlier, to limber up, and get acquainted with the new people. I arrived before Ken. I was telling everyone what a fun person he was, and how good-looking. Just then he arrived, very low key. He gave me a little wave but not that happy-go-lucky smile I had experienced the night before. I thought, "What happened to that charming person I was drinking wine with last night?" He was surveying the "situation," I later learned.

The girl singer was always ready to create a happening, and this was one of them. She recruited four members of the crew to help her with her "shenanigans!" They created a makeshift litter that would hold her. She could do her Cleopatra bit. The doors swung open, and the crew lifted her up and carried her into the green room in a very provocative pose. She was lying on her back, waiting for applause.

She saw Ken sitting on the side, and she was out to get him. She got off the litter, walked over to him like Mae West, bent down, grabbed his head, and pulled it into her boobs, which almost covered his whole head. She is not a 36B. What a way to welcome a new performer.

There were two choreographers in 1999. One was Ric, she and Ken had worked together at the San Gabriel Playhouse, they had a great working relationship. During rehearsal, she asked him to assist her. Ken is not only a great dancer and singer, but also an excellent choreographer. Believe me, I've seen his work. He choreographed several of my finale routines. He knew my style, and I didn't feel I was doing a "dancing school routine." He did this for me, for gratis, may I say. He was so easy to work

226

with, such energy and creativity that I could see him choreographing the Follies. He would have given it a fresh look, but you can't fight "City Hall." That was wishful thinking on my part. I even gave Lala his choreography tape. Ken was so versatile and imaginative, I thought, "He could bring new ideas to the

Ken and Dorothy, on a ten minute break, 1999

show." I thought she might put in a good word for him, but I'll never know if she did or not.

She came back and told me in her dominating, off-handed way, "I don't think he and Mr. P, would get along." What happened to talent? I didn't know she was also a decision maker. I don't think she gave it to him. The rumor going around was that she would "have" Ken by the end of the show. You figure it out. Did she mean for dinner? She was a showgirl, and she is making decisions on who should be the choreographer?

A few years later, she talked Mr. P, into hiring a friend from Orange County to choreograph the tap. I liked this young lady, but I did not find her choreography, for me great; and after all, isn't this a show that should have the best of the best when you're paying ninety dollars a ticket? You

On with the show, 1999

see, Lala needs attention, and Ken didn't give her the attention she was hoping for, so she talked him down. In the last few years, she was telling the choreographers what she liked, and what she didn't like, and who should be in the front line, besides her. And of course, if you have seen the show, she is center front in every number. At times, I could not believe what I was hearing.

We would be doing a step, and she would turn to some of us and say, "Do you like that?" Then she would go to the choreographer and say, " we don't like that step." I could not believe the choreographer would let her get away with it. The other choreographer had worked the biggest hotels in Vegas. You don't tell the choreographer what to do. I remember one of the cast members, he had been in the Follies from the very beginning, and he wondered why he was in the back line for almost everything. He asked why.

The choreographer told him," I have nothing to do with the placement of the people. I do what I'm told." As much as I hate to say it, Mr. P, likes women choreographers that he can control. The men give him a problem. Women just cry.

After the first day of rehearsal, I got home, had a little dinner and hit the couch. I heard a knock on the door. I wondered who was knocking at my door at this time of night. I opened the door, and Ken was standing there with a bottle of wine. Our friendship started that evening, and has continued so far, for fourteen-years. We have lived together going on twelve years. I would say, "The Best Years of My Life." I've had a few other "best years," but these stand out at a time when I needed them most.

We started the rehearsals with lots of energy, and dancing with Ken, "Mr. Energy," kept me going at high speed. During our lunch break, he would say, "Hi Dot, want to go to lunch?" And off we would go to Ruby's, and have the best time talking; mostly about who, what, and where in the business we had worked. Then back to rehearsal. We had our nightly wine, cheese and crackers and found we really did enjoy each other's company.

Ken was married at the time he came into the show to Ginger Prince, a cute little red head who did Broadway, and was very talented. They were married for 25 years. Ken helped raise Ginger's two daughters. They lived in New York. I got to know Ginger when she came out to see the show, and we did a few things together, but I did feel that their marriage was in jeopardy. I wasn't quite sure what was happening, but within the next few months, it was over and Ginger had a new relationship. They divorced.

Ken was not happy working in the Follies. It was all too consuming. It is the most controlling job I have ever had. Unfortunately, most of the performers at their age knew that Mr. P, had them over a barrel, and he knew it too. Their favorite saying from the Follies was, "Where would you be, if you didn't have this job?" This is very insulting to performers who have worked in Hollywood, TV, nightclubs, theatres, and Broadway. He was lucky to have their talent, so he could make his twenty million a year. Where would he be without them?

Ken talked to me about leaving the show. He said, "This is like amateur night in Dixie." Believe me, Mr. P., was learning from all of us. He had never done a show like this, but he did work at it and came up with a winner.

Ken decided to stay until the end of the show in May. I'm forever grateful for his kindness to me. Christmas was coming to the Follies, we would all be on hiatus for ten days, and, may I add, without pay. Picture At the time, Donald O'Connor was the headliner, and we were selling out every show. Look who we had as the Star! When I heard Donald was going to headline the show, I was really excited. He was my favorite dancer. I loved Fred Astaire, Gene Kelly, and all the great men dancers, but I loved Donald more. He could do it all: comedy, acrobatics, and what a tap dancer. He opened in the show in October, and I was a little disappointed that he mostly sang. I wanted to hear those great taps. I don't think he was feeling well at the time, but he just kept going. He was so nice to be

Our Christmas Party, with Donald O'Connor, and Gloria O'Connor, 1999

around. He was a star without an ego. Donald had a nice wife, Gloria, who really looked after him and tried to watch his diet, which is a plus when you're not well.

Three weeks before Christmas, I woke up and promptly fell out of bed. I was dizzy! The whole room was going around. When I stood up, I lost my balance and had to sit down again. I got to the phone, and called the Follies and told them my problem. I thought Mr. P., would say, "Just lie down, we'll call in the doctor," but instead he asked me to get to the front door, open it, and try to get dressed. "I'll send the car," was his answer.

The driver arrived and helped me into the car. We went directly to the Follies. Riding in the car and walking from the street to the Follies green room was a challenge. I was so dizzy, and ready to "up chuck." I hit that bathroom, just in time. The cast was called in, and already rehearsing with the understudies. Ken was choreographing a finale number to replace the one I was doing.

He was not my understudy, but the pro he is, he can jump into any situation. By the time the show started, Mr. P, had decided that I was not going to get any better, so his words: "Take her to the doctor."

When I arrived at the doctor's office, I had to walk up to the second floor. I was thinking to myself, "There must be an easier way!" He told me to sit on the examining table. I jumped up. Did I say jump? No help from him. In a very uninterested way, he told me I had vertigo. "It comes and goes," was his big diagnosis. "Have the driver get you motion sickness pills," he said in a detached tone, and that was that. I got down from the table, asked the driver to help me, and we were off to the drugstore, after I paid my $60.00. Boy, that's my kind of doctor.

The driver took me home, and I hit the couch with my pills. When I would lie down, I'd be okay, but as soon as I sat up, I felt ill and dizzy. Now we start with the phone calls from Mr. P, every hour on the hour! I don't know if he thought I was faking it and might be out having lunch, or that I would have a miraculous cure, and get back to work. But he was an annoyance. I would fall asleep, and the phone would ring. It would be him. He would say, "Kloss are you ready to come back? There's an empty hole in the show."

"No," I finally told him. "Stop pestering me. I'll let you know when I'm ready to come back."

"Well you know, you could do "The Pretty Girl,"" he coaxed.

"No," I insisted, "Do you want me to fall off the stage?!"

The one person who really did care was the new guy on the block, Ken. That first night I was out, after the show, he came right over to my apartment. He called to ask what I needed, and checked on me. We only had one more week of shows before the Christmas vacation. I was feeling a lot better, but my balance was still off.

Before I took sick, Ken and I had talked about having a Christmas party. We thought a "progressive" one would be fun. Since most of the people lived at the Villas, we could go from one house to another, starting at one cast members for hors d'oeuvres, then on to another cast member for fish and wine. Ken was bringing the turkey to my apartment, so I could spend the day basting it, since I was still at home. We also had mashed and sweet potatoes, cranberries, dressing and whatever was a Christmas delight. Two cast members lived next to me, and it would be great fun, to go from one condo to another. The turkey was sensational. We finished dinner, and started walking and singing Christmas carols on our way to the next condo, for dessert and Hot Rum, where it ended. It was fabulous, and the cast loved it. Donald and Gloria came, and had "seconds," so I guess it was good. Believe it or not, even Mr. P came. That was a big surprise.

The show closed. I left for Philadelphia to visit my kids, but it was not a happy trip. I guess the flying didn't agree with me. When I got off the plane, my balance was still off.

The dizziness would return on and off. It put a damper on my Christmas and I'm sure on Craig and Joni's festivities. When I got back, Ken picked me up, and I was feeling better. I did go back to work when the show re-opened. It took awhile for me to get back to normal. The dizziness would come back ever so often.

After the New Year, we had another few days off, and then a two-day rehearsal. We would replace the Christmas segment, before we opened again for the spring show. I'm not exactly sure, but it wasn't long afterwards that Donald became ill, and was out of the show. He did come back, but only for a few weeks at the end of the season, as I remember. He is no longer with us, but I sure did enjoy him while he was here. Donald really did "Make them Laugh!"

It was my best year at the Follies, because of Ken. He was fun, and would come to the girl's dressing room, and yell, "Dorothy, come into my office!" which was by the steps and water fountain. He was, and still is, so full of conversation. He makes my life bright all the time. It's Christmas every day. What a gift.

The season was coming to an end. Ken had mentioned that he would not come back to the Follies, so I thought he would be going back to New York. We talked about it and he decided he would stay on in California, so we moved in together. From the start, it was Happy Time in the "old corral." My life was no longer all about the Follies, even though I was on the same schedule. They always say, opposites attract. I've always wondered who "they" are. Not true! Ken and I are alike in many ways. I guess that kills that theory. He is ready to go on a moment's notice. Me too. He loves to converse on anything that tickles his fancy. Even at my age, I have learned so much from him. He has made me accept myself, and my talent as something special.

Many years ago, when I was teaching dance at Sacred Heart, a nun who had been observing me, passed me in the hall. "Oh, Dorothy," she said as she met me, "I would like to talk to you if you have the time. We can sit right here." I knew she meant business; she already had the seat reserved.

"Yes, Mother what can I do for you?" The nuns were addressed as Mother back then. I was puzzled. She spoke in a kind, soft manner, "Well my dear, it's what I can do for you. I find you have a hard time accepting a compliment. When someone mentions what a good job you did, you always say how you could have done better. You do a good job, so accept it, and just say thank you." It was the best advice I ever received. From then on, I waited for the time I could say, "Thank you!"

I Got Rhythm, 2007

Dancers are not always happy with the choreography they are given, but most of the time, they just accept it and move on. I had just accepted it the Follies way. Once I saw Ken dance, I knew I would love his choreography, and he would be so easy to work with. I decided to give it a shot in the dark, and ask Mr. P, if I could choreograph my own routines. To my surprise, he said yes. I didn't tell him that Ken was working on the routine with me, because he would have taken back his yes. I rented a studio during the summer. Mr. P asked me what music I wanted for the Eleanor Powell number. I told him "Fascinating Rhythm," the music she danced to in the movie *Lady Be Good* in 1941 (MGM). I would really like to dance to the same music.

After the show closed for the summer, I got a call from the Follies telling me to pick up the CD for my number. Off we went to the studio to start the number, and to my surprise, the music on the CD was "I Got Rhythm!" That was the part of the Follies that was most frustrating to me. If you wanted something, you had to go in the opposite direction, and if you were lucky, you might get it. I should have asked for "I Got Rhythm," and in all likelihood I would have gotten "Fascinating Rhythm." I watched

232

so many of the cast put together a routine or vocal number and ask to audition it. None of them were accepted. I mean they were good numbers, and ideas that would have been an asset to the show. I can't remember one number that anyone auditioned, was ever used.

I do remember, one cast member who, incidentally, was married to Juliet Prowse, a great dancer. He could really work a hat. During our 40-minute "coffee break" during the show, he was kind enough to teach those of us who were interested some hat tricks.

I loved learning how to twirl a Derby or Straw hat in the air. One break he started a dance and hat routine. It was so clever. We thought it would stop the show. I suppose Mr. P, was only interested in numbers that didn't stop the show; just slow it down. Anyhow, he showed it to Mr. P, and all he could say was, "What if you drop the hat?" My reaction would be: Pick it up. Jugglers are always dropping whatever they're juggling.

One cast member had it all. She was a cute redhead with a great figure, charming personality, and a lovely voice. She had seen the Follies and wanted to be part of it. She and I were both friends of Barbara McNair. Barbara was in the show at the time, and this gal asked Barbara how to get an audition for the show. Barbara told her to call me; I would give her all the information. She called, and came to the desert from Sacramento to meet me for coffee. I know it's a long ways for coffee, but it did lead to the job.

She had a great resume. She had done 180 national television commercials, and she was the original "Ginger" on the *Gilligan's Island* pilot. She and her husband Dennis moved to the desert, and she joined the Follies cast. After a few weeks of rehearsal, the hat man had his eye on her, and their eyes locked. And that was the beginning! It was like *An Affair to Remember*, but not on a ship; this affair was on stage. After three years in the Follies, she had gotten a divorce, and he was trying to get one, or so he said. He had been in the Follies for five years, but no matter; they were not invited back the following year. They moved to Las Vegas, where he had spent many years working, they could get a fresh start or so they thought. Unfortunately, they were only there less than a year when Eddie had a heart attack and passed away.

She came back and auditioned for the Follies again, but they did not take her back, which I never quite understood. These two people were not causing any problems; they were just in love. I do think there was prejudice against this red head. She never really got the vocals she deserved, and I know, 'cause I was her understudy for "You're Eather Too Young or Too Old." What a fiasco that was; they decided to change the lyrics to, "Either Too Young or Too Gay!"

Now we all know that this desert is a gay town, and if you didn't, now you know. Even the gays were offended. The choreographer set movements for the number. If you're a singer, you need to feel free to move naturally, not be restricted, and not have a movement on every word of the song. Some of her moves were fine, but you have to have that little bit of freedom to sell any number. Poor cast member, she really hated the number, but she did it.

The "Show Me and Perform" day came along for the understudies. It was my turn. I started the number, and tried to stay with the chore-ographed movements as much as possible, but my free spirit took over. I threw in a couple of my movements. The cast was laughing 'cause I tried to make it a comedy, especially with the title. The choreographer was talking to Mr. P, when I finished, he called, "Kloss, you know the choreog-rapher has a trunk full of movements she would like you to do."

I said, "You see, I don't feel them with this lyric. Why don't you give the number to someone else?" I thought it was over and sat down. They went on to the next person.

The next morning before rehearsal started, the choreographer came to me. As she started to speak, I quickly said, "Please, just give it to someone else."

She said, "No, Mr. P,' said, tell Kloss to do whatever she wants to do with it." Case closed! Poor cast member was stuck with the original movements. The song was a disaster! The audience hated it, and neither one of us ever got applause.

About three years later, Lala said to me, "I think we will bring back "Either too Young or too Gay" for you."

I said, "I don't think so. "It was a flop three years ago. You want me to flop again? Give it to someone else." It was never revived.

The next year, the selection of music was about to begin. Lala said to me, "What music would you like this year for your solo?"

I thought, "Here we go again." But then I thought, "Take another shot." Many years ago, in my act, I tapped to "Zing Went the Strings of my Heart." I thought it would be such fun to bring it back, one more time, before my demise. I told her, "Zing." We had a music meeting. I asked Ken if he would put together a CD with stop time (intermittent chords with passages of silence to hear all the tap sounds). Ken had to ad-lib and "sing" the arrangement, since we didn't have the music. But he explained it on the CD. It would be given to the musical director and Mr. P, so they would understand what I had in mind. I gave the stage managers the CD and they listened. I could tell right off, this was not going to happen.

Stop time would be so effective. All the great tap dancers over the years did stop time; and since I have always had nice clean taps, I would not have to record them. Just do them. I can't tell you how many people I have recorded their taps. Some of them didn't even know it. We had never done stop time in the show, and I thought it would give the number a new sound and look.

"Well Dorothy, I don't think we can do that," said the "dance authorities." Okay. So I thanked them and said, "Whatever," and left. When the musical director finished the CD for me, there was no stop time. So I lived with it, and Ken gave me a knockout routine. When rehearsals started, I showed the number to Mr. P. It was TOO GOOD! So he said in his pretending to think way, "You know, I saw you in your red costume at the fitting the other day. I think you should do "The Lady in Red." I told him, "We rented a studio at twenty-five dollars an hour all summer working on "Zing." Now you want me to just chuck it and do a whole new number at this late date?

That would really be a stretch. "Well no," he said, "make 'The Lady in Red' the start of the number, and segue into Zing." Okay, back to the drawing board. We did just what he asked, and came back with it. All was well until three days before the show opened. I got a memo from him that they had changed my music to "Boogie Woogie Bugle Boy." In three days, we had to put together a whole new routine and I opened with it. I like a challenge, but this was ridiculous. He likes to wear you down. He does it all the time to keep control. He never did want me to do "Zing," but played with my psyche. If you think about it, this is stressful for people our age; but he could care less. Oh, I was 83 at the time.

We had a really nice new choreographer, I liked working with him, ' he wanted you to be comfortable with the choreography, so it wouldn't be a strain. He and I worked on a routine (before Ken), and it was good. I was doing a big solo in the finale. Lala and her best friend in the chorus were in Indian costumes and walking from one side of the stage to the other. Not much choreography there. They looked wonderful, but just walking. I was dancing up a storm.

When it came time to choreograph the bows, Lala and her friend had this big bow, along with the two featured singers and a couple of other people, but not me. I was furious and questioned it. Lala went to the choreographer and told him to give me a bow. Then she went to Mr. P, Let me just say, it was not the choreographer's fault. He worked me into the bows, and I was happy until the next day. Lala said, "Mr. P, would like to see you in his office." I entered, and of course the entourage was there. It's like he always needs a witness, for gosh sakes. It's just a bow we're talking about.

He went into his speech about how this was his show, "And Lala and I really don't care about anything, or anybody!"

Whereupon, I jumped in quickly and said, "Well I'm glad to know that. Now I don't have to care about anybody, or anything, either. And let me add that I know it's your show, and you can give bows and take them away. But at my age, I'm not sure how many bows I have left." He took the bow away from me, but the Indians came center front, ruffled their feathers without a dance step in sight and took a bow center front. What a guy.

I asked the musical director one day why he set the tempo so fast. I felt like I was in a race. He said, "I don't set the tempo. Mr. P sets it. If the show is too long he just speeds up the music." I didn't even know what to say about that. But I got my answer. And I'm glad I'm still breathing, with some of the tempos. And even with the speed up, the show is still over three hours long, most of the time. As one famous star quipped upon seeing the show one day, "Hell, I could have flown to London and back by the time this show ends!"

The Follies got to be a habit, like any other job. I guess the glamour of the business keeps you going back, even after you read the contract that would put you in Alcatraz if you broke a rule. It's like the army; three strikes and you're out. There is no explaining your side of anything. At the end of your meeting, trying to explain your problem to human resources, you are asked to sign a paper; they win again and you lose. The oldest cast member before me was eighty. She gave her opinion one day about something. Mr. P, looked at her and said, "You have no opinion. And remember, the unemployment line is very long." How mean.

Every year around January, I would look at the cast member sitting next to me in the dressing room and say, "I do believe this is the year to go." Then things began to pick up for me, and I decided to stay another year. After the "Today Show" spot in 2005, I realized I could not only walk and dance, but I could talk. The media had found me, and everyone wanted to know about the 85 year old woman that was reliving her career from the 1940s. I was delighted. I had interviews on the phone, off the phone, in my living room, in the lobby of the theatre, and wherever they wanted me. I was available. The Follies, of course, knew they had a good thing in me because of the interest the media was beginning to show. Then *The Guinness Book of World Records* gave me the distinction of "The Oldest, Living, Working Showgirl in the World, 2009." WOW! I decided old was not so bad.

One matinee, Betty Hutton came to the show. She lived in the desert, in a small apartment, and had fallen on hard times. She had been invited to attend the Follies, but every time she decided she would like to attend, she would back off, and say, "Sorry, I just can't make it." She was rather a recluse, I heard. But finally she came, and I was thrilled. She had always been a favorite of mine. I would see all her movies like *The Greatest Show on Earth* and *Annie Get Your Gun*. She had such energy, plus everything else to make her a star. A fallen star is so sad.

Army Archerd was a legend in Hollywood; he wrote a celebrity gossip and industry events column for *The Hollywood Reporter* for years. In 2007, he was writing a blog, he is Hollywood's "Original Blogger." He wrote a piece titled, "Backstage with Betty Hutton." Here is his quote: "Betty Hutton went backstage to congratulate the "girls" in the Follies, to the delight of the age-defying cast. Betty broke into a duet of "Doing What Comes Naturally" with the senior showgirl, Dorothy Kloss. Dorothy celebrated her 83rd birthday this year and goes into *The Guinness Book of World Records* as the World's Oldest Living, Working Showgirl."

I was singing "Doing What Comes Naturally" in the show, when Betty attended the matinee. And, of course, that was Betty's song. It really was a thrill for me to be mentioned in Army Archerd's column. Sadly, Betty passed away not long after that, at 86.

A wonderful magazine, *Reminiscence*, the magazine that brings back the good old days, approached the Follies to do an article on me. I was perfect for this magazine. I don't know if they wanted me for my age, or the good old times I've had, but it was a great article.

There was *Dance Magazine, Dance Studio Life, The National Examiner* (full Page and a thrill!) Doris Day, on the front and me on the back!.

The one I really loved doing was the AARP photo shoot with the renowned photographer/videographer, Dirck Halstead. His photos have appeared on the cover of *Time* Magazine 56 times. It was a three-day shoot in different locations, which made it fun. Dirck was so easy to work with; the time just flew by, even though I was still doing my Follies shows. After the shoot was over, I found his web blog, "The Digital Journalist, A Letter from the Publisher."

At the beginning of his column, he said, "I just spent three wonderful evenings last month at "The Follies" and came away with a video on 'The Oldest Showgirl.'" The video was for the AARP BULLETIN. After the video came out on the web, I received a wonderful email from him. Quote: "The AARP tells me they are getting zillions of hits on the video. You are nothing less than inspirational." Wow!

Then in December 2009, I received word that AARP announced: Big News Top 10 Stories of 2009. "Some incredible headlines led the news this past year." I was the second most hit or watched on the AARP web site, right after the Speaker of the House Nancy Pelosi and Health Care. Not bad for a city girl from the north side of Chicago. But you can't get too full of yourself, because you might take a fall.

I have always had a love of the south. I guess it's after reading *Gone With the Wind*. I never got over that one. It's just that the southern women are so graceful, and the gentlemen are full of charm. I had worked in Louisville, Kentucky, at The Brown Hotel, and The Kentucky Hotel, at different times. Also, The Henry Grady Hotel in Atlanta, Georgia and Shreveport, Louisiana at The Shreveport Hotel.

During one of the evening performances, while Mr. P, and I were bantering on stage, he stopped me in the middle of a line and said, "We have Mr. Grayson here tonight, he would like to present us with the highest honor awarded by the Commonwealth of Kentucky; that of Kentucky Colonel." Signed by Steven L. Beshear, Governor, and by the Secretary of State, Trey Grayson.

I didn't know this was coming, so I was flabbergasted. He continued, "Mr. Grayson is the Father of Trey Grayson, Secretary of State, and he is sitting center front." There is a large speaker center stage. On each side of the speaker are two open spaces. Mr. P, had decided we would lean over and accept the award from center stage, instead of asking Mr. Grayson to come on stage. I leaned over to take the award, and as I stepped forward, my foot stepped into the open space with the two awards in my hand. I fell backwards, flat on my back, and the awards went flying across the stage. My southern grace went right out the window. There was a big hush, and you could hear the audience murmuring. Oh!! "Is she okay?" they all wondered.

Once I got my head together, I started to get up on my own, picked up the awards, caught my breath, checked to be sure I was okay, and said, "Thank you." After the show, Mr. Grayson and his wife waited to see if I was OK, and then we chatted about The Brown Hotel and The Kentucky Hotel, and the Kentucky Derby. It was worth the fall to meet them, and to receive such a prestigious award.

Most everyone likes to shop. I, for one, was not familiar with Costco when I first moved to the desert. But one of the cast members from the Follies, with the seven kids, knew all about it. She was used to buying big! I, on the other hand, could be out of the grocery store in ten minutes. On one of our days off, she asked me to go to Costco with her. She said, "It's a great store, and you'll love it." I was impressed when I saw the size of the store, and what they had to offer.

She said to me, "Why don't we split a few things?" Everything was in large packages. I said, "Alright," and away we went down the many aisles. By the time we reached the cash register, she had bought big, and I was splitting big. Even a split was too big for me. We did laugh, but I went back to my ten-minute walk around.

Not long after that, I did become a member. My walk around became a little longer. It's so strange how life moves you on. Several years later, Costco decided to do an article on me for the "Costco Connection," a lifestyle magazine for Costco members. It was really wonderful, with a great photo on the back page of the September issue, 2009. Can you imagine the circulation for this magazine and how much the AARP spread gave to the Follies? I finally got a bow, and they got big publicity. I believe the Follies bow was bigger.

I had known one cast member since the Abbott days. She had studied at the Abbott School since she was a child, and when she hit the working age, she made it to the Empire Room of the Palmer House. She was a good acrobat and a good dancer. She decided to leave the Abbott Dancers, and go overseas with the USO, entertaining the troops. She met and married a gentleman, who would be the future spokesperson as Colonel Sanders, for Kentucky Fried Chicken. But that was years later.

She was my understudy for the "Zing" number, when I performed it in the Empire Room. After I left, I didn't see her for 40 years. She had moved to California, was teaching dancing, and had remarried. The Palmer House, around 1997, was celebrating their 100th Anniversary, and had invited all the people that had worked in the Empire Room to help them celebrate. She went to the reunion, and met another Abbott from our time, Marilynn. It so happened that Marilyn lived in the desert. She knew I was in the Follies. We had renewed our "Chicago days," and would get together for lunch. One day, Marilynn called. She told me she had gone to the Palmer House reunion. She was telling all the ex-Abbott's that I was in the Follies show, emphasizing that it featured performers over 55.

Our friend immediately said, "I'd like to know more about it. Do you have Dorothy's number?"

She called me, and I gave her the information. I was not sure she would make it, due to her size. She was short, but she did well in the audition. Mr. P didn't think she would work out, but the choreographer thought her size would be an advantage. They could do funny things with her, and so she was hired. Much to her credit, she could still do cartwheels. And in one number, with one of the male dancers, he lifted her above his head, and the audience was amazed; she was eighty. There was only one problem; the male dancer developed a bad back from the trick, she didn't want to come down.

She and I did not get on well. She thought she was the best dancer in the show, she never got over the fact she had been my understudy. No matter what I did, she would critique me. She would say to one of the cast, "I wouldn't do it like that!" I know because another cast member used to listen to her every show, when he was standing next to her, and he would say to me, "Gosh, I wish you could get it right!"

I finally had it. One show, I was doing wings, which take a lot of energy. I had recorded them, so you know they were my taps. Mr. P, called a rehearsal for three of the cast members to come in, and do the wings. He wanted to see which one would understudy me. They would use my taps if they had to fill in for me at some time. It was her turn, and when she finished, she looked at Mr. P, and said, "Dorothy fakes them anyway!" That is one thing you could never accuse me of; if I can't do something, I don't do it. But as Bette Davis' mother used to tell her, "The birds only pick at the best fruit!"

Chapter 23: A Laugh a Minute

It was not all doom and gloom at the Follies. Every year brought forth new people in the cast, and they tried to fit in as quickly as possible. Some did, and some did not. But most of the time, no matter whether they did or didn't, we were a tough group to invade. As one of the cast members use to say, "You need large shoulders to work in the Follies." Every person had their own personality, and that is how it should be, but there are always obstacles in the way.

A new girl in the show was very excited. I named her "Lady in Wonderland." She had a sweet personality. She wanted to be part of the group, so everything would be "wonderful" all the time. She didn't have as much experience in the business as most of us. And so she really wanted to do her best. Every moment, during rehearsals, she would be up practicing the steps. I find that commendable, but enough is enough. We had a ten minute break every hour, and she would jump up, and say to one of us, who were trying to catch our breath, "You want to go over that step?"

"No," we would say. "Sit down and rest! It's a long day." What she didn't understand was that the ten-minute break was for resting. She came from Washington, D.C. raised four children, and also, owned a dancing school for forty-seven years. No wonder she was in "wonderland," after being surrounded by all those kids for that many years, doing "point, point, pas de bourre."

She was very nervous her first year. She had a good attitude, and thought that "everything was right with the world." I remember an article came out in her hometown paper, telling about her joining the Follies. Her statement to the paper was about me, "If she can do it, so can I!" Of course, I was 85. Understudies have a grueling job, but she wanted to look good to the "boss" (Mr. P.), and let them know that she could do it all, so they let her. They gave her seventeen understudies, but then she did volunteer for most of them. When she mentioned it to me, I said, "You asked for them, so enjoy, or tell them you can't do that many." But she was concerned about the job. I'm sure she could make it into *The Guinness Book of Records* for the most understudies in the world. She was afraid if she didn't hold her own, she would be out. She accepted what they gave her, and remained quiet.

She said to me one day, "Gosh, I forgot that my granddaughter was being confirmed this week. My daughter called to tell me, so I rushed out to buy a card and send her a couple bucks."

I said to her, "You mean you sent her $2.00, Boy you're the last of the big spenders."

She laughed, "No silly, that's not what I meant. I sent her $50." Sometimes she got it and other times, oh well!

You always have to be ready for the comment of the day, or whatever comes up, depending on the circumstances. The cast was rehearsing the drum number, and it was not going well. It was not from *The Music Man*, let me just say. But then, they had just started the number, and many of the booms were bombs. Mr. P, came into the theatre to watch, and with a look of despair said, "You people look like a bunch of old people in the home playing with sticks!" What a great way to "rally the troops!"

Channel two came to interview Sammy King, and his famous ventriloquist dummy, "Francisco" (Don't let Francisco hear that I called him a dummy). We were interviewing in the hall up stairs. Suddenly the camera crew and there newsman started to question us. I looked at Sammy, and said, "Did you know, I have a date with Francisco?" Quick as a flash Francisco (Sammy) said, "Honey, I'd pluck you anytime!" Unfortunately, it came off on live TV, as F— you any time. Wow! All hell broke loose. The people at the station were trying to explain to the listening audience. "What did he say; it was pluck, pluck, pluck!" So much for my date, with Francisco and live TV. When Sammy left the Follies, he said Francisco wanted to retire to Mexico. I don't think he will ever retire. I hope not, 'cause he brings such joy to the world!

The oldest gentleman in the show had a wonderful career. He was in his eighties, and had a heart by-pass a few years ago, but returned to the Follies. He is still doing eight and nine shows a week.

He did have a few funny things happen to him, and we never let anyone get away with anything. Mr. P, for whatever reason I don't know, gave everyone in the cast and crew 12 silver dollars in a little bag. Without thinking, our oldest gentleman nearly broke his front tooth. He thought it was candy, opened the bag, and popped one in his mouth. Ouch! Always look, before you leap — or chew.

We were doing a Spanish number with very colorful costumes. The men wore large black hats with red balls hanging from them. Now, don't get ahead of me. His dresser made a note on the costume list of things to fix. It said, "His balls are loose. Please fix!" Poor guy!!

Before one show, back stage, waiting for the opening announcement and the start of the show, we heard a lot of commotion from the front of the theatre. Then came the announcement, "There will be a hold." Word came back that a gentleman in the front row had a heart attack. The paramedics arrived, and they lifted him up on the stage to give him air and try to revive him. Another announcement came, "Please be aware we have a problem. And if the audience would like to exit to the lobby, for a soft drink and popcorn, please join us until the problem is taken care of." Not one person left their seat. They were all engrossed with what was happening on stage, and it wasn't dancing. They were watching a poor man die. After about forty-five minutes, they lifted the man onto a gurney, and took him out. What a way to start a show! What a way to go, when you've come to see a show. The gentleman was with two other people, and of course their seats were empty when the show started. As the music started to play, they played our signature song, "Gonna Take a Sentimental Journey." As the saying goes, "One minute you're waiting in the wings, and the next your wearing them!" It was bizarre to put on a happy face, and know that someone just expired on center stage. I guess it's what's known as "knocking them dead." Literally.

Lala said to Mr. P, "Are you going to refund their money?"

He said, "That would be going too far."

To put a nail in the coffin, the next day Lala said, "Did you know a man had a heart attack at the McCallum theatre, at the same time as our man, but ours died?"

I said to her, "So is this a competition between the McCallum and the Follies?"

The ironic part of the story is, the gentleman that passed away had come to see me. He had been in the Eddy Duchin Orchestra. Say hello to Eddy for me! I know he's up there.

The hotline is a Follies tradition, or annoyance, as I like to say. If you like it or not, you're stuck with it, if you want to be part of the Follies. I found it a nuisance and frustrating. You are obliged to either call the hotline after the show, when you get home, or in the morning for a cast call. No other show that I know of has a hotline to get your schedule for the next day. It's called "the Follies owns your life."

You arrive at the theatre at 12:30 p.m. you finish at 10:30 p.m., and then dash home. In the real theatre, they have a call sheet when you leave at night. You check the call sheet for the next day. This is where the Follies control comes into play. Keep them on their toes at all times. It's like your bedtime prayer. If we were not on our toes, we couldn't do nine shows a week. It's just a lot of B.S.

I had been calling that stupid hotline for fifteen years. This year, 2010, they put a computer in the dressing room, and the dance captain and Lala were on it constantly. They would sit there, and would pull up the list of people that called in, and those that forgot. It was a day of reckoning for anyone who did not call in. I call it kindergarten. The dance captain would call out your name and say, "Why didn't you call in last night?" You have to give her a reason, and then she would e-mail it upstairs to see if they accepted your excuse. It's like a reprimand and embarrassing to the person singled out.

One of the most aggravating things is being brought in at twelve o'clock, which is a half hour earlier than our usual call of twelve-thirty for a fire drill. It's the dumbest thing I've ever heard. Some days they call it an "earthquake drill." No matter what they call it, if either one of those things should happen, most of the cast would be dead. It's stupid to have the drills. I'll explain.

The cast is in the basement of the theatre built in 1936. We go down twelve steps to the dressing room, and these steps are the only reliable exit to get out. But since by law, you need two exits, they had to find a way to abide by the law. I cannot believe that the fire inspector has let this go, when you have sixteen people in the cast, and ten or so dressers tending to our needs, all under ground. Under the right side of the stage, they installed a portable ladder. They cut a square piece out of the floor at the side of the stage, as an escape hatch. Now the logic is, when they yell "fire," we form a single line in the dressing room, and march towards the portable ladder and wait our turn. If you're not careful going up the ladder, you will get kicked in the face by the person in front of you. The first person to reach the top of the ladder will find the hammer next to the escape hatch, and he or she is instructed to hammer the makeshift hatch, so that the person above will know we are trying to get out, and then open the hatch, one by one, we climb the ladder to freedom. Think about this: if there should be a fire, the guy who is supposed to open the hatch will be long gone. We have had many discussions about this problem, and it has been ignored for my 15 years. I guess I've been lucky that nothing has happened. They always say, be prepared and have water. We had nothing, let me just say; our cupboard was bare. This is no laughing matter.

Back to the stupid "hotline." One two-show day, the list was pulled up, and three people were asked why they didn't call in. They all said they did call in, and what is the problem? The Follies had installed new equipment. "There must be something wrong with the system," the three argued, but there was still doubt. I mean, why would they lie? It's just a telephone call. After the discussion, Lala said, "I won't mention the people, but two of them wear hearing aids, and the other one is not always playing with a full deck.

One of the gals was in deep conversation with another performer, and just as we were leaving the stage, we heard her say, "I guess I just have to take care of me."

One of the cast, who was quick of wit, said, "So what else is new?"

When I first came into the Follies, the oldest lady in the show was in her eighties and a really nice gal. She was from Chicago, and had been a Colonel in the Air Force in World War II. She had been in the show from the beginning, and the audience loved her. I always remember her with fondness, and one of her most memorable performances.

The ladies of the ensemble were doing a routine dressed in evening gowns. They had life-size dummies dressed in tuxedos with their feet attached to the ladies' feet. One hand was stretched out holding the dancers hand, and the other was attached to the girls back. It was a ballroom scene. Six couples whirled around the stage in a circle. She hit a platform, and she and the dummy went flying, she landed on her back, the dummy on top of her. She couldn't get up, and the audience was roaring with laughter. She was shouting, "I can't get up!" The rest of the dancers just stepped over her, and kept going until the end of the number. Otherwise, they would have all run into each other, and everyone would have been down for the count. They all whirled offstage and left her with the dummy. They closed the curtain, and one of the crewmembers got her back on her feet. It only goes without saying, "never dance with a dummy."

The Christmas show was always special. This particular year, we were doing a Christmas waltz, with four couples. There was one girl in the center; it was a lovely number. The opening, preceding the waltz number had many parts to the costume, so this was a quick change. One wrong move, and you missed your entrance or went on without some part of the costume. One night, I came off and started my quick change. I saw my partner enter the stage. I had to jump out immediately to join him. We started to waltz. I thought I looked fabulous; I was waltzing beautifully. My partner had a strange look on his face as we started to waltz.

I said to him, "Is something wrong?"

"Oh, no you look fine," he assured me, looking down. Then he started to giggle.

I knew something was amiss, and by this time the cast was laughing, so I knew it must be me. When we came off the stage I saw the problem. I had my wig on backwards. I looked like Harpo Marx. It's a good lesson. Always keep your head about you

Ken, Kay Starr, Dot and Donald O'Connor, taking a rest, 1999

During my first year, there was always a lot of tension. The choreographer had gone back to Munich. So now, who would be the chosen one to take charge of the cast, or better known as the Dance Captain? Well of course, you guessed it: it was not up for a vote. The girlfriend of Mr. P had one goal in mind, to be the "chosen one!" And this was the first step to the top of the mountain. First, she became the captain of the cast, and within time, who knows? The duties of the captain are to oversee the dressing room, and rehearse the cast for their understudies, and the power would come later.

The most exciting thing about my first year at the Follies was working with Kay Starr. If you are around my age, you will remember Kay and her wonderful recordings, especially "Wheel of Fortune," one of her big hits. Before we had a green room and dance studio on the Follies property, Mr. P's office and the headliners were in little cottages, on the side of the theater, next to the wedding chapel. It was such fun in those days. The covered patio with tables and chairs, and we would sit out there and "kibitz" during the breaks and have a laugh or two.

I remember Kay coming out of her cottage a few days before the show opened. We were sitting on the patio just getting some fresh air. She had several gowns on hangers, and I said to her, "Leaving so soon?"

She laughed and said, "No, I'm going to see the boss. This is the first time in my show business career, I've had to audition my gowns."

One cast member was a kick. He had been in the show from the beginning. The patio next to the theatre was our home away from home. He and the other acts kept us laughing most of the time. The story I love about this cast member is priceless. When he came to work right after Thanksgiving, he sat down on the patio, and said, "Boy, what a dumb thing I did for Thanksgiving. A friend of mine called and asked if I would like to go to dinner on Thanksgiving. I said, "Sounds great, what time will you pick me up?" My friend said, "Oh, about one." I said "great, I'll see you then." Thanksgiving arrived and the two of us took off in his car

The cast member said, "Where are we going for dinner?"

His friend said, "To the homeless shelter, they put out a great spread for the holidays, and it's free."

Cast member said, "Are you nuts? We're not homeless, what if we get caught?"

"Oh, we won't get caught" his friend chimed in, and with that, they walked through the door of the shelter.

They welcomed us with "Happy Thanksgiving," and told us to get in the food line. We picked up a tray, filled it with holiday fare, and found a table." I was not comfortable with this whole situation, but my friend had the transportation. Just then as they were beginning to enjoy their complimentary homeless dinner, Cast member said, "Hey, we have to get out of here!"

He had just spotted a cameraman and reporter from the local TV station coming to interview the homeless people. The cast member knew most of the people from the media; they had interviewed him many times. He said, "If they see me, I can see the headlines: 'Follies Performer Now Homeless" or 'Is He Stealing From the Poor?'" Robin Hood wouldn't like that. So they hit the back door, and made a quick getaway to McDonald's.

Another cast member was in her eighties. She was from Texas, and taught dancing for years. She had three talented children who grew up to be stars in their own right. Her son was in the movie *Chicago*, her daughter-in-law was on Broadway in *Chicago*, and another daughter taught at the American Musical and Dramatic Academy in New York. Her daughter Sandy, a lovely dancer, is married to Jay Johnston, the talented ventriloquist from the TV Show *Soap*.

She was full of energy. In the Christmas show, she and another cast member were chipmunks. She would jump into a split, and fling her head back with all the power she had. Believe me, she knew how to fling. This one particular performance, she not only did a fling, but she flung her head so hard that her wig went flying across the stage. She jumped up, grabbed the wig, put it back on her head, and continued the routine. Now that's a pro!

I love this Las Vegas story. Nino Frediani, the great juggler, and Sammy King, were going to Vegas on their two days off. They were driving, and she asked them if she could follow them since she would be alone. The trip started out with her behind them. They were taking it easy, so as not to make her nervous. Suddenly, she passed them with a hand gesture, that read to them, "You're going too slow, so I'll see you later," and she put the "pedal to the metal" and was not to be seen until she got back from Vegas.

She stood up in the dressing room one matinee, and announced she had written to the USO in Washington, to volunteer her services as a dancer and singer. She would like to entertain the servicemen in Iraq. We all looked at her and thought she was joking, but don't underestimate her. She did mean it. She was waiting for a reply. I said, "You're doing what?! people are getting killed over there, and besides, those young guys don't want to see us old gals!" But she was adamant and said, "If they want me, I'll go." Unfortunately, she went someplace else.

The most amazing thing about her, she lived every moment for the moment. The show had just closed for the season, and we were all at the Ramada Inn for the closing night party. The last thing I remember was her walking by our table and saying, "Well I guess I'll be on my way." Little did she know, how far she would be going. We all told her how beautiful she looked and off she went. She passed away the next afternoon. What a way to go. She had finished the matinee, attended the closing night party, and was gone — but again I say, what a way to go.

One other cast member, in her eighties, was very feisty. I really loved her. She didn't take anything from anyone. We were on hiatus for Christmas. I was on my way to Philadelphia to visit my kids. I arrived at the airport, and I met one of the other cast members, she was leaving around the same time. We decided to get a cup of coffee, and headed for the restaurant. There was our eighty-year old cast member having lunch, so we joined her. Not only was she having lunch, she was having a "hissy fit."

"Are you okay?" we asked.

"Not really," she said with indignation. "I'm so angry. I went through security and they took my gun!"

I said, "What are you doing with a gun?"

"I have to protect myself," she said as though we should know this.

I said, "From what?"

"Well, you never know," she retorted.

So I tried to make it fun, and told her, "You can't get a man with a gun!"

She didn't think it was funny. So we went on our way. Just to add a note: She and her brother, mother and father had an act together in the 1940s, and headlined all over the USA and Europe. But to me, I loved the fact that she played the Palace in New York. At this point, it was all "long gone," but not forgotten by show folks. Just to say you played the Palace was outstanding. What a memory. She would finish her "Pretty Girl" speech with "My Mother Thanks You, My Father Thanks You, My Brother Thanks You and I Thank You."

Mr. P took five of us on the Alaskan Cruise. We had just closed the show. It was my first year. He asked me if I would like to join the other five cast members to perform on the Holland America Lines. Three hundred Follies Favorites, meaning patrons of the Follies would be joining us. We would perform one show, and I would teach tap classes. Another cast member was asked to teach the ballroom.

I was excited about being one of the chosen ones. I got my seasick pills, packed my bags, and we left for Vancouver, where we were going to join the group on the ship. We hit the deck and were on our way. It was great fun, and we got to know everybody in the group. We had about 20 tap dancers; the other 280 patrons came to watch the tap class. I would "kibitz" with them as they drank their morning coffee and watched the class. Actually, the twenty tappers were pretty good, so I decided to give them a routine for the talent show, which was our last night on the ship. Besides teaching, we were "ad-libbing" every night in the bar, on the top deck. Everyone loved it. The last night, several of the passengers performed, and then the tappers closed the show. As each one took their bow, they gave their name; I'm Betty, I'm Jane, I'm Bill, I'm Jill, and so on. At the end of the line was Sandy, and she said, "I'm Sandy, and I'm tired." The audience loved it.

The ballroom class was in the afternoon. I was asked to help with the class. I said "Of course." So we showed up for the class and what usually happens when you have more women than men, the women danced with the women. The music was playing, and I was laughing and changing partners. I had this nice gal as my partner. She introduced herself and said she was from Chicago. Well, being from Chicago, we hit it off right away. She was at class the next day, and said, "I come to the desert to visit my new daughter-in-law every February. Would you like to have lunch when I come this year?"

I said, "Yes I would love to!"

I arrived back home and who do I meet but the ex of Mr. P in the hallway. She said, "I understand you met my new mother-in-law on the cruise, she had such a good time with you. She called, and said when she comes out to see the show, you're going to lunch."

I guess I looked confused as she continued. "You didn't know, but I just married her son." So for the next fifteen years, my new friend and I got together for lunch every year. When February arrived, I would say I was going to lunch with her and Lala would say, "I don't know what you see in that woman. I don't care for her. She wasn't very nice to me in the lobby."

I asked her what happened. She said, "she came up to me with a friend, and said, 'Oh this is the chorus girl that goes with Mr. P,'" Well??

Speaking of lunch, she was here for her annual visit one year, and we decided to go to Merv Griffin's for lunch. Merv had just bought the Givenchy Hotel, which had an elegant restaurant with magnificent grounds. We decided to sit outside, since it was a lovely day. As we were ordering lunch, I saw Merv coming through the door with his entourage, and I said to my friend, "Boy, today is our lucky day. Merv is here." she said, "I loved his talk show, and there was one song he sang I just loved. I wonder if I could get it."

Just then Merv was on his way back to his table. I called to him, "Mr. Griffin, may I ask you a question?"

Over he came, just as nice as you please, and said, "What would you like to know?" My friend has a question for you, and she asked him about the song. Then he asked us if we were visiting the desert. I said, "I live here but my friend is visiting from Chicago. She is the mother-in-law of the ex wife of Mr. P, from the Follies, and I'm in the Follies."

"Oh," Merv observed, "So you're one of the " lovelies." Just then, his group started taking their places at his table, and he left. When we were leaving, he beckoned for us to come over to his table. He explained to his guests who we were. I was a " lovely," and my friend was "the mother-in-law."

They all laughed, and then I said, "Mr. Griffin, have you seen the Follies?"

He said, "No," kind of apologetically.

I said, "Why not?"

"Well, you know," he explained, "I live in La Quinta, and it's a distance for me to come in."

Whereupon I was not going to let this go, so I said, "Mr. Griffin, we'll send a car!"

He looked at me with a big grin and said, "Dorothy, I have a car." What a pleasant man.

The luncheon became a yearly event, and several other fans and friends were added to our group. The date was St. Valentine's Day, and we would all get together for lunch: Doris Bennett, Alberta Stout, Jean Gabriel, Lisette Haigler, Alice Peterson and me. Every year, I would find a new restaurant, and we would have a grand time.

Bob Hope was one in a million. He and his wife Dolores had a home in Palm Springs, on top of the highest mountain. They would come to the Follies every year with their family and entourage of friends. They usually had the first two rows, with Bob and Dolores center front. It was fun to watch their reaction to all the numbers in the show. During one particular show, a cast member and I entered from stage left, and crossed to stage right. The curtain was closed behind us to set up for the next number. We came out singing, "Don't Fence Me In." As we started across the stage, another voice could be heard joining in. Guess who? It was Bob. He was singing his heart out. We saw Delores nudge him, and say, "Stop singing Bob, it's their number!" As they say, "once a ham, always a ham." We can always say that we sang with Bob Hope, or maybe more accurately, Bob Hope sang with us.

The ensemble was doing two routines back to back. The problem was, one number was tap and the other was jazz, so there had to be a shoe change. But there was no time; it was decided not to put taps on the shoes. Just fake it. Who would know? Well, somebody knew! You guessed it: our good friend Bob Hope. After the show, Bob came to Mr. P, and said, "If you're going to do a tap number, put taps on the shoes. The audience isn't stupid." He got that right.

The Rio Brothers were a great acrobatic act. They were only in the show a short time, due to a dispute they had with Mr. P. They decided to cancel their contract. They told him, "You didn't buy our act you just rented it."

The desert has always been, a celebrity town. They've been coming here for 60 years or more. The difference between then and now, they live in gated areas. President Ford and his family lived here for many years. Never in my wildest dream did I think that he and Mrs. Ford would attend the Follies, but they did one evening, with all of their security throughout the theater. It was very exciting to know they were in the audience, and little did I know they would exit by the side door of the theatre leading backstage. The other cast member and I were standing in the hallway, taking our microphones off, when the door opened. They came in with a gentleman ahead of them and one behind them, being sure all was clear. It was empty except for the two of us. The Secret Service men stepped aside as the President extended his hand, and gave us a hug. Then Mrs. Ford also gave us a hug, and told us how much they enjoyed the show. It was hard for us to move on. We were still in shock. Show business does have its wonderful moments, and it was a special one for us.

Howard Keel, 1997

Howard Keel was just the best. He had a lovely wife, Judy, who we got to know. Howard sang all the great songs from his movies, like *Showboat* with Kathryn Grayson, *Calamity Jane* with Doris Day, and many more. Who would not remember him in *Dallas* on TV, as we were all glued to the set to see what Howard, as the husband of Miss Ellie, and father of J.R. and Bobby Ewing, would do next.

It was a joy to work with Howard, and fun, may I say. Howard and I would be backstage waiting for our cue to go on. He loved to talk and reminisce, and I loved to listen. He told me about when he was a young man, married to a ballerina, and of course I was intrigued. One day, the cast received a memo saying that there would be no talking backstage. "If you are caught talking to a dresser or anybody else, that person will be let go and you can live with it," was the edict! I came up to wait for my number, and there was Howard, ready to tell me another wonderful story. But I cautioned him in a whisper about the memo. Well I guess I hit a nerve!

"Well my dear, you may not be able to talk to me, but I sure as hell can talk to you, anytime, and I want to right now," he boasted. And so he did, loud and clear. I do believe they could hear him in Poughkeepsie. I loved it.

The Mills Brothers, or should I say, The Mills Brother, were another star act. I talked about them before. There was only one original Mills Brother alive: Donald. It was just Donald and his son John, but with just the two, they still had that wonderful sound. The audience loved them. While working at the Follies, they received the exciting news they would receive a lifetime award in New York. They needed three days off, and so Mr. P, had to fill the spot. He called Howard Keel, who lived in the desert, and asked if he would fill in for the Mills Brothers. He was happy to do so, and arrived for a microphone check and music rehearsal. As he was rehearsing, Mr. P, made his entrance, looked up at Howard, and started to tell him what to do.

Quick as a flash, Howard said, "Mr. P, go over and sit down. I'm saving your ass, and don't need comments from you!" Unfortunately, it was heard all over the theater. The microphones were "live!" Don't tell a pro what to do. And one who is performing a favor to boot!

Downtown Theatre, Revue

Downtown Theatre, Chicago

It was not a good time for Howard. We thought we had lost him at one point. It was a tragedy waiting to happen. We did not rehearse the finale bows, they had been changed. Howard thought he knew the routine. Before, Howard would come to the front of the stage to take his bow, no one told him to stay back. When Mr. P, announced Howard Keel, he started to walk center front, but unbeknownst to him, the elevator at the front of the stage had gone down, but did not come back up. We had a big hole in the middle of the stage. It was an eight-foot drop into the elevator. Howard was heading right for the hole. He was walking forward and looking at the audience, he didn't see the hole; John Byner, a wonderful comedian in the show yelled, "Howard, jump!" And he did, right into the hole. John, and one of the cast members, jumped in and got him out. Without John shouting at him, he would have gone in headfirst. Thank goodness he was okay. Just remember an old Chinese proverb: "Look before you leap," or in this case, "jump!"

That elevator has had its moments. Once before, it had gone down and they couldn't get it up. What a dilemma. The cast was waiting backstage to go on, and the elevator was stuck in the down position. Mr. P, came out and said his famous line, "You know, we have 12-year-olds working here. They can't seem to get it right. So I guess we'll just have to fill in until they do!" He was great at ad-libbing, so he hit the stage and pulled a couple of jokes from his joke book. Out of the blue, Gene Barry, the star of *Bat Masterson* of TV fame, was in the audience. He came up on stage, and said to Mr. P, "I thought I'd help you out while you wait." Gene was full of conversation and stories. The audience loved it, but Mr. P was getting annoyed and trying to get him off. He would not go. Mr. P said, "Let me tell you, this man is not a man of few words, but then look who's talking."

He was very funny, but he had taken the spotlight, and you could see Mr. P was trying to get it back. It was hilarious. Finally, after 20 minutes, they decided we had to do something to get on with the show. So Mr. P, asked us if we could dance around the hole, and we did, to spectacular applause. Gene went back to his seat, and gave us a standing ovation all by himself. He was still "on." Truthfully, he did a great job, and it was an unexpected moment for the audience.

One of the cast members was in the lobby shaking hands, when a gentleman came up to her and asked, "Where is the 86-year-old? I'd like to meet that one."

She replied, "Oh, Dorothy doesn't come out to the lobby anymore!"

There was a pause, and he said, "That's okay, Could you get me the name of her doctor?" I don't know if that was a compliment or not, but I'm going to take it as one!

Another gentleman came up to one of the girls in the lobby and said, "Where is she, the 86-year-.old? I want to see the documents. I don't believe she's that old."

I really like that gentleman. The cast member told him, "The certificate is on the wall over there, as proof." He walked off towards *The Guinness Book of World Records* document.

Always competition. Did I know I would beat the Pope, you know the one in Rome? I know he has a great act, and everyone wants to see him. He can do things I can't do, like bless you. I mean, I could do that, but it wouldn't work. Someone up there is always looking after him, but the same person that is looking after him, is looking after me, too.

In March 2005, I was asked to be on "The Today Show" on NBC! WOW, I was excited! They sent this adorable pregnant gal, Melissa Stark, and Amanda Marshall, the producer from the New York office, to conduct the interview. The camera crew came from Los Angeles. Melissa interviewed me in the theatre, and then we went on stage, and I gave her a tap lesson, pregnant and all. She was quite good.

They also sent a camera crew to Yardley, PA, where my son and his family live, to interview my granddaughters, Jamie and Megan. It was a big thrill for me to have them on and give grandma a plug. I must say, they did a great job, and I was so proud of them.

The segment was called "Extraordinary Seniors." The day it was suppose to air, April 5, 2005, I had big competition. The Pope had been elected, and everyone in the world was glued to the TV set, waiting for the confirmation. We had been given a time for our segment, and holding our breath, that it would not be preempted, by the Pope. Well, my prayers were answered, "Extreme Seniors," with Dorothy Dale Kloss, was aired.

There was great feedback from NBC; I was thrilled. One blog that came in said, "Dorothy Kloss, on *The Today Show* this morning, is in a heck of a lot better shape for her age than the Pope will ever be." Many thanks, to the blogger.

The Jovers were two very funny people. Fe and Wilf! Fe was in vaudeville, and Wilf was in the circus as a young man. They met, married, and became a comedy act. They were from England, and played all over the world. We became good friends, and I had many laughs with them. Their stories about their years in the business always cracked me up. They lived in Surprise, Arizona. What a surprise that was! But then, that would be the perfect spot for them. One of my favorite stories was that Fe was in Germany with her parents. They were back stage, visiting some other show folks. She heard that Hitler was in the audience, so she peeked out the curtain to see him. I don't know how I got it wrong, but I got her story confused with another story. I thought Fe was talking about the German girl in the Follies, and she was on stage dancing for Hitler, when Fe peeked out the curtain. I came into the dressing room, and said, "Gosh, it's really amazing, I said to the German girl, to think that you danced for Hitler."

She gave me a funny look, and said, "Where did you hear that?"

I told her that I thought she told me.

Christmas In Killarney, 1990s

She said, "No, I was only two years old at the time, and I was not peeking out the curtain to see Hitler. I was probably taking a nap."

So I said, "Well, would you have liked to? It would be great on your resume." And we all laughed.

I loved the brother act in the show. All their lives, they were a team. When I came into the Follies, they had already been there from the beginning. They were real pros, and knew the business forward and backwards. I was in my seventies, and they were in their early eighties, but when they hit the stage, they were back in their twenties again, full of energy and the old soft shoe, of which they were masters. I loved watching them; they were so smooth.

As time went by, the old age thing began to creep into their life, but not their performance. Mr. P, decided to team us together. I was thrilled to be working with these two pros. We were doing "Christmas in Killarney." We looked like three leprechauns right off the boat. Unfortunately, the oldest brother had macular degeneration, and he had a hard time seeing, I really looked out for him during the performance. Since I was in the middle, I put my arm around him, so I could guide him to wherever he needed to go. I was just fine with this until one show: the other brother said to me right before our entrance, "Dorothy, I just want to pass this by you. I'm having a little

256

problem. When I look down, I get dizzy. I may hold on to you a little tighter than usual." Talk about two old smoothies; one couldn't see and one had vertigo. Boy was I in trouble, but I held on to them as best I could, and we got through the Christmas Season without a fall.

John Davidson came into the Follies, with his good looks and dimples. He had a fun act singing and playing the banjo. The audience loved him. After his last song, John would walk over to the side of the stage, where there are five steps going down into the audience.

Dorothy, Gloria De Haven, and Angela Paige, 1990s

Mr. P always stood there during the performance to announce the next performer or talk to the audience. In this show, he would wait for John to walk over, hand him his banjo, and John would continue his act. But this time, John reached for his banjo, and with a thud, Mr. P, lost his footing and fell flat across the five steps, and landed on top of the banjo. The audience gasped! John and an usher helped Mr. P up. You don't fall down in a tux. He broke the banjo. John was standing there, with his broken banjo wondering what to do, and finally said, "I guess that's the end of my act." He took his bow and left. He had to drive to L.A. the next day to have it fixed. Thank goodness it was our day off.

If you remember Gloria De Haven from her fabulous movie days, then you would remember all those great movies she stared in with Peter Lawford, Gene Kelly, Judy Garland and the likes. When Gloria arrived at the Follies, I couldn't wait to meet her. She was one of my favorites. First of all, she is not only beautiful, but one of the nicest ladies in the business. Before the opening show, she was a little nervous. She sent her dresser down to our dressing room to ask if we had a glass of wine, to settle her

257

down. We laughed, and told her, we're not even allowed a cough lozenge, only water. But we would love to have a glass of wine with her, only not in the theatre.

Gloria would be in the green room talking to everyone. Most of the gals in the cast would be discussing the $15.00 store, next to the theatre. Everything in the store was $15.00. Gloria found out it was our favorite store and paid a visit there, so that she knew what we were talking about. On her closing show, she sent each girl in the cast $15.00, and a card that read, "Have fun in the $15.00 store, Love, Gloria." That's a classy lady.

One cast member has that big wonderful Mae West personality. She is always creating something to take the boredom out of the long days and nights in the dressing room. Her dressing area is at the end of the dressing room, against a wall. It's perfect for her. She is in her own little world. The wall is her little haven for solitude and reflection. Every holiday, she would decorate the wall with holiday cheer, be it shamrocks, or a Latin motif for Cinco de Mayo. She brought sunshine into our lives.

One year, she had her son Danny, visiting her. He was also known as "Son" when she would talk about him. "Son" did this, and "Son" did that. I finally said to her one day, "does 'Son' have a name?" Yes, he did have a name, she informed me, and he was a stunt man in the movies. She asked Danny to build a "window" for the wall, with a faraway scene of a lovely brook and flowers, she could pretend to look out on. It was hysterical. She would sit there, and gaze out the window like she was waiting for a cool breeze to sweep in. As we passed her dressing table, on our way to the bathroom, we always had something to say, "How's the weather today?" or "Do you think it will rain?" or "The grass is always greener on the other side."

Then she would laugh and say, "You can say that again. I think I see someone coming down the road."

She loved to write poetry, and she was quite good. One day, I brought in an article from a magazine. The title was, "Would you like your poetry published?" I gave it to her, and said, "Here's your chance to become a famous poet." She was always up for a challenge, and even though I was only kidding, she sent her poetry in hoping they would consider it. Now, you know this was just a come on. Several weeks later, she came in to the dressing room and said to me, "You didn't think I could do it. Here is proof of my great accomplishment. I am now a framed published poet," and with that she pulled out her poem in a gold frame. "Talk about getting framed. It cost me $50.00!! Thanks a lot, Dot!"

I once received a nice letter from a gentleman who had seen the Follies. He complimented me on my performance. Since it was a very nice letter, and I always answer my fans, I sent him a note thanking him for the kind words. We started corresponding. He lived in Arizona. He told me how he loved to fly his plane. In the next letter, he sent me a picture of himself standing in front of the plane. I was in the dressing room with the picture, showing it to the girls, and may I just say, we were always kidding about finding a man. I said, "I hit the jackpot this time. Not only is he nice looking, he has his own plane. Maybe I have found my Howard Hughes. The gas alone is a fortune. The next time he flies to the desert, he says he would like to see me."

We were all laughing, and then I said, "You know, maybe I'll take flying lessons." The next time I wrote him, I asked what kind of plane he flew, and had he been a commercial pilot? The following letter was the kicker.

Dorothy, Ken, Joan and Neville King, in Mexico, 2002

Here is his answer to my question. "I fly for a living. Most of my trips are to your desert, and back to Arizona. I deliver dead bodies to their final resting place."

Now, I have no problem with dead people having a last ride to their final resting place, but I did not want to take it with them. Boy, did the girls love that one.

Speaking of the dead, and then we'll let it rest. My mother and I were walking alongside a cemetery when I was about nine, and it gave me the creeps. I said to Mom, "Why don't we walk on the other side of the street?" She answered back. "Dorothy, the dead will never hurt you. It's the living you have to watch out for!" And ain't that the truth.

Neville King was from London. He was a master ventriloquist who toured all over the world, and he was a star in the famous "Black and White Minstrel Show" in London for eleven years. He also had the honor of performing for Queen Elizabeth and Prince Philip. He was the funniest man I've ever known. He and his beautiful wife, Joan, were here for the run of the Follies. Ken and I loved the two of them. They made their home in Nottingham, where Robin Hood "resided."

Neville had one son, and he and his wife came over the "big pond" coming from England, to visit his father and Joan. They had never been to Mexico, so Ken and I said we would take them. It was a time to remember. We also had two other friends, Barbara, and Jean, with us. The eight of us got in the SUV and headed for Tijuana, Mexico. The whole trip, Neville and Ken kept us laughing with stories and jokes. On arrival at the border, Ken said to Neville, "I want you to behave yourself going across the border into Tijuana. We're parking the car on the U.S. side, and taking a bus across. No funny business! The police would think nothing of picking you up, and tossing you in the "hoosegow." He gave Ken one of his naughty looks, and got on the bus. We were sitting in front on the side seats facing each other. The bus driver was waiting for the other people to get on. The driver said, "We'll be leaving in five minutes."

Without opening his mouth, Neville said, "Yeah I bet!"

The driver looked around and said, "Who said that?"

Neville, looking right at him, said, "Who wants to know?"

Ken was giving him the elbow to shut up, but to no avail. He kept it up, until we crossed the border into Tijuana. Neville was on the loose. He sat there so innocently. The driver had no idea he was a ventriloquist. When we were getting off the bus, he stopped and said to the driver, in his British accent, "I say young man, I wonder who that smart a— was? Some people are so rude! But you did a grand job getting us here. Cheerio."

After shopping, it was time for a margarita, and so we went to "Caesar's Restaurant" in downtown Tijuana, where the Caesar salad was invented. We were drinking margaritas and feeling no pain. The Mariachis band came strolling in, strumming their guitars, and Neville just couldn't let it go. He pulled out a tip to give them, and said, "Jolly good, but could you play *God Save the Queen*?" Unfortunately, it was not one of their numbers. We had such fun with them. The next year, Ken and I went to London, and went to visit Neville and Joan in Nottinghamshire, a village just outside of Nottingham. As we went into the "first" pub, Neville pointed to a woman who looked like she was feeling "no pain!" He said, "I say, I heard she joined "Weight Watchers" last week, drank a fifth of scotch, and LOST three days!" That was Neville!!

A former cast member joined the Follies in 1999. She had worked on Broadway, and in Las Vegas, with her husband Bobby Sherwood and his band. She had a good sense of humor and sat next to me in the dressing room. When we were called in for fittings on the pretty girl costumes, I was ahead of her to be fitted. Daniel Storey was the costume designer from Vegas. Daniel had a small platform that he asked me to stand on, to try on the butterfly backpack (an oversized piece of costume that sits on the back of "show girls" as they parade). He put it on my back, and it was so heavy, I fell off the platform. He said, "I know you can carry it; just balance it better," he coaxed.

I told him, "No, I can't! It's too heavy!" But he was going to force me into it.

So he said, in a threatening way, "I'll have to call Mr. P."

I said, "Fine."

Mr. P came in and said, "So Miss Kloss, you can't wear the backpack?"

And I said, "No!"

The other cast member was sitting there waiting. He turned to Daniel and said, "Give it to her. She can carry it."

She was a stronger built girl than me, and so she became the butterfly. She really made it work for her on stage. She would walk forward, look at the audience, and in a Jewish accent say, "So, you never saw a Jewish butterfly before?" The audience roared.

A cast member and the one mentioned above did not get along. The one gal had hearing like an elephant. We would be sitting at our dressing table, at the other end of the dressing room, talking very softly. And if she heard her name mentioned, she would shout, "Did I hear my name?"

Finally one day, she got on our nerves, and we shouted back at her, "You know, you must have a chip in your ear, just let it go."

When our first black girl joined the show, it was a new experience for the cast. We didn't give it much thought. We had all worked with black performers; she was just the new kid on the block. I liked her right off, and we did want to welcome her into our fold.

It was a couple days after we started rehearsal. I was in front of the theatre on my way to lunch, when I saw this very handsome black man standing a short distance from me. I walked over to him and said, "I bet your our new girl's husband," and then continued on with how happy we were to have her in the show, and how much we enjoyed her singing and dancing. I guess I didn't give him a chance to answer me as I rambled on. He was looking at me rather oddly, but just gave me a smile and moved on. After lunch, I was back in the theatre and I said to her, "Oh, I met your husband, what a handsome man."

She said, "Where did you meet him, girl?"

I said, "Out in front of the theatre. He seemed rather shy but I guess you have the big personality in the family."

"Kloss girl," she mused, "I wish I had been there to meet this handsome man. But I have no idea who he is or what you're talking about, he's not my husband. I have no husband at the present time, but if you see him again, introduce me to him, okay?!" Oh well, I've always been friendly!

When I first started at the Follies, the head of wardrobe was this very opinionated gal, and believe me it was her way, or no way, she was never wrong. My pretty girl costume was a knee-length sequined dress with feathers on the bottom. It had been worn by one of the other cast members, and they recycled it for me. It was too big in the back, but had not been taken in. As I was getting ready for the number one evening after my day off, I stepped into the dress and could hardly pull up the zipper. I grabbed the zipper and tried, but it was a struggle. Just then, she came into the room, and I said to her, "What happened to my costume? It was too big for me and now I can hardly zip it up!"

Quick as a flash she said, "You're retaining water!"

I could not believe what she said. I came back with, "this is not a medical problem. You shrunk it!"

"No I didn't," she said, "I just dipped it in a light solution, and hung it up to dry. And anyhow, it fits you better now!"

It's a universal axiom; if you are talented, nice looking, hard working, and getting recognition — those around you (some), will find any reason to try and put you down. I was backstage during one of the Christmas sections of the Follies, and we were dressed as Christmas presents with matching headpieces and long white gloves. Well, in my usual exuberant manner, I was recounting some story, raising my gloves, using my fingers, and generally having fun telling about some incident. Little did I know that one of the "whiney" chorus girls, who was constantly finding fault with everything, and debating you at every turn, was watching me like a hawk. We finished the show, and the evening show rolled around. Well, there we were backstage again, in the dark, waiting to go on, but this time everyone was present,! "Miss Sneaky," at the top of her lungs, whined to the dance captain, "You know, during that last show, Dorothy gave me the finger! Is that harassment?"

Well, without hesitation, I answered, "You want to see it again?"

There was much laughter, and smirking, and "that was the end of that!"

One guy cast member could be very funny. During rehearsal, he and his girl partner were working on a step that was a little tricky. I don't know who was right or wrong, but you could hear her, wrangling and wrangling and wrangling. She was getting on his nerves. He stopped, walked over to my partner and I on the other side and said, "If she says one more word, I'm going to sock her in the nose. And that's what I love about the south.

Maureen Kluck and her good friend Margaret O'Brien

I was going to edit this piece out written by Maureen, but it was so complimentary, I thought what the heck, I'll leave it in. So hats off to you Maureen and thank you for my hat too!

My first sight of Dorothy Kloss was on the stage at the Follies! I knew immediately that this is a lady I would like to know! Her sparkling eyes and great personality came through every time she came in view! In other words she was a great package! Great legs, great smile and a great personality!! Dorothy always made you feel like you too were important! Always upbeat and smiling! Luckily once in a while after I left the Follies I would run into Dorothy and Ken at the local Mall!! Again she was friendly and smiling! Even though I was not a dancer there but rather taking reservations for the show, she always stopped to speak with me. I admired the

Maureen, as Walter Pidgeon's daughter Sara.

positive nature of both Dorothy and Ken and they were both the most "FUN" couple I knew! We shared show biz stories and found we had common likes and experiences.

My show-biz experiences came about because I looked a lot like Margaret O'Brien, the Oscar-winning child star.

Picture this: here I am sitting in my First Grade class at Culver City Grammar School in 1940. Suddenly My Mother comes into the room with the Principal and quickly dragged me out! I was not sure what was happening as I was put into a big black limousine and driven away. It turned out Mervyn LeRoy, the director, saw a photo of me in my Father's office and when he found I was the daughter said, "Go get her now!" From there to wardrobe and the back lot where I was put into a tin bathtub with Butch Jenkins' stand-in and off we floated in flood waters churned up by four airplane engines! The movie was Our Vines Have Tender Grapes. From then on I was an "MGM Brat" and worked as a Stand-in and Double for Margaret! My Father George E. Lee was a Property Master and had propped many of the landmark MGM movies including Mutiny on the Bounty with Clark Gable, The Wizard of Oz, Green Dolphin Street and many more! When he started he worked on all the early Johnny Weissmuller Tarzan movies. I was born in 1935 and he named me after Maureen O'Sullivan (Jane) because he adored the little Irish lass. The Tarzan crew gave me a cedar chest full of beautiful silk coats and dresses and other baby things. There was a brass plaque on the chest that read, "To Whatzit Lee from The Tarzan Crew"! I kept the little pink silk coat until it just shredded away. I was taken to the studio at age two to meet Maureen O'Sullivan while she was filming The Emperor's Candlesticks. I was treated to meeting the crew and ice cream and a photo shoot with Maureen. I stayed close until she passed away. She gave me Christmas presents, usually a dog or cat, and I met all her children and played with them on occasion. The most well known of her offspring is Maria Teresa "Mia" Farrow!

Her husband John Farrow offered to help me get into the movies but I was not really interested! I liked the technical aspect of the shoot, but I

never liked to have a camera pointed at me! I did enjoy being on the sets with my father and with Margaret and her mother. I loved all the things and memorabilia my father brought home to me! I actually had a pair of each of the original "Silver" and "Ruby" Slippers from The Wizard of Oz! He brought home the big rubber feet from

Margaret O'Brien and Maureen in The Secret Garden

Summer Stock that

264

Gene Kelly and Phil Silvers wore in the dance number "Heavenly Music"! I could write a whole page of the things he brought home, but it would depress me a lot! Why? Because my Mom gave or threw all of the things away when I left to get married at 16! We did not speak for about 5 years because in those items were all my dolls, including a life-size Shirley Temple doll, a Deanna Durbin doll, and of course a Margaret O'Brien doll designed for her by Madame Alexander, and a cloth French doll Margaret gave to me for my birthday! Two Dionne Quintuplets: a large set given to me by the mother of Myrna Loy and a small set still in the baskets with their clothes.

All the character dolls were autographed, including a Sonja Henie doll my Uncle Herb bought me at the Sonja Henie Ice Palace that used to be in Westwood! I had most of Madame Alexander dolls and the Story Book Doll Collection still in the Polka Dot Boxes. Oh, I can't forget the handmade Chinese Lion Dancer Doll in the glass case that Chiang Kai-shek sent to me because my Dad had taken care of his Chow-Chow when he was visiting

MGM with his wife! The dog had puppies in my Dad's office at MGM. But that is now "water under the bridge" and I am just grateful to still have Margaret O'Brien and her friend Randal Malone as friends. I cherish my friendship with Dorothy Dale Kloss and Ken Prescott. Dorothy, you are the best and the happiest person I know! Keep dancing, lovely lady!!

Maureen and Madame Alexander "Bride Doll"

Chapter 24: Building a Stairway to a Star

Let's go back to 2008. *The Guinness Book of World Records* proclaimed me "The Oldest Living Working Showgirl in the World." The certificate was presented to me on stage, during the "Living Better, Longer" symposium filmed at the theatre. I was on the panel. Mr. P. and Doctor Small from UCLA were the moderators. At the finish of the program, they asked me to come to the microphone and presented me with the certificate. A larger version was in a prominent place in the lobby of the Follies. It was amazing to me that at this time in my life, I would be in *Guinness*. My photo in costume was published in *The Guinness World Records,* 2009 on page 91. The paperback version is on page 134. It gives you a feeling of being number one.

Showgirl in Silver

The media jumped right on this, and the publicity for the Follies, and me, hit the ceiling. I made YouTube, Facebook, and many, many blogs all over the net. In the United Kingdom, *My Weekly,* a widely read newspaper, published a two-page spread and

Showgirl Clown

photo on the front page. "The London Daily Express" did a big article, and it even spread to Russia, and Canada in the *Winnipeg Free Press*. Everyone I would meet would say, "I know you!" It has been fun.

It's been a long journey. It's been full of excitement and adventure. I have loved every minute of the trip to the unknown. I've had hills to climb, and I've fallen off many times. But the start of a new climb always took me to new places, people and knowledge I never dreamed of. At the end of the Follies 2009-2010 season, I decided to resign from the Follies, due to a more lucrative offer. In fifteen years, no one had gotten a raise! That doesn't show much appreciation for your talent. That was, and

A Showgirl, "Waiting for Santa"

Red Showgirl

still is, the Follies! I will still be dancing and singing as long as I can, still clicking my heels even though the Follies have been telling people I retired, which is NOT TRUE. Before, this goes to press, let me just mention:

Stars in My Life

All the stars are not in the sky; they are all over the world shining brightly, on television, radio, Broadway, movie sets, and stages where they can make people happy with their talent. Every profession has its own stars, but mine comes under the heading of show business! Just to be part of it is magic, and here are some of the magical stars I have known.

Kaye Ballard and Me

Kaye Ballard! How exciting to know one of "Cinderella's step-sisters." Kaye loves to nickname people she likes, and thank goodness I'm one of them. She calls me "Tapper." Kaye wrote her book a few years ago, "How I Lost 10 Pounds in 53 Years!" Very funny and interesting! She revised the reprint, when it went to paperback. I met her for coffee one day, and she told me she had put Ken and me in the revised book. Under Acknowledgements. She said, "I took two people out I don't like anymore!" What a loss for those two people. Thanks for being in my life. Love ya, Kaye!

Dorothy and Rita Coolidge

Rita Coolidge has a heart of love and kindness. When she headlined at the Follies, we became great friends, or as we said "friends forever." Not only is she beautiful; she has this lovely voice that touches your heart. Especially when she sings "Amazing Grace" in Cherokee. You know the love she has in her heart for her heritage, and her people. Having Rita as a friend is having someone you can count on. One of Rita's hit recordings says it all: "Your love is lifting me higher." Call me!!!

Donald O'Connor was my favorite dancer, hands down. He could do it all with style, energy and comedy. When Donald came to star in the Follies, I could hardly wait to meet him, and tell him that I was his number one fan (and probably his oldest). Every show was sold out. Everyone from my generation remembered Donald from all the great movies he made: *Call Me Madam, There's No Business Like Show Business*, and of course, *Singin' in the Rain*. His star was shining brightly, until one night he took ill and had to leave the show. It was sad to see him go. He passed away a couple years later, but it was the highlight of my career to have worked and enjoyed such a legend.

Mary Wilson, of the Supremes, and "Friends"

Mary Wilson one of the original "Supremes," along with Diana Ross and Florence Ballard. She is my kind of gal. The audience couldn't get enough of her. Mary loves to laugh, and have a good time. With her energy, she rocked that stage like an earthquake. My friends Lisette and Boyd Haigler asked me to invite Mary for dinner. It was a small dinner party for Mary, and her friend Mark Bego, who collaborated with Mary on her book. So there were ten of us: Lisette, Boyd, Mary, Mark, Ken and yours truly, with their four adorable dogs. The dogs didn't join us for dinner, just looked and hoped. Before dinner, Mary said to Mark, "Make that great martini I like for Dorothy."

"Oh," I said, "This is really good, Mark!"

So, he took me at my word, and as I was talking my head off, he kept filling my glass. A sip at a time becomes nine. I didn't even notice until I went to the powder room. Now this house is fabulous, with wonderful white tile floors. Leading into the living room are three steps, with tiny lights on the steps to find your way. Of course, if you've been drinking, you probably wouldn't see the lights. At that time, with floaters and cataracts, to boot, I started down the steps, and the toe of my sandal bent back. They said, I fell in slow motion, and landed on both knees. Ouch! I didn't feel a thing. I got up with a little help, and Mary said, "Girl, you better put plenty of ice on those knees tonight!"

I said, "Mary, I'll just have a little more ice in my drink, and I'll be fine."

I haven't had a martini since. Mary gave a great closing night party. With all that energy she has, she is making the world a little better. She truly is a "Dream Girl."

Susan Anton has that great smile and personality to match. She wowed them at the Follies. She and I would stand back stage, and talk about her days in Vegas and growing up in Yucaipa, California, and about her mom. It was hard for us to stop talking, and get on stage for the finale. Of course we did, but in the middle of a sentence we had to cut it off, and head for the music. The next show, we would pick up right where we left off.

Susan Anton and her husband, Jeff

Julius LaRosa, what can I say, I loved Julius. He was the sweetest man in the world, and I'm not just saying that because he brought in a box of chocolates every day for the cast. That's a lot of sweetness. He was also a kind, sensitive man. My brother Vincent passed away during the time Julius was in the Follies. I was devastated when I received the news, and I left immediately for Beverly Hills. The funeral mass was celebrated at The Good Shepherd Church, and afterwards everyone had a lovely lunch at "Mateo's Restaurant," where Vincent use to meet his buddies. Need I say more? I left and drove back to the desert. When I arrived back to work, an envelope was on my dressing table. I opened it, and a large red rose was on the side of the page, and the most beautiful letter from Julius expressing his sympathy for my loss. It was a lovely moment for me, and I will always be grateful for his kindness and friendship.

Julius La Rosa

Anna Maria Alberghetti was born to be a star, and she certainly shined brightly on the Follies stage. What a magnificent voice. I remember her many movies. Among them, *Cinderfella* with Jerry Lewis and *Here Comes the Groom* with Bing Crosby. She played the Follies twice, and both times she was a smash. Everybody in the cast loved her.

It was Christmas time, and Ken and I decided to give a Christmas party for the cast and friends. Our condo happens to be right across from the recreation room, so it was perfect for a party. Anna Maria arrived, along with the other acts in the show.

Anna Maria Alberghetti

We had about eighty guests ready to raise their glass to wish each other a Merry Christmas, or just raise their glass and down the old hatch with cheer, along with turkey, ham and all the holiday goodies. One of the cast

members, who shall remain nameless, thought she was a great singer, and would sing at the drop of a hat. I would never sing, with Anna Maria in the group. However, this did not faze this person. Everyone was in deep conversation with vodka, or wine, in hand. I was standing next to this person, and casually said, without thinking, "We should have a little entertainment!" And without hesitation, "She" blurted out a number that would have made the cattle run for cover. Everyone looked over at Anna Maria to get her reaction, and the look on her face was like a call to arms. Coffee anyone?

Steve Anthony, Dorothy, Buddy and Lezlie Greco, Palm Desert, CA

Two of the most gracious people I know are **Buddy Greco** and his wife **Lezlie Anders**. They are "double your pleasure, double your fun" with their dual talent. Buddy at the piano, and Lezlie singing and kidding Buddy about his five wives. She has a natural wit, and they fit together so well. When they moved to the desert from Vegas, they decided to open the Buddy Greco restaurant. They had in mind the old days, when people stayed up after nine (in the desert it's the "Bewitching Hour"), and went to jazz clubs. Unfortunately, this is not the case here; they don't do jazz, they do golf. We loved going there for the dinner show and the friendly atmosphere. After a couple years, the restaurant closed, and the last time we talked they were getting ready to move to London. Before they left, they did a great show at the Annenberg Theatre called "FEVER! A Tribute to Peggy Lee." Rave reviews!

The Four Aces

The Four Aces are timeless. They are Follies favorites, and brought back by request several times. They have had more than thirty "Top Forty"

The Modernaires, and Dorothy

recordings, and I loved all those wonderful songs from my time: "Love Is A Many-Splendored Thing," "Three Coins in the Fountain," just to name a few. Fred, Danny, Harry and Joe were the "Aces," and what a group of fun entertainers. I was always happy to hear they were returning to the Follies. Hope we meet again.

"**The Modernaires**" came to Follies Thirteen, Paula Kelly, Jr., Martha Dickerson, (Paula's sister), Bill Tracy, Alan Copeland, and Joe Croyle. We were all friends, and had some fun times together. Can you imagine the original Modernaires with Glenn Miller 60 years ago? And now the next generation still singing "Kalamazoo," "Chattanooga Choo Choo," and "Juke Box Saturday Night!"

Bill Tracy was full of stories about the good old days, and that's hard to come by in this day and age. As a kid, he was one of the original "Mitchell Boys Choir" that appeared in the Bing Crosby movie, *Going My Way*. He would come over to our condo with other friends, or meet us at Coco's Restaurant, in our corner booth. We would talk for hours. I'm sure

Mary Tyler Moore, Dorothy and Bill Hayes

they wished we would leave, but we always left a good tip. "The Modernaires" were working in Arizona when Bill took ill, and never recovered. We were devastated. One evening not long afterwards, Joe Croyle called and we met for dinner. He asked Ken if he would be interested in taking Bill's place, and join the group. Ken did join the "New" Modernaires, with Paula Kelly, Jr., Julie Lancaster (Paula Kelly's younger sister), and Joe. Unfortunately, Martha had passed away. Julie, Paula's younger sister, came out of retirement to take her place. Ken sang with them for about two years, and then returned to his first love, choreography, and doing his act.

Bill Hayes joined the Follies for their thirteenth season. He had his own audience. His fans from *Days of our Lives* filled the theatre every performance. Ken and Bill had worked together in 1975, when they did *Oklahoma* together. Bill played "Curley," and Ken was "Will Parker." They would kid each other about anything that came to mind. During the middle of Bill's engagement, he decided to put in a tap number; he loved to tap dance. It was cute, but he was not Gene Kelly. Ken happened to be in the green room, waiting for me and had watched his act on the monitor. When Bill came off Ken said to him, kidding, "Bill, did you stop the show or just slow it down a little?" Bill just laughed and headed for his dressing room.

I remember the early years of **Tony Martin**, when he was working nightclubs, like The Chez Paree in Chicago. Of course, he also did movies, television, theatre, and now like the rest of us in the Follies, he was Follies age — 55+. He was very nice and always friendly. He was married to the great dancer, Cyd Charisse. I had admired her dancing for years, and I thought I would finally meet her. Not to be! She was very

Tony Martin

unfriendly, and did not speak to anyone in the cast. I don't think she even talked to Tony. She was rude as she passed us on her way out the door from Tony's dressing room, with her head held high like we didn't exist.

Peter Marshall

My thinking: "If you're so good, why can't you be nicer?" Oh well, her loss.

Mr. Show business himself: **Peter Marshall**. I do believe Peter has worked with every performer in the world, and has a story for each one of them. He has a darling wife, Laurie, who he is crazy about, and they are a fun couple. He played the Follies twice, and he was a real favorite with the audience. He has that wonderful way of talking to the audience like they were best friends. That's a gift. Peter produced a new show called *Old Faces of 2002*, which Ken choreographed. You will probably recall Peter's long running television show, "The Hollywood Squares!" The show, *Old Faces of 2002*, was filled with his old buddies from show business, who were stars in their own right, like Kaye Ballard, Tom Poston, Bill Dana, Artie Johnson, and the Modernaires. They did a takeoff on *The Hollywood Squares*, as well as featured in their own acts. It was a good show, but like a lot of good shows, it didn't go anywhere after playing

Frankie Lane, and my granddaughter, Jamie

the McCallum in the Desert. Peter is still out there as of 2012 talking, singing, and making people happy.

Twenty-one Gold Records including "Mule Train," "Rawhide," "That's My Desire," and "Lucky Old Sun." Those were just some of his great hits,

Carol Lawrence cooking up a storm, with Tony Pastor, Ken, Dorothy, and Peter

who else, but **Frankie Laine**. He brought that "Lucky Old Sun" with him to the Follies, and they were lucky to have him. He was such a nice man, but his time with us was short lived. He was unable to complete his contract. How ironic he had just made a new CD "Ain't Over 'til it's Over!" Is that timing for you or what? He passed away shortly afterwards.

I love tap dancers, and **Carol Lawrence** is one of the best. She's from my hometown, Chicago. Carol was in the Follies twice, and what a talent. I'm sure you remember her from "Westside Story" as Maria, with that lovely voice. At the Follies, Carol did her own act. This is where tap dancing comes into play. Carol not only captivated the audience with her singing and tapping, but she captured several gentlemen from the audience to come on stage. They were ready and willing. She taught them a few tap steps, and then at the end, showed them how to pick her up in a lift as a finish. One evening, Ken, Tony Pastor, Jr., the son of Tony Pastor Sr., from the Big Bands area, decided to see the show. Afterwards they were meeting Carol and I for a drink. We were going to "Melvyn's," the landmark restaurant here in the valley. Again, "Life happens when you're making other plans."

Funny Man Bill Dana

One of the gentlemen who picked up Carol twisted her leg, and the pain shot to her head. But being the trooper she is, she just smiled, took her bow and waited to scream when she got to her dressing room. The show finished, and Carol had put ice on her knee, and was ready to go, but she had to keep the leg straight, or it hurt. Ken had a SUV and he helped her into the front seat, propped her leg up on the dashboard, and away we went. We made it to "Melvyn's," had our midnight snack, and all was well. Carol was back on stage the next matinee.

Oh, before I forget, that girl can cook. Tony had us over for dinner one evening with other friends. He was in the kitchen, doing his thing, when suddenly Carol joined him, and said, "I think you need some help!" They cooked up a storm. Carol did write a wonderful cookbook, "I Remember Pasta, Mama's Secret Recipes." On closing night, the entire cast received an autographed copy. Thank you, Carol, for your talent and kindness.

When I first came to the Follies in 1995-1996, Mr. P. was not the comic relief. He came on stage and did a minute and a half, as opposed to his forty-minute monologue of today. He was just getting the hang of it. He was, and still is, a fast learner. My first show was with **Bill Dana**, a very funny man. Then in the following years, there were other comedians like **John Byner**, who took the house down, and **Dave Berry**, who had a joke

John Byner

a minute. Dave had done the Follies a couple of times, and had this cute little wife of many years. They were like Velcro. She could do his act in a minute, and if he took a breath, she jumped right in and finished with the punch line. They were shopping one afternoon at our local mall, and as Dave was getting out of the car, another car came out of nowhere, and hit Dave. He was crushed between the two cars. When we heard about it, we were all very concerned. And, of course, we were wondering, "Is he alright? Will he be out of the show?" The next day, he was in a wheel chair, and made his entrance from stage right. Can't keep a good man down.

Then there was **Babe Pier**, who was not only funny on stage, but kept you laughing off stage. His act was terrific. He had the ability to imitate voices of celebrities. He kept himself busy not only doing eight or nine shows a week, in his spare time, he would go to the boxing club and go a few rounds. He and our dear departed friend, Bill Tracy, would come over to our place and kibitz all evening about their days in Vegas and elsewhere. What fun!

Seeing, is believing! **Nino Frediani** knows all about that. Nino is so nearsighted, he can't drive, but his exceptional accuracy and speed gave him the title of "World's Fastest Juggler!" Ken and I have stayed with Nino, and his lovely wife Kuniko, in their fabulous home in Vegas. Nino built the most beautiful little chapel in his backyard that I'm sure he did out of love. He is one of a kind, He also taught my granddaughter Jamie to juggle.

Nino Frediani, teaching my granddaughter, Megan, to juggle

A new friend in our life is **Brad Cummings**, and his friend "Rex," the dinosaur. Not only does he speak for Rex, but you also wonder which one is the human! He is just sensational. He came into the Follies my last year, and Ken and I are so glad we got to know him and his beautiful wife, Rineka. Now it's the e-mail to keep in touch, as we have gone our own way. In the last one we received, he told us that he and "Rex" were on a cruise ship making the passengers laugh.

Speaking of ventriloquists, **Sammy King** and "Francisco" came into our lives several Follies seasons ago. Sammy has had several return visits to the Follies stage by popular demand. He and Brad, and "Francisco" and "Rex," have been friends for thirty years. So it was great for them to meet again and renew old acquaintance.

*Dorothy and
Sammy King*

*Ken and Brad Cummings,
the ventriloquist, 2009*

Chapter 25: It's Magic

My stairway to my star was a few short steps from where I was performing, The Follies, but it took many tap steps to get there. I'm referring to my very own star on the Walk of Stars, May 29, 2010, in front of the Theatre and the Follies.

Let me tell you how it happened. I met Lisette Haigler at the opening night party for the Follies a few years ago. I was sitting at a table looking

Craig and me, on my 85th Birthday

into space, when this very pretty woman walked over and said hello. She told me she was a friend of a cast member. She loved the Follies, and had seen the show at least three or four times a year. I liked her right off. She invited Ken and I for Thanksgiving, but we had another engagement. I said, "Maybe we can have coffee sometime," and that was the beginning of our friendship.

Lisette and Boyd Haigler are a very generous couple. We began to see a lot of each other. Boyd is from South Carolina and Lisette from Belgium. They live in this wonderful, whimsical house that makes you smile when you come through the front door. When I hit eighty-five, Ken said, "we're going out for a nice dinner, but it's a surprise." The evening arrived, and as we were leaving he said, "I have to blindfold you!" I thought that was strange. We got in the car and the next thing I knew, Ken was leading me up some steps. A door opened, and a hundred people sang "Happy Birthday." I can't tell you the warm feeling that went through me. I was really surprised; The Follies cast, along with every photographer in town. Sitting at the white piano was Joel Baker, playing "Happy Birthday." Ken had everyone organized and in place, which is one of his great gifts. Make them laugh, sing a song, tell a joke, and give them what they want. He just amazes me. Kaye Ballard, Buddy Greco, and his wife Lezlie Anders, were also there. And then the big surprise came: my son Craig flew in from Philadelphia to spend my birthday with me, as did my

Ken and Dorothy with Lisette and Boyd Haigler, 2011

niece Brandy and her husband Richard from Carmichael, California. It was a spectacular party.

Not long after that, the plan was already in the works for me to get my star on "The Walk of Stars," only I didn't know it. Ken and Lisette were very busy with lists of people to invite. The event was a fundraiser for the star, the cost $10,000. They had already contacted Bob Alexander, the President of "The Walk of Stars," to nominate me. The word came back that it had been a unanimous vote. WOW! Ken and Lisette immediately made out the invitations; the party was on February 7, 2010. What great fun. Our friend John Salerno played the piano, and sang an opening number to me. Nancy Osbourne, who is a great singer, also entertained with several lively songs. Unfortunately, Ken had laryngitis and could hardly speak, but he put up a good fight, and kept the crowd entertained with videos of me performing, and one of Ken performing in his Big Band Show in Myrtle Beach, S.C. that ran for a year. To my amazement, they raised the money in one night and the star was mine.

Star Ceremony

*Bob Alexander, President of The
Palm Springs Walk of Stars, 2010*

*What a story I have to tell,
Dorothy's Star, 2010!*

283

Hot, Hot, Hot! Bill "Bulldog" Feingold, Dorothy, and Kaye Ballard, 2010

Rita Coolidge, saying nice things about me. Love that girl!

Jamie and Megan, with Grandma Dorothy, 2010

My own Star, 2010!

*My granddaughters Megan
and Jamie, 2012*

*What a great day for me!
2010*

*Ken and Dorothy arriving
at the reception, following
the Star Presentation, 2010!*

*Boyd Haigler and
Dorothy, in the
Car of The Day, the
1957 Pink T-Bird*

*Dorothy, Lisette, and
Rita, Star Party, 2010*

The date for the unveiling of the star was set for May 29, 2010. Mine was the 330th Star, and the placement was in front of the Theatre where the Follies perform. I thought that was so fitting. Kaye Ballard, Rita Coolidge, and Bill "Bulldog" Feingold were the speakers. And now I have a wall full of wonderful tributes from The California Legislative Assembly 64th District, Congresswoman Mary Bono, Mayor Steve Pougnet, Supervisor Jon J. Benoit 49th District, and many kind words from the Board Members of The Walk of Stars. Many thanks to all you wonderful friends and fans for giving me such a wonderful gift.

On a negative note, Mr. P was not invited since he had told me the Follies could not be involved. So I did not involve the Follies, except for a few people in the cast who did attend. The Follies closed on May 16. 2010. I sent Mr. P a letter informing him I would not be returning the next year. I had a better offer. I wished him a happy 20th Anniversary, but my time at the Follies was over! I want to spend the rest of my life without stress, and do what I love to do: DANCE. I had always said, "I had a life before the Follies, and I'll have one after the Follies," and so I have. My first priority was to have my cataracts removed, and that took most of the summer, along with writing this book. It is now November, and I just returned from performing at "The Magic Castle" in Hollywood. It was a sensational week. I worked with several great magicians, but they didn't show me any tricks! They treat everyone with such respect and profes-sionalism. Dinner was set up every evening, back stage in the "green room" for the cast, and they had makeup artist to do your makeup every evening. What a treat. We did three shows a night, but it was a piece of cake due to the jolly atmosphere. I had such fun with "Mr. Dead," Mat Plendl. He and I did a little monologue, and then he introduced me as *The Guinness Book of Records'* "Oldest Living, Working Showgirl in the World." I did a big tap number, and the audience went wild; it was terrific!!

Back in September, I auditioned for the new Paula Abdul show, "Live to Dance." I arrived at the rehearsal, and hundreds of dancers where there. But they had already seen a tape of me, and had checked out Facebook, YouTube, and Follies publicity, so they were waiting for me. I was directed to a room to wait. Unfortunately, there was no place to sit, but they told Ken they would get me on very soon. We asked if there was a dressing room, and they said, "No, you have to change into costume in the unisex bathroom." I walked in, and it was 8x10 with a sink, toilet, and shower. Filthy dirty. I had to change in the shower as several people came and went. I said to Ken, "I don't think I want to do this."

But he said, "Hang in, you'll be fine." They kept coming back and telling us that it would only be a couple minutes. Well, three hours later, I finally moved into the studio with the producers and agency people, sitting at a long table. They asked me a few questions, and then I went into my dance. When I finished, they stood up and applauded. They said they could not believe how I looked and danced at 87, and I would be hearing from them. A week later, I received a phone call from the agency saying they would like me for the callback, at which time Paula with the other judges would be there, but in the meantime, they were sending me a contract to be returned in three days. The contract arrived and was about 30 pages long. We read it. No way.

They were not responsible for any injury during your performance. They have the right to videotape, audiotape, film, and photograph. You cannot perform without the producers release for two years, and no residuals. Ken called them and said, "Count Dorothy out. She cannot sign a contract like that. You must be nuts to have someone tied up without work."

They did a whole big thing that "we really like Dorothy, and you don't have to sign the contract." A few days later another call came in, asking for the music I would be using. It had to be 90 seconds. We said okay, but they were on the phone every day. Finally they told us that the big audition (in front of cameras, Paula, two other judges, and an audience) would be on Sunday, the 31st of October! Ken talked to the gal again, and told her, "Dorothy cannot be standing around at her age," and they told him, "We will take care of it when you arrive." The next call, they had me coming in at 7 a.m. for the audition. Ken said, "No, she cannot do that after three shows a night at the Magic Castle," so they would fix it.

They came back, "Would 1:30 be okay?"

Ken said, "Fine, but we have to be out by 5 p.m. for her first show at the Castle."

"Oh, no problem," were their words. Wanna bet? We arrived at 1:30, and were ushered to a big white tent, on the grounds of Dodger Stadium. It was filled with hopefuls. We signed in, and they gave us a form to sign. Ken said, "I have to read it first, I'll be back." No place to dress again. The other dancers came in their costumes, or found a corner or in the outdoor potty. As we were sitting waiting, a young guy came in who had just finished his audition, and saw Ken. They both had worked dance conventions together. He said hi and Ken asked him about the audition. He said, "Did you see the contract or release they want you to sign? I wouldn't sign it, so I'm out!"

They had asked us to sign it when we arrived, but we said no at that time. It was now three o'clock and I said to Ken, "I think we should go." He talked to the one gal about the release, and she had said, "Don't worry about it."

Ken said, "I'd like to speak to the head gal," and they sent for her. She gave us this big, "It's going to be okay, and don't worry" routine. "Paula really wants to see Dorothy."

Just as we were about to leave, they came to say we would be next, and moved us to another tent, closer to the big tent. Remember, I'm 87, and it felt like another year had passed. It had turned freezing cold, and my feet were beginning to cramp. It was 5 p.m. They did several interviews with me, and finally I made it into the big tent where Anthony, one of the "hosts" interviewed me again, and then said, "Please sign this — it's just a release." We would not sign the original contract, and that was the death sentence. I walked on the stage and there they were: Paula, and the other two judges. The two judges voted me off. Paula was very nice and complimentary, but you see, we would not sign that contract. It was another experience I could have lived without, but what the heck, it certainly filled my day, and I can say that I danced at Dodger Stadium.

So as they say in baseball, "One, Two, Three strikes you're out!" Good Move!

Chapter 26: Stop the Press

Just when I thought I had told it all, my brain said "Hello again," so I thought I would share my new adventures with you before we go to press.

March came in like a lamb and went out with a bang for Ken and me. The phone rang one morning and I heard Ken say, "What date? Okay, sounds great." He turned to me and said, "Pack your bag — we're on our way to Vegas. It's a perfect gig for us to break in our new dance act." A week later, we were on our way to the South Point Hotel Casino, to perform for the Breck Wall Tribute. If you have spent any time in Vegas in the last forty years, you would remember "Bottoms Up," a great show that ran for many years. Breck produced and performed in it. Now he is performing on that heavenly stage.

We arrived in Vegas on Friday, a few days before the show on Sunday, that way I could hit the shopping mall and visit old friends. On Sunday our call time was at one o'clock for rehearsal, and the show was at three. One rule in show business: be on time, don't waste time, and be considerate of your fellow performers. At twelve forty-five, we arrived in the show room. Kenny Kerr, a very funny man, and the other acts were waiting their turn to either check the stage or sound. A group of showgirls were on stage rehearsing. Their choreographer was a gal named Mistinguett, who came dashing in at one-fifteen, already late. When we heard her say "take it from the top," we all said to the man in charge, "Tell her to get off," but all he said was he would try. Kenny Kerr said, if she is not off the stage by one-thirty, he was leaving, and he did.

She got off the stage at two o'clock. Consideration for the other performers — I guess not! We finally rehearsed, and then back to our room to makeup and dress for the show by three o'clock. It was fun; we met Senator Harry Reid and the Mayor and his wife. Kenny, of course, is always ready for a laugh. Oh, did I forget to mention he is a female impersonator? He was in drag with a silver gown and a blond wig, looking very fetching. When Kenny saw the senator's security men, he decided to have a little fun with them. He sashayed over to them with a twinkle in her/his eye and said, "So boys, would you like to frisk me?" You could see a little smile on their face as he sauntered off to the stage to perform. I guess you had to be there.

Kaye Ballard was unable to attend, due to another commitment, and asked Ken Prescott not to be confused with Kenny Kerr to read her thoughts on her long friendship with Breck. Then Ken sang "I'm Flying High, Got My Eye on the Sky." What an appropriate number when you consider why we were there. Now it was my turn. Ken introduced me and I made my entrance. We talked for a few minutes before we went into our tap number. We had very little space to dance, and it was a little scary doing a circle of turns with a lectern stand on one side and a piano on the other side. I did notice when I came on stage that in front of the piano was a large flower arrangement with a pin spot. I didn't think much about it when I made my entrance. I was looking at Ken. We started our routine, and as I danced to the right side of the stage I saw the urn with Breck's ashes in front of the flower arrangement with the pin spot. I'm tapping my heart out next to it, and let me say, one wrong step and I would have been doing the old sand dance, but our music was appropriate, "Shakin' the Blues Away."

After the show, we were invited to a fabulous birthday party for Tony Sacco, a great entertainer who also has a very popular TV show in Vegas. It was at the Turnberry in a wonderful condo on the top floor overlooking Las Vegas. We went through security and then took the elevator. Music was playing and the place was jammed with people. Tony's mom was singing. She is eighty-seven years old and I loved her; after all, she is the same age as me and we're still doing it! Ken sang and I danced in my high heels, which was not a smart move, but what the heck, you have to get into the mood of the moment. The entertainment was great and the laughter was infectious. The host of the party imports pate, and believe me, she must import a lot to live in this condo. I should have stayed in the kitchen longer and made pate instead of tapping my heart out.

I was beginning to fade when Ken said, "Grab your coat, we're going to another party." We arrived at The Lakes, a lovely area with magnificent homes. One we passed was a palace. I guess the person who resides there has dreams of Camelot, so why not? A short way down the road we turned into the driveway of a lovely home on the lake. The view was magnificent from every room in the house. Our host took us on a tour of the house and then we continued our quest for merry-making.

The next morning we met our friends from Los Angeles who had come to see our show. We had breakfast and hit the road back to Palm Springs and sanity. I love Las Vegas. It's an entertainer's town, and it's been good to all those wonderful showgirls for years. I may not have been a Las Vegas showgirl but I am the oldest showgirl in the world. You see age has its rewards.

Miguel Padro, and Roger Freeman, sponsored the Loretta Young Star, 2011! On right, Margaret O'Brien, Elinor Donahue and Chris Lewis, Loretta's son.

Actress Loretta Young made many movies in the 1930s and 40s. She won an Academy Award in 1947 for her performance in *The Farmers Daughter*. In 1953, her TV show *Loretta Young Presents*, hit the TV screen and it was an immediate hit until 1960. She made over 280 episodes. One of the best -known personalities on television, she gained the reputation as one of America's best-dressed women. Loretta lived in Palm Springs for several years, but unfortunately she had never received a star on the "Walk of Stars." Loretta is still remembered here in the valley with great affection. Rodger Freeman and Miguel Padro decided her star was way overdue. They contacted the two gentlemen that own the house that Loretta and her husband Jean Louis shared until her death in 2000 at age 87, and on April 16th they had a fundraiser to bring their dream to fruition. Let me just say, stars do not come cheap at $10,000. They asked Ken and me to participate. We, of course, said yes for this lovely lady of the screen. Ken choreographed the entertainment segment with

Loretta Young's Walk of Stars fundraiser party. Creating her famous entrance from TV were Jennie Inch, Dorothy Kloss, Barbara Rogers, Susie Cadham, Olga Morales, and Joan King, 2011.

six beautiful gals swinging through the door in their lovely gowns. It just

Dorothy paying tribute to Loretta Young in Loretta's former Palm Springs home.

happened that Joan King, the wife of Neville King, the great ventriloquist who lives in Nottingham, was crossing the big pond for a visit with us. Unfortunately, Neville passed away in 2010. I called Joan before she left and told her to bring a gown. I thought this wonderful event would cheer her up, and it did. Champagne does wonders for people. We read excerpts from Loretta's movies and then Ken introduced some of the celebrities, including Kaye Ballard, the funniest woman alive. Elinor Donahue from the TV show *Father Knows Best*, who also appeared on *The Loretta Young Show*, as was Margaret O'Brien from *Little Women* and Loretta's son Chris Lewis. He told wonderful stories about Loretta and what a wonderful mother she was to her children. The entertainment began with Eric Dege presenting each of the six lovelies through the living room door as Robert Johnston played the theme from her television show. Each lady read an excerpt from one of Loretta's movies and then Ken sang "There Will Never Be Another You." Ain't that the truth.

Creating her famous entrance from TV were, Jennie Inch, Dorothy Kloss, Barbara Rogers, Susie Cadham, Olg Morales, and Joan King, 2011!

Loretta Young's daughter, Judy Lewis, and ME! 2011

The entertainment continued with both Margaret and Elinor relating stories about working with Loretta and how kind and generous she was to everyone. Greg Fedderly, a handsome young man who has a wonderful voice and sings at the Met, sang "Because of You," and the audience loved it. After the entertainment, the silent auction began. The room was filled with donated memorabilia that was quickly snatched up. The click of the champagne flutes could be heard a mile away as everyone toasted Loretta. The music continued and the conversation throughout the room was about Loretta's beauty, charm and love of her Catholic faith. It was a splendid event, and Ken and I are happy we could share in celebrating her life.

A sad note: Judy Lewis, Loretta's daughter by Clark Gable, died of a brain tumor just a few weeks after Loretta's Star Ceremony 2011.

Jane Russell, with Ken and Dot, 2006

Gentlemen Prefer Blondes

Gentlemen don't always prefer blondes. Jane Russell was a beautiful brunette and I'm sure most of you remember her from the movie with Marilyn Monroe. I had a chance to meet Jane on a few occasions, and each time she was a delight. My first meeting was a party hosted by Ed Martica in his lovely home. Ed gives wonderful parties and loves to dance the Polish Hop; me too. It was in honor of Jane. Most parties start out slowly and then after a martini or two they liven up considerably. This party was no exception. The baby grand piano was the focal point of the living room, dead center and one level up from the floor. It gives the illusion of a stage.

As Jane and I and a few other music lovers gathered around the piano, we asked Jane to sing. She graciously gave the pianist her key and started to sing, what else but "A kiss on the hand might be quite continental but diamonds are a girl's best friend." What a thrill to be standing next to Jane Russell singing that famous song. When Jane finished, someone in the group said, "Dorothy, give us a little soft shoe!" Always one to oblige, I moved center stage, and the pianist started to play "On the Sunny Side of the Street." I started out great, then halfway through decided to do a grapevine across the floor, forgetting there was a step down to the floor. As you know, what goes up must come down. I should have stopped while I was ahead, but I went right to the end, missed the step, and hit the wall. WOW! I pulled myself together, stepped up on the upper level and did the grapevine back to the center, took a bow and said "Carry on."

Jean Gabriel and I have been friends since I moved to the desert. I met Jane through Jean's daughter-in-law Daryn. Jane is her godmother. The day after the party, Daryn called with an invitation from Jane. She wondered if I would like to join she and Daryn for lunch while she was still in town. Now, who would not want to have lunch with Jane Russell? I met them at Spencer's and we talked the afternoon away. Jane was considering the Follies, but after asking me about the eight and nine shows a week, she lost interest.

Jane passed away in February 2011 at 89.

Earlier in the book I mentioned Georgia Carroll and working with her at the Strand Theatre in New York. Georgia was married to the famed bandleader Kay Kyser and sang on his popular radio show *The Kollege of Musical Knowledge*. After their show business careers ended, they settled in Chapel Hill, North Carolina. Kay died in 1985. Georgia passed in 2011 at 91. What is interesting is that Jane Russell also sang with Kay Kyser in her early career.

Melinda Reed has a wonderful talk show here in the valley. She called to ask if I would be on her show. Ken accompanied me to the studio. The lovely young producer Stephanie Denny greeted us and walked us to the studio. What a joy to work with such pleasant people. Melinda was there and we started chatting. She told me that Carol Channing would be arriving, and she would follow my interview. I arrived in my favorite leopard

Dot with Melinda Reed, Talk of The Desert *TV Show, 2011*

print dress and thought I looked stunning. Stephanie looked at me and said. "I have a leopard dress and I love it." After that statement, she left the room. A few minutes later, as Melinda was explaining the run-down of the show, Stephanie returned. She swung into the studio wearing her leopard dress, did a turn and said, "We do have good taste." It looked much better on Stephanie.

We were off to the interview. Melinda is one of the best. I was so comfortable in the chair next to her. She has an amazing way of asking you a question, and she actually lets you answer it, unlike some

Accepting my Golden Halo Award, Southern Motion Picture Council. Daniel Wright, Barbara Hale, Gigi Perreau, Margaret O'Brien, Dorothy, and Tim Clark, 2011

interviews I've done. No matter how long it takes, she tries not to interrupt your flow, unless there's a commercial. After we finished, we walked out of the studio and there was *Hello Dolly* herself. Carol has a laughing face and she always welcomes you with a big smile. Her husband Harry was there and was trying to tell her to brush her hair back. She gave a sigh and said to me, "Dorothy, how do I look?"

"Carol you look fine," I told her.

Then with a chuckle in her voice she said, "I always like to hear the truth."

Margaret O'Brien and her friend Randal Malone, the President of Southern California Motion Picture Council, invited Ken and I to the Council to celebration their 50th Anniversary. After lunch, it was show time, followed by several awards being presented. Barbara Hale, I'm sure you will remember as Della Street on the *Perry Mason* show, was one of the recipients of the Golden Halo Award, as was Gigi Perreau, a former child star. To my surprise, Randal introduced Ken. He jumped on stage and started talking about my life and career and then asked me to join him on stage. I was still in shock as Margaret presented me with The Golden Halo Dance Achievement Award. To make it even more special, Randal told me many famous dancers through the years including Fred Astaire and Ginger Rogers received this award. Boy was I in good company.

Peter Ford, son of Eleanor Powell and Glenn Ford.
A photo moment for me, Christmas 2011

As I finish writing this book, the 2012 Christmas season is fast approaching. It's one of my favorite times of the year, and Ken's favorite. Our condo looks like a Macy's department store!

Let me just say, when I first started this book, I actually didn't think that it was within my reach. But, in whatever driving force in the universe you believe, it has guided me along, and amazingly, allowed me to

The Magic Castle, Hollywood Ca. Marilyn Manson, Dorothy, "Mr. Dead," and Frank Oliver.

remember an incredible amount of incidents that have made my life interesting and rewarding.

All kidding aside, there aren't many "still performing entertainers" at 88! I have seen decades, of fabulous shows, and starred in Vaudeville, night clubs, theatres and on TV. I have been fortunate enough to perform alongside some of the biggest names in the entertainment industry, and I have seen the amazing change in audiences and their tastes over the years. But one thing still remains: the demand to be entertained is paramount. And fortunately for me, I can still deliver. I have gone from Eddie Cantor and Eddy Duchin to Kay Starr and Kaye Ballard, and was even sought out to say "hello" to Marilyn Manson, who asked to meet me at the Magic Castle.

I am truly grateful to have not only had an incredible past, and present, but a bright future as well. So what's next, you ask? Well, this book was on my "to do

Dot and Matt Plendl, (Mr. Dead), 2010

list!" Done, and I hope you enjoyed reading it as much as I enjoyed writing it. I have many interesting, and exciting things on the boards, and as for retirement, well what would I do? Clip coupons? I don't cook. Go to the senior center? No! Or just sit and rock — I told you I had vertigo — all that motion wouldn't be good!

I teach dance every week, jazz and tap classes. I go to dinner, have a few drinks — just remember "a little vodka couldn't hurt," and of course, my all time favorite pastime (besides dancing), is SHOPPING!

So look out for me — as they say, "It ain't over 'til the fat lady sings," and since I am thin and physically fit, it's definitely not going to be over soon, if I can help it. I just can't wait to get going on all the wonderful things that await me!

Just remember, age is a number! Okay, okay, it's an old number, but — IT IS JUST A NUMBER. Life is a gift. The past is the past, the future is the future, and the present — well they call it that for a reason, because it is just that! A PRESENT! Open it, take it out of the box, and get crackin' on what you want to do for yourself. Life is not a dress rehearsal, as the saying goes. So go out there, and for heaven's sake, "star" in your own show. No one else can, and no one else will, except you.

Dorothy with famous magician Christopher Hart, 2010

My final words: as Auntie Mame said, "Life is a banquet, and most poor S.O.B's are starving to death!"

For every star that falls to earth,
a new one grows,
For every dream that fades away,
a new one grows,
When things aren't what they seem
You must keep following your dream,
So while my heart, is still believing,
I'll say good-bye.

There's No Business Like Show Business — THE FINALE!

It only takes a moment to be touched by talent, humanity, and the joy of friendship! Here are just SOME of those special people that have crossed my path!

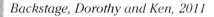

Backstage, Dorothy and Ken, 2011

California Dancin' *with Gwen Verdon, and Jim Horvath, my student from Chicago.*

Celebrating Carol Channing's Birthday, 2011

Mel Haber (Melvyn's Restaurant) and Dorothy. Performing at the Angel View luncheon 2011

Beautiful Rhonda Fleming with Dorothy and Ken

Dot and Anacani from TV's The Lawrence Welk Show

Racquet Club
Palm Springs, 1999
Dot, Linda Christian,
Barbara Proctor
and Ken

Mary Wilson's
Goddaughter, Dorothy,
and Trina Parks

Ken, Dot,
Judy Bell and
Tony Butala
from The Lettermen

Stefanie Powers at her book
signing, 2010

Dorothy, Suzy Cadham,
and Nancy Sinclair,
"Golddiggers" from the
Dean Martin Show

Barbara Van Orden,
her husband Elton, and
their Christmas Guests,
at Carol Channing's
Christmas Show, 2011

Randy Jones, "The Village People"
and Dorothy, 2011

Steve Tobia, Dot, James
Bacon, Cindy Jordan, the
"José Cuervo" Girl and
photographer Linda Lazar.
James was promoting
his book James Bacon's
Hollywood is a Four Letter
Town, *1977.*

New York, class with
Ken and me with
Luigi, the great jazz
teacher. I'm hoping to
make it to 2013.

*Ken's Jazz Class,
with Guest Margaret
O'Brien*

*Family reunion with
my niece Brandy
and her daughters,
Allison and
Stephanie, 1999*

*Beverly Burgess and Dorothy
celebrating seventy-years
of dancing and we're still here!*

Dorothy with Bridget Kelly
One of my dance students from
Sacred Heart forty years later
in 2008. Love that girl!

Roz Converse,
a Samuel Goldwyn Girl in the 40s
with daughter Laura, 2011

GUINNESS BOOK GRANDMA

When you think of "Grandma," do the words "old," "slow," and "wrinkled" come to mind? Well, not for my Grandma. Dorothy "Dale" Kloss is 85 years old and was featured in The Guinness Book of World Records *as the World's Oldest Performing Showgirl. She is currently tap dancing for the Follies in California. She puts on two shows every day, from September to early June. There are about 18 men and women who perform for the Follies, all from ages 55–85.*

Almost every other year my Dad and I fly out to California to see my hilarious, animated, and encouraging Grandma, who is in better shape than I am. When we go to see her in the show, we are introduced to the audience by the MC. Then during the three-hour show, I can spot dancers winking and waving at me, along with a dazzling smile from my Grandma when she is introduced.

In every single act, the costumes that the Follies girls wear are outrageous. You would never imagine seeing older ladies in sparkly, sequined, brightly colored costumes. Along with the amazing fashion wear comes tap shoes sporting two inch heels. But my Grandma, she's got special costumes. Since she is the oldest performer, most of her costumes are tweaked to stand out during the performance, and it adds a great emphasis to her solo.

My Grandma Dorothy is not your average old lady. She is inspiring, and has the mind, heart and soul of someone years younger than she. Obstacles have never been a problem in her life; they are just bumps in the road on the way to success. God outdid himself when he chose her to be my Grandma. I can't wait to go see the show and whisper to the person next to me, "Yeah, that's my Grandma."

The above, written by my Granddaughter, Megan Kloss for a school project. She lives in Philadelphia. I have missed so much of her everyday happenings, but then I am not the only Grandma with their Grandchildren a million miles away and I miss her and her sister Jamie more than they know. Megan will be sixteen in November and Jamie will be twenty-three in February 2013. They have grown up on me these two beautiful, bright young ladies that I am so proud of and I'm so lucky to still be around to see and hear their accomplishments. You see, old is not so bad.

Megan was eleven when she sent me the above copy and I have carried her words in my heart from that day forward. Now I have a chance to let her know that God out did himself when he gave me such a precious gift, and her name is Megan.

Love ya,

Grandma Dorothy

My Bucket List

I have never given much thought to the future, just the present. When a friend inquired, "What do you see yourself doing in the next few years," it cracked me up. I said quickly. "Stayin' Alive would be a good thing."

First of all there are no guarantees unless your Doctor gives you a time frame. He could be wrong, but you've done nothing but think about it, and pushed yourself to do the things you should have done up until now, and if you haven't done them by now let it go, you wouldn't enjoy them anyhow since you always have that time frame lurking in your mind. I'm leaving my time frame to the man upstairs.

Great old song.

You have to give a little
Lose a little and
Let your poor heart break a little
That's the glory of,
That's the story of love.

So I'll continue to give a little, lose a little, let my heart break a little and try to keep that Glory of Love the best way I can and so, here goes!

- Have dinner with Robert Redford
- Fly to Paris with Ken Prescott
- Take my granddaughters, son and his wife to London
- Have tea with the Queen at Buckingham Palace and if William and Kate would find the time to stop by that would be a plus. Harry too!
- Do a show on Broadway or even Off Broadway would be OK
- Dance at The White House for the President. The politicians have been dancing around there for years. I'd like to join them. I guess that invitation will not be forthcoming after that remark.
- Take piano lessons again. The one thing I regret, not making the time to pursue.
- Go back to that toddling town Chicago and visit my old memories that are still there.

None of the above will probably happen but I can live without them. I just hope this book sells so I don't have to go to the home.

My bucket has always been full of things to make my life interesting, old friends and new friends.

Just remember, if you give love, you'll get it back twofold. I have. Try it. You might like it.

Love,

Dorothy

CPSIA information can be obtained at www.ICGtesting.com
Printed in the USA
BVOW011328140213

313264BV00005B/10/P